THE
SAGAMORE

AN OMNI CLASSIC RESORT

**The Sagamore Resort
Bolton Landing, New York**

THE GREAT
AND THE GRACIOUS
ON MILLIONAIRES' ROW

THE GREAT
AND THE GRACIOUS
ON MILLIONAIRES' ROW

Lake George in its Glory

By
KATHRYN E. O'BRIEN

North Country Books
Utica, New York

THE
SAGAMORE

AN OMNI CLASSIC RESORT

Dedication

The Great and the Gracious . . . is gratefully
and affectionately dedicated to
Mrs. Russell (Kathleen) Smith, librarian at the
Bolton Free Library, Bolton Landing, New York,
who first said, "There ought to be a book—"

Her library expertise and enthusiasm, her interest in,
and love for the Lake George-Bolton Landing area
and its people, past and present, have been a source of
continuous and vital inspiration to the author during
the research and writing of this manuscript.

CONTENTS

PRELUDE

It doesn't seem possible that it was only three and one-half years ago when I first encountered a stranger who has become a very close friend.

It was in the spring of 1975. I looked across the desk of the library in Bolton Landing and heard the same request which I had heard so many times before. The woman who stood there, quietly waiting, wanted information on the former Beckers estate for an article, commissioned by the magazine, ADIRONDACK LIFE. Regretfully, I had to give her the same answer I had given to so many others: while many great and famous people had once owned palatial homes on that ten-mile stretch of road between Lake George Village and Bolton Landing (Millionaires' Row), and while townspeople could tell many tales of these individuals, very little had been written up, and that little, only sketchily. I bewailed this state of affairs to Kathryn O'Brien, as I had done occasionally to others, but this time, my words fell on fertile ground. By the time I had guided Kathryn to the Chairman of the Bolton Historical Society and the two of us had helped her, quite literally, to dig up the facts she needed, a book had been born.

It has been more than just a privilege; it has been a great pleasure to work with Kathryn and to watch her—again and again—probe with tireless energy for the facts needed to put together in one place the answers sought by so many others. I am sure that her book, THE GREAT AND THE GRACIOUS ON MILLIONAIRES' ROW, will answer the inquiries which libraries, historians, and Chambers of Commerce in Lake George Village and Bolton Landing are forever receiving about the colorful individuals who once lived on Millionaires' Row; and that these almost-legendary people will take their rightful place in history as symbolic of an affluent America.

Kathleen L. Smith
Bolton Free Library
November, 1978

ACKNOWLEDGEMENTS

The author wishes to express deep appreciation to those who have given assistance by providing information, either directly or indirectly, in the writing of THE GREAT AND THE GRACIOUS. Without their memories, experiences, knowledge, and generosity in sharing, this book would not have been written. Among the many who have helped are:

Mr. and Mrs. Robert Barnett, Mrs. Emily Beals, John Alden Beals, Mr. and Mrs. Lyman A. Beeman, Sr., Georg Behr, The late Ralph F. Bixby and Mrs. Bixby, John Bowman, Mr. and Mrs. Milton Brickner, Gilbert Burton, Mrs. Leo Campbell, Brian Clements, Mr. and Mrs. Malcolm Cormack, The late Mrs. James Cotherman, The Cullinan Family of Blenheim on the Lake, Sally Bixby Defty, Mrs. Elizabeth De Long, Mr. and Mrs. Walter Dombek, Mrs. Earl Elmore, Mr. and Mrs. Gardner Finley, Robert A. Flacke, Mrs. Ross French, Mrs. F. L. P. Gilmour, Mr. and Mrs. Charles Horne, (Evelyn Tuttle), Dr. and Mrs. John Kelley, Mrs. Cecil Lamb, Michael Lamb, Mrs. Edward Lamb, Mr. and Mrs. Phillip Lamb, Mrs. Howard LaRose, Robert W. Leavitt, Sr., Mrs. Joanne Luke, Mrs. Susanne Lustyik, Mrs. Robert Mackintosh, Mr. and Mrs. Edward Malcolm, Helmut C. Neumann, Mrs. Margaret Norton, The late William Palgut and Mrs. Palgut, The late Delbert Pratt and Mrs. Pratt, Mrs. Thomas Pratt, Julius A. Roethke, Judge James Ross, Mrs. Maude Sampson, Mrs. Sheila Satterlee, Ruth Seaman, James A. Schermerhorn, Joseph "Trip" Sinott, Dora Smith, Joseph Smith, Mrs. Milos Spatney, Mrs. Christo G. Starche, Elsa Steinback, William Stevenson, The Rev. and Mrs. Ernest Van Rensselaer Stires, Rose Stitchman, Mrs. Victor Strom, Mrs. Thaddeus Thomas, Mrs. Robert Thomson, Mrs. Margaret Tucker, Mr. and Mrs. J. Croswell Tuttle, Esko Virta, Mr. and Mrs. Homer Walkup (Charlotte Tuttle), Mrs. Dorothy Webster, Ronald Welton, Mr. and Mrs. Walter Wescott, Hugh Allen Wilson, The late Cyrus Woodbury.

Mrs. Helen Knoblauch, Barneveld, N.Y.; Father and Mrs. George Conger, Ellenville, N.Y.; Mrs. Louis Stires Curtis, Lexington, Mass., Ernest McAneny, Bronx, N.Y.; Dr. Arnold O'Brien, Westford, Mass.; Dr. and Mrs. Jean-Maurice Poitras, Towson, Md.

Reference Librarians: Mrs. Russell Smith, Bolton Free Library; William Crawshaw, Crandall Library, Glens Falls; Mrs. Joyce Henry, Lake George Library; Mrs. Betty McAndrew, Head, Reference Department, Crandall Library, Glens Falls; Sara K. Ruger, Troy Public Library; Ms. Marion Taub, Saratoga Springs Public Library; Mrs. George Truesdale, Hillview Library, Diamond Point.

Historians: Mrs. Philip Walker, Bolton Landing; Mrs. George Truesdale, Town of Lake George; Mrs. Edith Bailey, Village of Lake George.

ADIRONDACK LIFE, Bruce Carman, Ed.; Blue Mountain Lake Museum, Craig Gilborn, Director, Marcia Smith, Asst.; General Electric Company, Schenectady, N.Y.; Glens Falls Historical Society, Joe King, Director; Hyde Museum Personnel, Glens Falls; Lake George Institute, Mrs. Cindy Corbett, Director, Joan Wade, Asst. Director; Clergy of St. Mark's Church, Brooklyn, N.Y.; Department of Parks, New York City; Union College, Schenectady, N.Y.; University of Georgia Press, Malcolm M. MacDonald, Asst. Director and Editor; Sleepy Hollow Chamber of Commerce, Tarrytown, N.Y.; The Isabella Stewart Gardner Museum, Boston, Mass.; The U.S. Geological Survey, Albany, N.Y.; Warren County Publicity Bureau, LeRoy Akins, Director; The Yaddo Corporation, Saratoga Springs, N.Y., Curtis Harnack, Executive Director; Office of the New York Times.

To my late husband, Thomas O'Brien, I owe special appreciation for his infinite patience and cooperation during the writing of the major portion of this book.

And to all others who showed interest in THE GREAT AND THE GRACIOUS, please know that your contribution, no matter how small it may have seemed to you, is deeply appreciated by

THE AUTHOR

INTRODUCTION

In the Post-Civil War period, the rise of technology brought great changes to the American economy: manufacturing in the industrial East was intensified; wagon trains went West carrying settlers bent on making new lives for themselves; inventions revolutionized train-travel as iron rails were replaced by steel, the new Westinghouse air-brake came into being, and Pullman's sleeping and dining-car service became available. Riches poured from the mines, fields, and streams of the great West and were transported East, where New York City held the greatest concentration of power and population.

As America turned from an agricultural past to an industrial future, great fortunes were made by those who were intelligent, energetic, far-seeing and often, ruthless. Fortune played no favorites, welcoming alike the robber barons, the greedy opportunists, and their opposite—the occasional man with the vision to see his own place in history as a catalyst in the distribution and use of resources and power.

There was wealth enough for all who dared to claim it; and, inevitably, those who had garnered great wealth were regarded with awe in the eyes of the less fortunate. With wealth, these persons favored by fortune, could also afford Beauty—perhaps the greatest goal of their striving—in art, and in their surroundings, bending nature into a man-made harmony. In summer they left the cities, which guarded their fortunes, for the ocean, mountains, springs, or lakes. Some came to Lake George in Northern New York State—a lake famed for its beauty since 1642 when Father Isaac Jogues, Indian captive, first saw the shining body of water and, holding up his mutilated hand in blessing, named it Lac du St. Sacrément.

The credentials of the Lake George coterie was impressive, including in their number philanthropists, statesmen, doctors, opera singers, artists, scientists, sportsmen, publishers, financiers and occasionally a spectacular law-breaker—all of national and international reputation. Over the years, these, and more, came to the Lake George area and, since the majority in this migration possessed great wealth, the site of their mansions—the ten-mile shoreline between the villages of Lake George and Bolton Landing—became known as Millionaires' Row.

With a few exceptions, the newcomers' early struggles had awakened in them a social conscience, and the area with its outlook on the world, was made richer by their presence.

If the new arrivals needed an apologist for their wealth, they had one in William Graham Sumner, Professor of Political and Social Science at Yale, who said,

1

"The Millionaires are a product of natural selection acting on the whole body of men to pick out those who can meet the requirement for certain work to be done . . . they get high wages and live in luxury, but the bargain is a good one for society."[1]

But when the vanguard of millionaires appeared at Lake George, some of the old residents were not sure that they had a bargain. A Senior Citizen remembers that her father, watching the building of still another palatial home, complained:

"Daughter, if these summer people keep coming and building along the shore, none of us can even fish in the lake without trespassing on somebody's property." And she had answered happily,

"I don't care; they'll need lots of servants, and I'm going to work for them." Serving the millionaires, musicians, artists, and professional people who resided on this ten-mile drive became the chief summer industry of the area, and men and boys, girls and women, gravitated to their service.

Rewards extended far beyond the sometimes-inadequate salaries. "We never thought of any difference between us and our employers," says our Senior Citizen. "They always included us in any special entertainment and remembered us on holidays. It was hard work, but it was fun, too."

There was no television then to bring the world into the living-room, and those who worked on the estates had the enviable opportunity of seeing—sometimes even meeting—the great men and women of the day. Many village residents made careers as trusted servants of these celebrities, with the assurance of a pension at the end of their years of service.

Further, the wealthy, the beautiful, and the talented, were glamorous in a work-a-day world starved for glamor. Legends that sprang up around them could have come from the pen of that then-popular author, Mary J. Holmes. Some of the legends had their basis in truth; others were pure fantasy, and the two have intermingled until the view of what these people were really like has become blurred.

Today's summer visitors, staying at motels built where elegant mansions once stood, are readily caught up in the spirit of romance and often start their own research by asking innumerable questions. They haunt the local libraries and historical associations seeking answers, and may find that, while some information is available, the answers only spawn more questions.

Out of the desire to know, has come THE GREAT AND THE GRACIOUS. Information not generally known has been found in privately printed, as well as published material. Senior Citizens have supplied reminiscences of the golden decades; members of the present generation

---

[1] The U.S. of America; a history. Vol. II, Dexter Perkins and Glyndon G. Van Deusen, The Macmillan Company, New York, 1962, pp. 128 and 129.

have offered data on their ancestors, and history—minded men and women have given encouragement.

Due to the limitations of space, only a comparatively few can represent the many. Guidelines for their selection indicated: *the place,* Millionaires' Row with Lake George Village as its beginning and Bolton Landing its ending; *the time,* the turn of the century or before, when families had established their residences. Inevitably, there are exceptions: Charles Evans Hughes, a gigantic personality, is included although he was a renter, and not primarily an owner. Harry Watrous, living beyond the arbitrary boundaries, rates mention in *Sidelights* because of his legendary "Monster." Great musicians and world-renowned scientists who socialized with the Wealthy and then returned to relatively humble lakeside dwellings, are an important part of the story.

And so, THE GREAT AND THE GRACIOUS joins the ever-increasing roster of books with a Lake George theme. As long as lake and mountains endure, people will be irresistibly drawn to Lake George where there is beauty to inspire the artist and writer, with the halo of sunrise rimming the mountain-tops, and the glory of sunset on its shining waters.

CHAPTER I

Dr. William Gerard Beckers
Harry Kendall Thaw

(Villa Marie Antoinette)

Driving on the ten-mile stretch of Lakeshore Drive between the Villages of Lake George and Bolton Landing, one sees a succession of motels, often, in mid-summer, displaying the "No Vacancy" sign. It seems incredible that these motels, available to all tourists, stand on sites that were once vast estates owned by people of wealth and prominence, and that the road itself was known as Millionaires' Row. Then, the sign would have read "No Trespassing."

Most of these lakeshore empires made their appearance soon after the end of the Civil War and extended their reign into the 50's, but it was World War I that saw the building of one of the greatest of these opulent mansions. The builder was a native-born German, Dr. William Gerard Beckers, and his creation was an exquisite palace named, for his wife, Villa Marie Antoinette.

Hostilities at the beginning of World War I brought casualties never dreamed of in the economy of the United States; a shortage of adequate dyes. Without the chemicals formerly imported from Germany, American-made dyes were inferior and would literally wash out in the rain. A joke of the period was,

"Is this dye *fast?* You should see it *run!*"

The quiet hero of the hour who revolutionized American dye-making was Dr. Beckers. Born in Germany in 1874, he had graduated from Heidelberg University and served as Professor of Chemistry in the Royal Dye School. As required by law, he served in the German army for a designated period, holding the rank of First Lieutenant. Coming to the United States in 1901, he established a business in the manufacture of dyes, and became a naturalized citizen in 1910. During the war years, the time of America's greatest need, Dr. Beckers' knowledge of dye-making became invaluable. A few years later, his Company merged with four others to become the world-famous Allied Chemical and Dye Corporation.

Now wealthy and successful from his dye business, Dr. Beckers decided that, like the residents of Millionaires' Row, he, too, would build a summer place at Lake George. Searching for the most beautiful spot on the lake, he finally chose a tract of approximately 90 acres on Huddle Bay between Bolton and Diamond Point. Here, between 1916 and 1918, he

5

built his mansion, making it one of the most beautiful and ornate estates in an area of palatial residences.

This was a period in United States' history when war sentiment was acute: the war-fever was spreading and Americans were suffering and dying on foreign soil, or enduring privations at home. German-made goods were destroyed in patriotic fervor; persons with German-sounding names had them legally changed; the German-born, although naturalized, were regarded with suspicion. We can only speculate on the reception Dr. Beckers received in the Adirondack resort community, but rumors, still remembered, show suspicion of the former German Army Lieutenant.

Rumor had it that Dr. Beckers' father was a manufacturer of dyes in Germany, and that Dr. Beckers himself had stolen the dye-making secrets and sold them to the United States Government; that Kaiser Wilhelm had sent the dyeing secrets to the United States with Dr. Beckers, intending to abdicate and come here himself, and that Villa Marie Antoinette was being built as his residence; that there were secret passages on the estates built for evil purposes—probably a cache of arms and ammunition. As for those visitors who occasionally appeared with the builder, they were probably German spies.

There were those who saw only the Heidelberg dueling scar on Dr. Beckers' cheek, his stern "typically Prussian" bearing, and the way he bowed from the waist, clicking his heels in the German military tradition. Others recognized in his building of Villa Marie Antoinette, another side to a complex personality. To them he was not only an industrial chemist, but a man who dared to dream great dreams and make them come true. His Castle in Spain was an actual Spanish villa from which his mansion was copied. There was high adventure in bringing together rare treasures for his creation—fatherly pride in placing the likeness of his daughter, Elsa, in a stained-glass window.

To the disappointment of mystery-lovers, the Kaiser never claimed the Villa, but had he done so, he would have found the mansion, with its magnificent view of Lake George, a suitable retreat. Over $4 million was spent on the estate including the outbuildings and landscaping; approximately ¾ million went into furnishings; the stone wall, which cost $200,000 to build, enclosed acres of green lawns, flower gardens and fountains; Huddle Brook was allowed to follow its natural course across the estate to the lake.

The great house, of stone and concrete construction with stucco overlay, was built around an open courtyard with an ornate fountain. There were 40 rooms in the mansion including 8 baths, the latter done in milk-glass tile brought from Germany. Even in those troubled times, workmen and artists were brought from Europe to carve fireplaces, paint murals, and decorate walls and ceilings. The walls of the conservatory, called the flower-room, were covered with canvas on which views of Lake George were painted. Many floors were of white Italian marble.

The dining-room, said to be the only Wedgwood room in the United States, gleamed with ceiling and wall-panels of delicate porcelain; the carved fireplace, built with lava from Vesuvius, had a screen and andirons of sterling silver; the cut-glass chandelier was purchased at a cost of $12,000 (averaging $10 per prism). Over-all, the dining-room was reputed to have cost $85,000. Throughout the house, ceilings and walls were embossed and decorated with gold-leaf.

In Dr. Beckers' study, the carved fireplace, representing the seven champions of Christendom, was a reproduction of a fireplace in Westminster Abbey; an Estey pipe-organ carried music to every room in the house; curtains made in Italy, and heavy, irreplaceable draperies framed the windows; solid gold sconces decorated the walls; an Aubusson rug, considered priceless, covered one of the largest areas; and, in every room, there was a cut-glass chandelier made by Czechoslovakian craftsmen.

In the library, a tapestry valued at $20,000 hung above a heavily-carved prayer bench; a hand-carved cabinet bore the date 1603. Among rare books and first-editions, was the unique and valuable "Book of Hours," a parchment manuscript illuminated by a 14th-century monk in letters of gold.

Two bowling alleys were constructed in the basement; there was a billiard room; the wine cellar held 1,000 bottles of choice vintages; the heavily-beamed gatehouse was a stable built to hold 20 horses. And, there *were* two underground passages: one led to the lake, the other to the gatehouse.

With the completion of the Villa, Dr. Beckers now considered Bolton his permanent home, and he proceeded to take an active interest in the community. He secured a Post Office for Bolton and, for five years, served as its postmaster; he was instrumental in incorporating the Bolton Rural Cemetery; he built a dam on Huddle Brook, developing a hydro-electric plant designed to serve every home-owner in the community with water; he assisted in re-building and enlarging the Sagamore Hotel destroyed by fire in 1914; he helped organize the Bolton National Bank, and was a developer of the Sagamore Golf Club. He served a seven-year term as first vice-president of the Lake George Club.

All his activities were not on a grandiose scale, and old residents who remember, still tell of his assistance to needy neighbors. It was ironic that one of this empire-builder's most cherished dreams—to change the name of Bolton to Beckersville—would have cost nothing, but this desire found no favor with the community. Mute evidence of his hope and subsequent disappointment was found by later owners in an abandoned sign lettered "Beckersville."

Dr. Beckers lived to see the second World War between his adopted country and Germany and, in 1942–43, he sold the Villa to a most unlikely purchaser, Harry Kendall Thaw.

The new owner was not a quiet man; he was flamboyant. In the early

Dr. W. G. Becker's beautiful estate,
Bolton on Lake George, N.Y.

Entrance—Marie Antoinette Villa

Evelyn Nesbitt (Mrs. Harry K. Thaw)

Marie Antoinette Villa, built by
Dr. William G. Beckers

9

1900's, he had made lurid headlines with the murder of Stanford White but, by 1942, after several sojourns in and out of prison, his presence in Bolton created little interest. Another generation had grown up since his day in the newspapers; another World War had to be dealt with. Only old-timers remembered the aging man as the century's most publicized man-about-town.

Thaw's victim, Stanford White, was an architectural-genius who had designed, among others, the old Metropolitan, the Memorial Arch at Washington Square, Madison Square Garden, buildings at the University of Virginia, and the famed Sherry's in New York City, where elegant women and powerful men made their appearance. Stanford White also had ties with Lake George. He had been commissioned by George Foster Peabody and Spencer Trask, financiers, to design Wakonda Lodge, part of the present Wiawaka Holiday House, Inc. complex. At the time of his death, he was also designing a unique structure on Triuna Island for the Trasks.

White's protégée, Evelyn Nesbit, had started her career at 16 as a model for Charles Dana Gibson, artist, and creator of the Gibson Girl, the Ideal American Girl of the period. She was also one of the girls in the highly publicized Floradora Sextet, a feature of the top hit then playing at the Casino Theater. On stage, six young ladies wearing frilly dresses and picture hats and coquettishly twirling parasols, were joined by six dapper young men in grey cutaways and top hats, singing,

"Tell me, pretty maiden, are there any more at home like you?" and the girls replied, singing,

"There are a few, kind sirs, but simple maids, and proper, too."

Proper or not, Stanford White had been most generous with Evelyn, her mother, and brother. He provided them with a suite of rooms near the Casino Theater, and sent Evelyn to the DeMille School in Pompton, New Jersey.

Due to the popularity of the Floradora Sextet, it was inevitable that the girls in the line would be pursued by wealthy young men, a group which included Harry K. Thaw of Pittsburgh. Heir to a large railroad-and-coke fortune, but with no discernible aim in life, Thaw succeeded in meeting Evelyn; soon after, over the objections of his family, they were married.

Sometime later, Thaw, brooding over Stanford White's former attentions to his wife, planned to remove his hated rival from the scene. The murder took place in 1906 at Madison Square Roof Garden in view of the elite of New York City. Elegant diners looked on in horror as Thaw, approaching White's table, fired three shots at close range and his victim fell to the floor, mortally wounded. Fifty years later, this episode was vividly portrayed in a movie, "The Girl in the Red Velvet Swing," starring Joan Collins, Ray Milland, and Farley Granger.

In the ensuing trial, the red velvet swing figured prominently as evidence of Stanford White's extravagant life. He had lived in the tower of Madison Square Garden; in a hideaway, two flights up from his apartment, was a swing where one could swing up to the ceiling. Drawings showing several red velvet swings, now appeared in the scandal sheets. As imagined by the artist, scantily-clad girls, their laps full of fruit, swung over a long banquet table where White and his friends lounged in satyric splendor. Never before had the public been so entertained by the "goings-on" of the wealthy.

Testifying for the defense, Dr. Britton D. Evans asserted that Thaw had been the victim of a "brain-storm or mental explosion" when he shot White. Ironically, the shots fired by Thaw, while blotting out Stanford White's genius, popularized the word "brain-storm" which has become part of the English language. A less permanent addition to speech was the catch-phrase, "Who's loony now?" which surfaced during the trial and, for a time, was an inescapable part of every smart conversation.

Evelyn, called as a witness, was effective in her wide-eyed innocence. Her appealing beauty, the huge sums of money spent by the Thaw family, and sordid details allegedly describing White's private life, were powerful weapons in the defense. The Jury acquitted Thaw of murder, but committed him to Mattewan on an insanity charge. Nine years later, he was acquitted of all charges.

Opinions varied on the acquittal. One clergyman remarked publicly, "Thaw had the courage to free the world of a moral hypocrite." Others doubted Evelyn's innocence and mourned the loss of White's genius. A professional analyst labeled Thaw a sadistic paranoiac.

The label seemed justified: vicious acts perpetrated by Thaw against both people and animals resulted in his again being judged insane, and he was committed to the mental ward of Pennsylvania State Hospital. During those years when Harry K. Thaw, millionaire, was living in confinement behind iron bars, another millionaire, Dr. William G. Beckers, was building a magnificent estate on the shores of Lake George, which Thaw would one day purchase and occupy.

After spending several years in the State Hospital, Thaw again secured his freedom and, in the early '40's, came to Villa Marie Antoinette as lord of the manor. With the mansion as his headquarters, he enjoyed the resort's entertainment facilities to the full, distributing extravagant tips wherever he went. Townspeople have reported that, every Friday evening during the summer, a New York City bus would bring a number of beautiful girls to Bolton. Met by Thaw, the girls were escorted to the Villa for an eventful weekend. They also tell of a gray-haired Thaw entertaining party-going young men and women at the Sagamore Hotel, and making a grand exit with his usual large tip.

Thaw also became part of the community to the extent of attending church suppers. Gallantly waiting for the church ladies who were serving, he would join them at their table and later cheerfully wash dishes in the kitchen.

"We knew he was half-crazy," admits one of these ladies, "but we liked him."

Villa Marie Antoinette was held by its aging owner for about five years. After his death, in 1947, the estate with its elegance and its memories succumbed to a new day, and it was sold to Earl T. Woodward, Lake George realtor, for a fraction of its cost. A year later, Dr. Beckers died. The end of a period of lavishness was in sight, but Villa Marie Antoinette would still carry on.

Mr. and Mrs. Walter Dombek of Forest Hills, L.I., intended to purchase a summer cottage at Lake George "when the right one came along." One day while they were relaxing on a beach, the "right one" came blowing past in the real estate section of a New York City newspaper. The couple became interested in properties listed by Mr. Woodward, investigated and, some time later, found that they were owners, not of a summer cottage, but of a great mansion named Villa Marie Antoinette.

Because of the organ in the Villa, they chose "Melody Manor" as the name of the restaurant and hotel which the mansion now became. People came here to dine, partly for the excellent food and service, and partly for the experience of seeing the Wedgwood dining-room which had known wealth, power, and finally, madness. However, the Dombeks soon found out that accepting over-night guests was another matter: there were only seven usable bedrooms, each one as big as an average apartment. In the master bedroom, the bed was hung with irreplaceable damask with matching damask draperies at the French windows. Richly embossed doors led to an adjoining tile bath fitted with gold fixtures, and to a mirror-lined dressing room. The other bedrooms were equally lavish, and all had access to sunporch and terrace.

With paying guests occupying the rooms in the Villa, maintenance became urgent and costly. For example, Tiffany asked $750 to clean the dining-room chandelier; all other expenses were in proportion. Even the 40 servants once employed at the Villa could not have handled the work involved in serving the public. Regretfully, the Dombeks decided that Melody Manor, as it then existed, must go. There was some hope of turning the mansion into a museum, but with high taxes and no Foundation to give financial assistance, the idea was abandoned.

An auction was held August 27–29, 1953; all furnishings were for sale, and everything rare, beautiful, and priceless passed into the hands of shrewd buyers. Then the wrecking crews moved in and, finally, the great house died a violent death by explosives. Music died, too; an estimate of $35,000 to move the Estey organ with its complicated sound system was prohibitive so, inevitably, the organ became part of the sacrifice.

Around Bolton, they still talk about the auction. Someone wonders where the furnishings and art objects are now; someone else recalls that one of the gold and Wedgwood door-knobs brought a bid of $250. In retrospect, the door-knob becomes symbolic of the passing of time, for on that August day in 1953, a door to the past was closing, and the auctioneer's cry, "Going . . . going . . . gone!" marked the End of an Era.*

*This chapter, which appeared in somewhat different form in *Adirondack Life,* Fall, 1975, copyright 1975 by *Adirondack Life,* is reprinted by permission.

CHAPTER II

Two Great Hotels:

(The Fort William Henry—The Sagamore)

For generations, a hotel stood at the head of Lake George; and during the same period, another hotel stood at Bolton Landing, the end of ten miles of shore line, and the beginning of a forbidding pass over Tongue Mountain.

In the early days of the 19th century, hotels, or inns, served a vital purpose for men in the lumbering business, for the drivers who carried lumber to the mills, the businessmen who dickered for lumber, or the laborers who wielded the axes. Those who worked needed food, drink, and rest, and they wanted plain accommodations without frills. Gradually, the inns added visitors to their registers, then vacationists. The lumber business dwindled, as what had once been an abundance of lumber became scarcity. As far as one could see, the hills were stripped of trees, in fact, before a conservation movement began, the Adirondacks had been cut over, from three to five times.

Lavish hotels had already made their appearance in other parts of the country, and at Saratoga Springs, the elegant hostelries provided every conceivable form of luxury for their patrons. Traveling further north for recreation, summer tourists at Lake George demanded and finally got, the latest in conveniences, the ultimate in decor, and the serving of the most exquisite food.

In 1854–55, a hotel was built at the head of Lake George. The builders had formed a stock company headed by a Mr. Thomas, and the hotel was called Fort William Henry after the fort of French and Indian War fame that once stood near the site of the hotel. The new establishment opened in 1855 under the management of Dan Gale and was an immediate success. Several years later, Dan Gale, as sole owner, sold the hotel to T. Roessle & Sons of Albany, New York, at a price reported to be $125,000. The new owners proceeded to enlarge and reconstruct the existing structure in line with the overwhelming hotels in other summer resorts.

The new version of the Fort William Henry was from four to six stories in height; there was a tower at each end, and the edifice was capped with a flat-and-vertical roof that extended over the edge, the invention of M. Mansarde of Paris. The porch where, on pleasant days, the guests gathered, was 25 feet wide and extended the entire length of the hotel, a distance of 343 feet. An observation balcony in the center of an upper story afforded a view of the lake down Northwest Bay and into the Narrows, a site chosen later by Dr. William G. Beckers, a resident of Millionaires' Row, as the most beautiful view on the lake.

In the foyer of this huge hotel, the decor was white and gold. Many of the necessities of civilized life were available here; stage companies dispensed tickets and time schedules; there was a telegraph office to serve those tycoons and plungers who kept in close touch with their various businesses and stock market quotations were received hourly; cigar shops and book stands served the hotel patrons, and an immense dining room faced the northeast with a view of lake and mountains.

The furnishings were massively carved, in the heavy, dark wood of the period. Rooms were lighted by that miracle element, gas, and the gas was manufactured on the grounds of the hotel. Everything possible was done to make the stay of the visitor pleasant and relaxing; and when he was leaving, a stage coach on one of three daily runs, drew up to the door to take him to his destination.

The hotel management planned many activities for the enjoyment of their guests. For the gentlemen, there was a billiard room, cards, and always, the bar. The ladies gathered on the famous porch to discuss themselves, their gowns, and each other, or to promenade between each of the three hearty meals. (The bar was, of course, off limits to the ladies.) For both sexes, there was the three-times-a-day diversion of watching new arrivals dismount from the stage coach, the excitement of appraising him or her, and estimating the visitor's probable place in hotel society.

Steamers took passengers on daily excursions down the lake, and there were frequent dances and balls arranged by the management of the hotel. Romance flourished at the summer hotel, and usually there was a discreet amount of flirtation in progress. The atmosphere was ideal for husband-hunting, and to that end, there was constant dressing up among the ladies, in the billowy, bouffant style of the day. Another diversion was the novel experience of drinking tea on Tea Island. On sunny afternoons, patrons of the Hotel were rowed about a mile down the lake to the Island. Here they were welcomed to a small tea-house built near the shore. It was reported, perhaps by a canny manager, that General Abercrombie of French and Indian War fame, had buried treasure on the island; this conversation piece often inspired the guests to dig, seeking in vain for the cache.

Other pastimes included a ride in a lumber wagon up Prospect Mountain for a picnic and the view, or a visit to the ruins of Old Fort William Henry on the hotel grounds, a relic of the French and Indian War with the outlines of the old fort still visible. Another relic of the "French Wars" was the old well built by Rogers' Rangers in the mid-1700's to serve the soldiers at the fort; inevitably, to the guests, it became a wishing well.

On Thursday evenings, the hotel management arranged a grand hop which was an event of great importance to young ladies and their hopeful mothers. An orchestra played for dancing, and refreshments were served with style and grace. Between 9 and 10 o'clock, the doors of the great dining room were thrown open and a number of servants entered with trays of ice cream and cake. The luxury, the view, and the assurance that people meeting each other here belonged to the same social strata, attracted a large and exclusive clientele. The price of elegant rooms, sumptuous meals, and planned social events was probably quite high by standards of that time. For comparison, a list of prices charged at Lake George hotels in 1872, gives the rates at Trout Pavilion, oldest hotel on the lake, as $10–$15 per week. On the same list, Fort William Henry's rate is marked "special"; this could only mean that its rates were somewhat higher than average.

But with the hotel's clientele, their fortunes fluctuated, and millions were made or lost over-night. "Old" money became "New" money in the closing years of the last century. Men who had made quick fortunes came to the hotel, often advertising their wealth by the jewels worn by their wives and daughters. Sometimes such a patron failed to return the following summer, and the men in the bar marked the absence of poor old-so-and-so who had, unfortunately, guessed wrong in his investments and, had to sell his wife's jewelry to meet his mortgage payments.

The hotel burned in 1908, but was rebuilt as soon as possible and the Fort William Henry which now arose was a model of elegant simplicity. Smaller and less flamboyant than its predecessor, its outer construction was white stucco with a red tiled roof. A vast marble-pillared porch faced the lake; under its hospitable roof, tea was often served so that guests might sip their tea and enjoy the view at the same time.

A unique feature of the new Fort William Henry was the pergola. To reach the pergola with its cement and marble construction, the hotel visitor followed the walkway leading from the porch of the hotel to a landing built over the road, its walls bright with geraniums and trailing ivy. Short flights of steps took him to the pergola itself, extending over the water. Here, framed in colonnades and arches, he could catch vistas of the lake, order refreshments from a hovering waiter, or, finding a partner, dance to the strains of the resident orchestra. He, or probably, she could stroll through a block of exotic shops that edged the lake and were accessible from the pergola, finding rare and expensive articles for sale. It was generally understood that the pergola was primarily for guests of the hotel, but the public was not unwelcome. Perhaps the high prices charged for the goods and services were considered sufficient to ensure the quality of the hotel's clientele.

In the fall of 1913, Albert Thieriot, manager of the Fort William Henry, asked himself, "Why not keep the hotel open all winter?" The most evident "why not" was the indisputable fact that compared with other winter resorts, Lake George's snow supply is often scanty; but that year proved the exception, and young men and women flocked to the hotel for the fun and excitement of skating, reveling in 15 foot snowdrifts, sleighing, and often, for the plain, old-fashioned rites of getting warm before a blazing fireplace and sipping hot drinks.

"There is little doubt," exulted the *Lake George Mirror* published June 27, 1914, "that for many years to come, the 'Fort House' under the auspices of Jack Frost, Albert Thieriot, et. al., will be a year 'round hotel and attract to its doors some of the best people of the land, thereby bringing fame and profit to the region." But, due to the outbreak of World War I and less snowfall, the hotel's management never again experienced the rush of that first enthusiasm. However, over the years, the "best people" referred to by the Mirror, continued to patronize the Fort William Henry.

But exclusiveness was going out of style. Following two World Wars, a quiet revolution had set in. With the spending power of the multitudes increasing, it was evident that no longer would the shores of Lake George with its mansions and luxury hotels be reserved only for the super-rich. In haste, mansions were remodeled, or ruthlessly torn down to make room for the more democratic motels; establishments in the lake shore villages blared with the raucous noise of their "attractions." The leveling process had set in, and only the lake remained aloof and serene.

Today, the grounds of the Fort William Henry house a row of motel units. Fortunately, the hotel, which was partially razed, has kept its beautiful old-style dining room where several hundred people can be served at one time; and the view of the lake, seen through its wide windows, is still a thing of beauty.

THE SAGAMORE

The reputation of a hotel is often built on the personality of its manager. Myron O. Brown, manager of the Mohican House on Lake George had made such an outstanding success of his position that, when he was unable to renew his lease on that hotel, he found backing for his own venture. Four millionaires from Philadelphia, E. Burgess Warren, William B. Bement, Robert Glendenning, and George Burnham, who had spent several summers at the Mohican House, decided to finance him in a hotel of his own.

The choice of a site fell on Green Island, close to the shore at Bolton Landing. The island had previously sold for $600, but with the growing demand for Lake George property, the price had advanced to $30,000. The four men who had formed the Green Island Improvement Company, bought the site, and Myron O. Brown started building his hotel. Another investor, John Boulton Simpson of New York City, joined the group and ultimately became president of the Company.

Opening on July 1, 1883, the Sagamore attracted the wealthy and famous from all over the world. Spaciousness and luxury were emphasized in the hotel's construction. The architecture was vaguely reminiscent of 16th century England, but its great size was expansively American. The hotel, several stories in height, was built on a number of different levels, so that the view from the windows and numerous porches was always changing; the corridors connecting the levels were wide open to the sun and to the view. The interior construction showed massive beams, both ornamental and useful; the many fireplaces were made of terra cotta; walls were tinted in delicate colors, and the dark, polished woodwork suggested elegant simplicity. The general office, grand hall, and luxurious parlors were on the first floor. Windows framed lawns and flower-bordered walks shaded by tall trees and, beyond, an incomparable view of the lake and its islands. The upper floors contained the sleeping rooms lavishly furnished with conveniences available at that time; some rooms opened on private balconies.

All this luxury was available to the public for a mere $17.50–$25.00 per week; but with clerks earning from $1.25 to $6.00 per week, the prices were still exclusive.

The investors had built their own cottages on the island, and more would follow. "Bellvue" was completed and would later be occupied by Col. T. E. Roessle of Albany, owner of the Fort William Henry Hotel. John Boulton Simpson's "Nirvana" was a showplace; E. Burgess Warren had built "Wapanak," and George Burnham's summer home was generally called the East Cottage. The term "cottage" was a whimsical misnomer used by the very wealthy in Saratoga and other leading resorts to designate an ornate mansion in a rural setting.

Ten years later, on June 27, 1893, the Sagamore burned. There was no way to stop the fire which, starting in the hotel's laundry, roared through open corridors, and more leisurely devoured the hotel's massive wooden construction. Due to the slow spread of the flames in some quarters, it was possible to rescue a quantity of personal property and some of the furnishings; but the luxury and beauty of Sagamore I, a smoking ruins, was gone forever.

Work on Sagamore II began at once and one year later, another hotel opened its doors on the former site. The new Sagamore rose to three and four stories with a roofed-over porch on three sides of the structure. Dormer windows, fluted chimneys, balconies, and even a tower, suggested that magnificence had returned to the hostelry at Green Island. Spaciousness was again emphasized, with other sections of the hotel added on at the back, equal in size and height to the main structure. A curving driveway swept up to the front of the hotel past small, newly-planted trees and others somewhat larger that had survived the former fire.

The builders had taken the opportunity to install then-modern conveniences. These were listed in a later advertisement appearing in the Lake George Mirror on August 6, 1898. Myron O. Brown was given as Lessee and Proprietor, and improvements to the hotel included electric

The Sagamore, Lake George

A VIEW OF
THE SAGAMORE
FROM THE WHARF

18

THE TEA TERRACE

A CHILDREN'S PARTY

At the Sagamore

19

lights, steam elevators, private bath rooms, billiard rooms, bowling alley, reading rooms, and ladies' parlors. Evidently Mr. Brown was fulfilling his pledge to make the new Sagamore the finest resort hotel in the world.

Sagamore II carried on for 20 years and, on Easter Sunday morning, 1914, burned with a loss of $350,000—a third of this amount was covered by insurance. The Lake George Mirror, issue of June 27, 1914, mourned ". . . That it will ever be rebuilt in its former spaciousness and magnificence is very doubtful; in fact, quite unlikely."

Careless smoking was blamed for the fire; there was also a rumor of arson. The members of the Corporation steadfastly refused to accept the latter theory, believing that no one could possibly want to destroy a hotel of such magnificence and beauty. Another doubt arose at this time: it was generally believed that the building of another Sagamore hinged on the Corporation's ability to construct a golf course for the use of hotel patrons. This was a definite problem, since most of the land in the vicinity was unsuited for a golf course, and any land that was suitable was unavailable.

There was one bright spot in the whole disaster, and the management found some hope in utilizing it: during the previous year, a large building had been erected on the island for the use of the help. This building was equipped with most facilities, and while it was plain, it was acceptable. The enterprising members of the Corporation, sparked by Mr. Brown's presence, undertook the task of fitting up the building with a kitchen and dining room for the use of the summer colony; there were even a few rooms for over-night guests. The summer patrons accepted the makeshift arrangement gratefully, and life went on with some adjustments. The question of where to build a golf course was answered by purchasing land on Federal Hill a few miles from the Sagamore and constructing an excellent course.

One member of the summer colony who was dissatisfied with the makeshift accommodations was Ernest Van Rensselaer Stires, son of the Rt. Rev. Ernest Millmore Stires. In the belief that the summer residents deserved something better in a clubhouse, young Mr. Stires launched a campaign to erect a more suitable—if smaller—Sagamore.

At that time, John Boulton Simpson was a heavy stockholder in the Green Island Improvement Company and he, too, was anxious to build. Impressed by Mr. Stires' enthusiasm, he suggested a spectacular business deal: Mr. Stires would take over the Green Island Improvement Company for the duration of the project and post a completion bond. If he could have the hotel finished and open for business by June 20, 1922, the bond would be returned and the stock would be his.

Ernest Stires had worked as an architect in an uncle's office, and his interest in the proposed building was genuine. He accepted the terms of the agreement with the support and encouragement of his father, and, in order to supervise the work, rented the Burnham Cottage on Green

Island. As consulting architect, he worked with Robert Rhinelander, Architect/Contractor of Glens Falls, and the work went forward. By mid-June, 1922, Mr. Stires had fulfilled his part of the bargain and received the promised stock. By the fall of that year, the hotel had a $6,000 profit with which to pay the interest of the stockholders.

Those who flocked to the grand opening found a new clubhouse of 100 rooms with 50 or more baths. The spacious lounge measured 30 x 54 feet, the porch was 15 x 55 feet with a number of 24-foot columns, 20 inches in diameter. The clubhouse was handsomely furnished with mahogany furniture, carpets and drapes, all installed by M. L. C. Wilmarth, owner of a furniture store in Glens Falls and a summer resident himself. The dining room had a view of the lake on three sides and was joined by a children's dining-room.

One who considered the new clubhouse only as a start in the right direction was Dr. William G. Beckers, owner of Villa Maria Antoinette, a palatial summer home at Bolton. With firm belief in an ever-expanding future for the area, he foresaw the need for a large hotel to serve the public as well as the summer residents. A few years later when the position of manager of the clubhouse was open, Dr. Beckers, now a major stockholder, took the opportunity to summon Karl Abbott, a hotelman famed for his successful operation of both Northern and Southern hotels, to come and survey the situation.

Mr. Abbott, used to the grandeur and luxury of Florida hotels and the sheer size of Northern resorts, inspected the property and indicated that he preferred managing a larger hotel; but he was a man who liked a challenge, and he suggested to Dr. Beckers,

"I'll run this place for a season. If I make as much profit as you have lost in the past season, it's agreed that you will build me a 200-room hotel on this site, and I'll manage it. How's that?"

"Fine," Dr. Beckers agreed heartily, sure that members of the Corporation would concur. To him, the future of the Sagamore was worth any gamble.

That summer, a catering service was inaugurated at the Sagamore providing food for parties, picnics, and banquets. The superb cuisine delighted the party-giving residents, and the profits accumulated. Mr. Abbott had won the bet as he had anticipated, and on October 1, 1929, the work of enlarging the clubhouse to double capacity began.

The building progressed daily and towards the end of October, the frame of this huge structure was up. It there had been any indication that the greatest stock market crash in history was about to occur, work would have been slowed, or perhaps would never have been started. On October 29, 1929, the Stock Market Crash marked the end of post-war prosperity. In panic, 16 million shares of stock changed hands in one day; for many, their savings, resulting from their life's work, had been swept away. By the end of the year, the value of stocks would decline $15

Old Fort William Henry

812 Fort William Henry Hotel & Cottages, Lake George, N.Y.

The "Porch" at the Ft. William Henry, 25' by 343'

billion; over two years, the losses would amount to $50 billion. It was the end of opulence for many who had considered themselves fabulously wealthy.

Construction on the Sagamore stopped; there was no money with which to buy materials; credit suddenly tightened.

"The building has to go on," Mr. Abbott told himself. Once involved in the project, he was determined that it would be finished. Resolutely, he went to see Dr. Beckers in New York City. He found that the Doctor was neither shocked nor panicked, but cautious. Taking a practical view of the situation, he told Mr. Abbott that construction on the Sagamore would have to wait.

Mr. Abbott pleaded his case: without immediate action, all the money and labor that had gone into the building so far would be lost. The enlarged hotel was needed for the prosperous times that were sure to return to the resort area. Dr. Beckers considered, then said thoughtfully,

"Go ahead and order the materials; they will be paid for."

Mr. Abbott didn't ask how. He merely said, "I admire your courage, sir," and left.

His next move was made on impulse. He was in the train station near the ticket window when a stranger rushed up and bought a ticket for St. Louis. Something clicked in Mr. Abbott's brain . . . St. Louis. William H. Bixby, son of the millionaire summer resident of Bolton lived in St. Louis. The hunch impelled Mr. Abbott to buy a ticket for the mid-western city, and once there, to search out the office of Mr. Bixby.

He found the wealthy man receptive, sympathetic, and also cautious. The Lake George area held great meaning for him as the place loved by members of his family, generally known as the Bixby Clan. He considered the problem from every angle, then said kindly,

"Come back tomorrow and you'll have the money."

What messages went back and forth over the telephone lines between Mr. Bixby in St. Louis and Dr. Beckers in New York City, Karl Abbott never knew. He only knew that the next morning, a check for an amount large enough to finish construction of the Sagamore was waiting on Mr. Bixby's desk. Later, he heard that stock in the Sagamore Corporation owned by Dr. Beckers had passed into Mr. Bixby's hands.

Work progressed all that winter, and by spring, Sagamore III was nearly completed. Elegant and inviting, it seemed, outwardly, a worthy successor to the two hotels—and a clubhouse—that had gone before; but inside, 100 additional rooms stood bare of furnishings of any kind. The depression had tightened its grip, and both credit and money were scarce. Once again, fate intervened in the person of M. L. C. Wilmarth, who came forward to furnish the bare rooms with elegance, good taste, and, on generous terms.

In the next few weeks, the hotel was finished and furnished, and the grand opening of a new and beautiful Sagamore took place on July 1, 1930. To the summer colony, the Sagamore was a second home; to the boating populace, the huge white hotel with its massive pillars was a landmark—a palace shining in the sun by day, and glowing with innumerable lights at night.

Among the residents of the area whom Mr. Abbott welcomed to the Sagamore was George Foster Peabody. At this period in his life, Mr. Peabody still held property at Warm Springs, Georgia, although he had sold the springs themselves to Franklin Delano Roosevelt. The sanitarium and cottages at the old health resort were shabby and run down, but Mr. Roosevelt had firm faith in the curative properties of the waters and approached Mr. Peabody with an idea . . .

One day, early in the Presidential Campaign of 1932, Mr. Abbott received a call from Mr. Peabody, which may have gone something like this,

"Karl, Mr. Roosevelt and I are thinking about building a hotel here at Warm Springs. This used to be a great resort before the Civil War, and we think it could be built up again. We'd like to discuss plans with you . . ."

After Mr. Abbott had hung up the receiver, he considered: "Suppose Roosevelt is elected president; he'll have only a four-year term; then he might lose interest." And here Mr. Abbott's fine instinct for successful ventures deserted him. "Dealing with a politician is too uncertain; I'd better refuse the offer," he decided.

Later, he mourned over his lost opportunity, "If I had only known that FDR would be elected for four terms—"

The Sagamore continued to serve the public: those who were famous and those who came to look at them; those who wore their wealth quietly, and those who wished to be thought wealthier than they were.

Not all the hotel's activities were sophisticated, however. In the late 30's, the Sagamore staged a week-end house party that had all the nostalgic trimmings of the Good Old Days. Now the hotel became Ye Olde Sagamore; costumes came from New York City, and the guests came from wherever they happened to be.

"We wouldn't miss it!" they exclaimed, arriving by horse and buggy. The electricity was turned off by choice; oil lamps and candles furnished the illumination. The powder room became a "water closet," and the guests took part in hay rides and barn dances; they popped corn and played charades in the big parlors. The fun time was reminiscent of Mr. Abbott's own boyhood—a tribute to his early days in a small New Hampshire hotel.

Although the Sagamore was open to the public, it was also a place where the elite of Millionaires' Row chose to entertain their friends. For example, glancing at the social column of the *Lake George Mirror* for August 1, 1931, we find that,

*Old Tallyho which ran from Glens Falls
to Lake George—Ft. Wm. Henry Hotel*

Foyer—Old Ft. William Henry

Old Minne-Ha-Ha

What is left of Ft. William Henry Hotel

A weekly putting contest on the Sagamore lawn was a successful event. Observers, sitting at tea tables under flowered umbrellas, were served tea after the game;

An informal party was given in the hotel grill by Dr. William G. Beckers of New York City, who was spending the summer at his beautiful home, Villa Marie Antoinette;

An informal dinner party was also given by Dr. Willy Meyer, the famous New York surgeon, for his close friends and relatives;

The Saturday night dance, a weekly event, was a huge success, with dancers spilling out on the stone terrace;

And a seven-year-old youngster had been given a birthday party complete with a gorgeously decorated birthday cake.

Obviously, at the Sagamore, members of the summer colony relaxed with their families and friends. Harmony was achieved by the management through careful screening so deft that the general public hardly realized they were being screened. The word, "discrimination" when used, then followed the dictionary meaning, "the power of making nice distinctions." A society whose membership included Adolph S. Ochs, Alfred Stieglitz, Dr. Jacobi, Dr. Willy Meyer, and others of the Jewish faith, would have been horrified at the thought of a discrimination based on prejudice.

Yet, Mr. Ochs may have been acting in the best interest of other Jewish people when he advised a certain cultural group to entrench themselves elsewhere. Evidently, he believed that an influx of one segment of the population could initiate prejudice against them all.

Customs, attitudes, and laws have undergone wide-spreading changes, but the Sagamore has weathered them all. Today, the hotel still stands on Green Island facing an always-incomparable view, and in its vast dining room where mirrored walls still reflect sparkling chandeliers to infinity, the aging hotel retains the power to charm the most jaded convention-goer.

CHAPTER III

Col. Walter W. Price

(Upper Price Place—Lower Price Place)

Walter W. Price was born in England in the early part of the 19th century. He grew up with the indifferent education available to boys whose families were on the fringes of poverty, and as a young man, worked as a laborer in the exporting business. He married, then at some point decided to come to America alone—a decision which became desperate when a young woman began causing him difficulties. He escaped by taking passage on a ship bound for the New World and its glittering promise of wealth which, in his case, proved to be true. Ultimately, he became one of his country's most financially successful—but notorious—exports.

In New York City, he found work with a coal company, selling coal from door to door. Work in a brewery came next. The Company was thriving, and Walter soon found an opportunity to exercise his aggressive talents. Finding a $3,000 mistake in the books, he so impressed the president of the Company that he gave the bright young man a better position with a raise in salary. Using his new position as a springboard, in six months, Walter Price owned the Company. In a short time, he was exercising a monopoly over all breweries in a wide area and established The Empire Brewery. His new status brought him in touch with a number of desirable ladies—probably wealthy—and according to Court records, he married several of them in succession. The records also show that, in correspondence with his wife in England, he professed to believe that his English marriage was invalid; later events cried out "bigamy,"—a circumstance which caused newspapers to brand him "the Bluebeard of North America." Yet this was the same man who gave $50 to any child whose parents named him "Walter Price."

By the mid-1860's, the Adirondacks had become fashionable as a playground for the very wealthy. Luxurious mansions were built deep in the mountains where tycoons, their families, friends, and servants could carry on the rustic life in luxury. Price chose Lake George as the site of his estate, and commissioned the famous architect, Isaac Hobbs, to design his mansion overlooking the lake. Price Manor, also called the "Upper Price Place," is now the site of Twin Birches, a summer resort. A fountain formerly on the Price estate is still in use here. The Lower Price Place, an English Tudor house built by William J. Price, Son of the Colonel stands impressively at the junction of the present Northway and the Bolton Road; it is privately owned.

At the time of the Colonel's arrival, T. Roessle and Sons of Albany, New York, and Washington, D.C. were negotiating with Dan Gale for the purchase of the Fort William Henry, a hotel at the head of Lake George. The deal was consummated at a price reputed to be $125,000, and a building program was instituted which, when completed, made the hotel outstanding in size and lavishness. Documents show that Price's money underwrote the project; he was also backer of the historic Arlington Hotel in Washington, D.C.

The Upper Price Place became a show-place. In Stoddard's Guidebook published in 1873, the author writes glowingly of the magnificent residence:

> "Now on the left at the water's edge, is a gaily painted pagoda-like summer-house; following up the graded lawn to the west, near the summit of the hill, we see the elegant summer residence of Col. W. W. Price, one of the finest buildings of the kind in the country."[1]

The title "Colonel" was a mark of distinction, not necessarily signifying military service. In Price's case, he had earned the right to be called Colonel by outfitting an entire Company in the Union Army.

The last Madame Price, Constance (Bridget) Fallon, was said to be an upstairs maid in the Price establishment whom the Colonel married and elevated to the position of hostess. Two daughters born to them, were said to be deaf-mutes. They were named Nellie and Lillie Minne-ha-ha.

"They were not deaf-mutes," insists Mrs. Robert Mackintosh, granddaughter of Lillie. "My grandmother was completely deaf, but I've heard her utter sounds which resembled words." She doesn't remember much about great-aunt Nellie; apparently this pathetic little girl who was disliked by her father, was ignored by the rest of the world as well. Lillie achieved a certain fame at an early age when a steamer, "The Lillie M. Price," bore her name. Captained by E. White, this was one of several steamers which, at that time, made excursions from Lake George Village through the Narrows and back to its starting point. According to Stoddard, specifications for the "Lillie," were: 6 ft. of draft, length 61 ft., and 14 ft. in the beam. The boat had become very popular with tourists.

As host in his mansion, Col. Price entertained lavishly, and at the sumptuous dinners which he gave, the wine flowed freely. As the years progressed, the Colonel began to drink more heavily, but none of his guests had the bad manners to notice or criticise. The term "alcoholism" and all it now implies was unknown. Good liquor was considered part of the good life, and wine was as common as tea. Possibly alcohol was at the root of one of his public quarrels with his wife, Constance. She had slapped Lillie for some misdemeanor, and to the embarrassment of their guests. Col. Price, furious, bellowed, "If you touch that child again, it will be your last day in this house."

---

[1] Lake George: Stoddard. Weed Publishing Company, Albany, New York, 1873, p. 66.

Price Manor—built by Col. Walter Price

Among the servants who worked closely with the Colonel, it was whispered that he was indeed acting strangely. Hadn't he caused a hole to be bored from the cellar into the dining-room above?

"Why did he do that?" the newest maid inquired.

"To watch his wife," was the whispered explanation. His method was to excuse himself from a banquet on the pretext of going to the wine cellar to select an excellent vintage; once there, he could survey the scene above from the peep-hole. From this vantage point, it was explained, the Colonel hoped to detect any hand-holding indulged in by Mrs. Price and the gentlemen seated at her right and left.

Apparently, the current Mrs. Price was in disfavor and about to lose her status as mistress of the mansion. One evening, in what seems to have been further indication of imminent change, the Colonel sent Mrs. Price upstairs with Nellie; he then left the house with Lillie, a driver, and a maid. Rumor says that the child was taken to a refuge in New Jersey. Later, Lillie was returned, and both children lived at Price Manor with their father during their growing-up years. Their mother, living at the Price residence in New York City, undoubtedly visited her daughters occasionally.

Following the Colonel's death in 1876, legal battles grew intense as numerous heirs, issues of his former marriages, appeared to claim their inheritance and the last Mrs. Price, although "illegal," made valiant efforts to obtain funds for herself and the two deaf children through the Courts. After many stormy sessions, she was successful, and a settlement was made on each of the daughters.

The tangled life of Col. Price is buried in legal documents, where the accusations of his opponents are hardly complimentary. His philosophy was evidently that of the exploiter and the opportunist, yet his contribution to Lake George in the rebuilding of the Fort William Henry Hotel was substantial. He must have given time and money to St. James' Church, as he was asked to become a vestryman, an honor usually reserved for leading citizens of unquestioned character. Evidently, he accepted the position as his name appears on the roster of vestrymen.

After Price Manor was no longer "home" to the Price heirs, it passed to other owners. In 1891, George Foster Peabody and his two brothers, Royal and Charles J., bought the mansion to make a home for their mother. Alterations heightened the beauty of the house and laid the ghosts of tragedy that still haunted it.

Here the story of Col. Price stops, but a romantic tale about Lillie lives on: a persistent rumor has it that Lillie, who was over 21 years of age in 1892, went to England where she married the Duke of Devonshire. Only a few years later, the reputable *Lake George Mirror* was pointing with pride to Price Manor as the place where the "duchess grew up."

Such a story was not hard to believe at that time. Many American girls were marrying royalty: Jennie Jerome and Lord Randolph Churchill were a notable example, and Lake George had its own royalty in the person of the Countess Mankowski, an American girl. But Mrs. Mackintosh, hearing only recently of her possible connection with English royalty through Lillie, was astounded, and quickly produced evidence to the contrary.

She insists that, in 1892, at about the age of 21, her grandmother, Lillie Minne-ha-ha Price, married Adolph Pfeiffer, a professional lithographer from Bavaria who had been in America long enough to achieve distinction. He was one of the founders of the Union League for the Deaf, and it was at this institution that Lillie and Adolph first met. Mrs. Mackintosh has in her possession the copper plate from which the Price-Pfeiffer wedding invitations were engraved. Old newspaper articles describe the wedding; there is also a receipted bill for a hotel room in Niagara Falls where the couple spent part of their wedding trip. A picture of Lillie taken at this time, shows a poised young woman with lovely features and stately bearing. She was also an artist, and Mrs. Mackintosh produced several china plates painted by Lillie which show definite talent.

While rumors were spreading in the Lake George-Bolton area about a foreign alliance, in England, events were also happening in the House of Devonshire. *Burke's Peerage* shows that in 1892, the eighth Duke of Devonshire, Compton Spencer, (b. 1833), married the Countess Louise Frederike Auguste; she died in 1911. Also in 1892, the 9th Duke of Devonshire, Victor Christian William, married Lady Evelyn FitzMaurice; he was Governor General of Canada from 1916–21. The rumor and the reality resemble a jig-saw puzzle with the question, where does Lillie fit into this picture, still to be answered. However, as puzzle-and rumor-fans will tell you, there is always one last piece or bit of evidence which completes the picture. Possibly someone may yet find the missing link which will solve the puzzle for everyone.

CHAPTER IV

George Foster Peabody

(Abenia)

He was tall and carried himself erectly; his aquiline and sensitive features were, in later life, partly concealed by a mustache and goatee, but his dark eyes sparkled with intelligence and intense love of life. He was reserved, but his very presence radiated power, and his self-confidence inspired confidence in others. Although the time of his greatest business activities coincided with that of the "robber barons," his basic honesty refutes the term, and he is best remembered as a contributor to the development of his country's resources. Following the Civil War, he amassed a large personal fortune, then made an additional career of giving it to worthy causes. Financier, philanthropist, friend of great men and women, he was also a romantic who loved one nearly-unattainable lady all his life.

George Foster Peabody was born July 27, 1852, in Columbus, Georgia, where his father ran a general store. Residents of the South at the time, both parents were transplanted Yankees who had come from Connecticut for business reasons. Young George had no formal schooling until he was ten years old; his mother taught him to read, and as a young child, he had read the Old Testament completely through. After his tenth birthday he was sent to a school which was operating in Columbus.

These were years when there was unrest and bitter dissension between the states on both economic and moral grounds. George was used to seeing slaves bought and sold; blacks helped his mother in the kitchen. All this seemed normal and natural to the child; it was the way things were done.

When the Civil War broke out, the life of the community changed. The mills in the area were making ammunition for the war; there was inflation, but it brought no great economic suffering for a time. Then the fighting pressed closer and, in 1864, Sherman marched through Georgia to the sea. On one day of horror, word came over the telegraph lines that Atlanta, 125 miles to the north, was in flames. Fear gripped the populace; small children, wide-eyed and uncomprehending, felt the anxiety; bewildered refugees started drifting into town.

George Foster Peabody never forgot that day; its effects colored his thinking throughout his life. The family had gathered around the table for a hastily-prepared meal: his father, the muscles of his face still under

34

firm control, his mother, tight-lipped, anxious, the children, healthily hungry, but with a sense of foreboding. Suddenly, the door was burst open and a company of Northern soldiers crowded into the room. There were several curt orders, a few hints of violence for non-compliance, then the soldiers sat down, ate, and finally left.

For two days, they heard the sound of fighting in the streets outside their home: the shouts of men, the rumble of wagons, sporadic shots, and the smoke of burning buildings filtered into the house. When the fury of the fighting had subsided, they went outside and found that their house was one of the few buildings left standing in the town. George's father went to check his store and found it looted, the building partially destroyed.

Despair did not keep them down very long. Through sheer necessity, Mr. Peabody and his neighbors started clearing away the rubble that had been their town and laying the foundations for new buildings. Neither did this set-back, serious as it was, alter the family's plans for George's schooling. In the fall of 1865, he and his brother, Charles, were sent to Danbury, Connecticut, where they were enrolled in Deer Hill Institute.

This experience lasted only a few months. Mr. Peabody soon found that, with the scarcity of goods, and high prices, he was unable to make a living with his store; the family moved to Brooklyn; the boys were taken out of school, and George went to work.

From that time on, the life of young George Foster Peabody could have been the inspiration for a Horatio Alger novel. Starting as an errand boy with a mercantile firm, he was made clerk, then bookkeeper. In two years, he was working for a firm based in Boston, importing luxury fabrics. He went through the financial panic of 1873, and learned economics from hard experience.

Realizing the necessity for an education, George sought and found a substitute for the schooling which circumstances had denied him. At the Brooklyn YMCA, he found a library and a place to read; there were lectures which he attended and absorbed. The phrase, "You can't keep a good man down," could have been tailored to fit George Foster Peabody. In his personality was a concentrated force that demanded expression.

Church attendance formed a great part of his developing life. Here one day, he met Gen. Armstrong of Hampton A & M Institute, and was deeply moved by the experience. On his suggestion, the Sunday School gave part of its funds to help the Negro Institute. This encounter began his life-long interest in the Negro and his fulfillment as an individual.

In Sunday School, George (now called "Foster" by his friends) also met two people who became an integral part of his life: Spencer Trask, a young man from an old, established banking family, and Kate Nichols, whose family circumstances marked her as one of the privileged. Foster's adoration of Kate was from afar; Spencer's was more pressing. Eventually, Spencer won the lady, and they were married in 1874. For the next year, Foster Peabody saw little of the couple. Then, one day, the two men met again, and their common destiny was assured. Probably Spencer went home and said to his wife,

"By the way, dear, I saw Foster today. Let's have him over for dinner soon; and I wish you'd pay special attention to him—he's a rather shy fellow—draw him out."

Young Mr. Peabody came to dinner; his friends were gracious; their philosophies of life were harmonious with his own, and from that time on, he saw a great deal of both of them, exulting in sharing their happiness and suffering with them through their tragedies.

The next five years were rich with the joys and sorrows of living for the three friends; Foster advanced rapidly in his work and, finally—a crowning achievement—he was asked to become a partner in the firm of Trask and Stone. He hesitated, on delicate ground; then, wishing to bring up a subject that might, later on, interfere with their relationship, he said frankly,

"Spencer, I am in love with your wife."

Spencer Trask had already appraised this man; he knew his integrity and respected his honesty. His response reflected his acceptance and his trust, as he answered cooly,

"I don't blame you, Foster; I'm in love with her myself."

Both men immediately dropped the subject and went on with the business at hand. Here, stated with unbelievable simplicity, was one of the great romantic triangles of history in which restraint, devotion, and respect were mingled in a deep and enduring friendship between three unusual individuals. Together, the three brilliant minds were a unit, united in their desire for world peace, for beauty in all phases, and with understanding and compassion for those less fortunate than themselves. In addition, an aura of romance surrounded Katrina and, like a Lady of medieval times, she was the inspiration of her two knights going forth to slay dragons; in this instance, they faced the very real dragons of an expanding economy.

Investment bankers such as the Spencer Trask Company, played a large part in the development of the United States. The Company's representative had to know the possibilities of a community, the needs of its citizens, and how they could best be met. He had to be shrewd in appraising an industry or operation so that his Company would profit by the association; further, he had to inspire investors with confidence in the integrity of his firm.

The West was opening up; the transcontinental railroad was in existence; coal and oil fields were being explored; gold and silver were being mined both in the U.S. and in Mexico; the expansion of public utilities was under way; and business ventures, such as the beet-sugar industry, promised large profits. It was an exciting and challenging period in which to live, demanding promotors with keen judgment, courage, and above all, vision—qualities which Peabody possessed in abundance. He listened, learned, invested, and profited hugely.

Although Mr. Peabody's business interests at Spencer Trask Company were diverse, he was most closely associated with the building and financing of railroads. Handling securities for the Company, he covered the main lines already in existence in the west and southwest, and promoted the building of others. The West was still wild and largely unsettled. Hostile bands of Indians menaced the railroad workers, and trains, crossing endless plains, occasionally stopped to let a slow-moving bison cross the track.

In the mid-1880's, Mr. Peabody met Gen. William Jackson Palmer, with whom he formed close personal and business ties. A former Civil War officer, Gen. Palmer was the principal builder of the Denver and Rio Grande Western Railroad System; he also constructed a network of narrow-gauge mountain railways which hugged the rugged mountains and were engineering feats in themselves. Obtaining permission from the Mexican Government, he organized the Mexican National Railway, and Mr. Peabody, representing the Trask Company, handled the securities. Lead, silver, and coal deposits lay along the route, and Peabody bought extensive mining property, investing much of his personal capital in Mexican interests. These ventures paid off handsomely.

Working with Gen. Palmer was an adventurous chapter in Mr. Peabody's life. They camped with the Indians, rode burros, and adjusted to a life that required the greatest physical and mental stamina. Always considerate in his dealings with others, Peabody endorsed the General's humane treatment of Mexican laborers, and his insistence that American workers use sympathy and tact in dealing with them.

Throughout these adventurous, exciting, and profitable years, George Foster Peabody, a man in love with another man's wife, remained a bachelor, caring for his mother and gradually providing her with necessities—then luxuries. In the style of the day, one of the luxuries of the wealthy was a summer home. Following the trend set by other wealthy men, in 1891, Mr. Peabody purchased the Col. Price (the Upper) place consisting of a large house and several hundred acres of land on the western shore of Lake George. Since Indian lore was one of his many interests, he named his summer home "Abenia," Algonquin for "Home of Rest."

He remodeled the house, which was already elegant, and made it a place of regal beauty. Abenia overlooked the lake, and he lined the porch with porch-rockers and even placed them on the roof so that his guests could enjoy the view. The influence of Katrina Trask was evident in individual touches: in the planting of geraniums along the edge of the roof, in the selection of the carved dining-room chairs, each one representing a knight from Tennyson's "Idylls of the King." The paintings in the mansion expressed Mr. Peabody's own taste which ran to madonnas and cherubs and, throughout the house, a profusion of flowers appeared daily from garden or greenhouse.

Each year, when spring came to Brooklyn, Mr. Peabody sent his household staff to Lake George, his mother following later in the season.

Abenia, George Foster Peabody

George Foster Peabody

38

Wikiosco—Royal C. Peabody,
now Blenheim on the lake

39

Gradually, he spent more and more time at Abenia, planting trees and shrubs, building stone walls, laying out walks, but still managing to preserve the natural beauty of the surroundings.

He entertained lavishly, bringing together people prominent in the church, in education, and in finance; and the influence of what was said and done at Abenia radiated over the entire country. Such diverse friends as Dr. Booker T. Washington, president of Tuskegee Institute, and John D. Rockefeller, Jr., oil tycoon, enjoyed his hospitality; relatives from the South came frequently. It was probably his favorite cousin, Pocahontas Peabody who gave her name to his steam launch, "Pocahontas." This craft became a familiar sight to everyone on the lake as it steamed toward the village every Sunday, stopping at the docks of neighbors to take them to church.

His accounts show that he enjoyed the luxuries which his money could buy, although the prices shown in his account books seem low by today's standards. In 1901, he purchased trappings for his horses, including a "Swiss style breast collar" $200. His fur rugs were a delight to the youngsters who visited the house, and included a tiger rug, $20; wolf rug, $10; Polar bear rug, $60; white bear skin, $40; two white fox skins, $10; and the purchase of a mink cape, (32 tails and 15 heads) for $200. The species, and the prices, reflect the abundance of wild life which were then available, but now unobtainable, or even prohibited, in today's living.

The gifts which he purchased for his friends would be collectors' items today: scent bottle, $55; four-leaf clover brooch, $6.00; gold and sapphire brooch, $15; baroque pearl brooch, $17; pearl and diamond scarf pin, $30. The accounts list several portraits by the artist Ferraris, including one of his mother and another of Katrina Trask. In 1902, he ordered a Knoxmobile at $1,014.95.

Gradually, he acquired more Lake George property, which eventually comprised 1,000 acres and included a mountain. Prospect Mountain, which overshadows the village of Lake George to the west, was and still is, a favorite climb for those who visit the area. In the late 1870's, a hotel was operated at the summit, reached by a carriage road. Destroyed by fire in 1880, the building which replaced the hotel was operated as a health resort.

Mr. Peabody had been a resident of Abenia four years when a cog railway, said to be the longest in the world, was built up the mountain. He was well aware of the thousands who used the railway and the hotel accommodations at the top. He became more aware when he heard rumors that gambling was being conducted at the mountain resort. In the early 1900's, he solved the problem—as few could afford to do—by buying the mountain; during World War I, the tracks were torn up and the steel used for the war effort. Old-timers in the region still recall that, for many years, light flashed from the top of the mountain as sunlight played on the windows of the abandoned hotel.

Eventually, the philanthropist gave Prospect Mountain to the State of New York along with Hearthstone Park, with the stipulation that both properties be operated for public use. Today, the State operates an automobile road up the mountain, joined by a steeper road with a Jeep available to take visitors to the summit. During the winter, snow-mobiling is encouraged on the mountain trails. The campground at Hearthstone Park is a popular place each summer as thousands enjoy the State-owned facility.

In former days, there were few tourists, and summer on the western shore of Lake George was a time of comparative quietness and relaxation with family and friends. Elvira Peabody was her son's official hostess, and the spacious house was also home to his two brothers and their families. Edward Morse Shepard, one of Mr. Peabody's greatest friends, also came to Lake George as a summer resident; and the Trasks' purchase of lake property completed his happiness. Later, his brother Royal built a magnificent mansion nearby called Wikiosco, and his brother, Charles J., bought the Lower Price Place which he renamed "Evelley."

He made many friends among the townspeople and especially loved the children of the village where, it was said, he knew the name of every child. The picnic which he gave annually for the children of the Episcopal Sunday School was a big event in their young lives. Going to "Mr. Peabody's picnic" meant that they were allowed full use of the vast lawns, carefully tended gardens, and the living rooms of the big house. One Senior Citizen still remembers the soft, cuddly feeling of her bare feet on the bearskin rugs of Abenia. His personal gifts in the village showed his concern for individuals; for example, he bought a home for two ladies who had spent years in teaching on St. Helena Island; he sent money to a clergyman who preached at Lake George during the summer, so that he might make the trip in comfort. When larger amounts of money were involved, he went over the request carefully, and sometimes refused to give when he felt that the case was without merit. When giving to communities or organizations, it was his custom to ask that they, too, contribute a sum to the project, thereby insuring their own involvement.

The panic of 1907 was a serious threat to the financial institutions of the country: fortunes were being swept away and the doors of business firms closed as the panic grew. Relying on their prestige and integrity, Trask and Peabody were able to pull the firm through the crisis, although they experienced losses in their personal fortunes. In spite of loss, Mr. Peabody was still a wealthy man whose fortune at any one time could not be estimated, as he was always in the process of giving it away. It was generally accepted that, among the residents of Millionaires' Row, he was "the one who had the most money."

Mr. Peabody retired from business life at the age of 54—the early retirement hastened by a near-fatal accident which occurred while he was traveling by train. He had taken the train at Saratoga Springs, headed for New York. Stepping into the aisle of the speeding railroad car, he was walking unsteadily to the end of the car when the train gave a sudden lurch. He was thrown to the floor of the car, striking his head and straining his muscles. Taken back to Yaddo, The Trasks' Saratoga home, he was put to bed and ordered to Abenia for a long rest. It was then that Mr. Peabody decided to retire from active business and take care of those activities which lay closest to his heart—his philanthropies. Due to his active temperament, retirement seemed to result in greater activity, and some of his busiest and most influential years still lay ahead.

With more time at his disposal in which to research the background of worthy causes and organizations, he extended the range of his philanthropy throughout the country. In addition, he underwrote the publication of several books which he believed had merit, and printed and distributed Katrina's writings on the subject of Peace, an ideal which both shared.

At Saratoga Springs, he, Shepard, and the Trasks were active in efforts to revitalize the springs and re-establish the area as a health resort. In May, 1909, their efforts resulted in legislation passed by the New York State Legislature, creating the Reservation at Saratoga Springs.

In the first hours of the New Year, 1910, Mr. Peabody was shocked and grief-stricken by the sudden death of his friend, Spencer Trask. The loss of Spencer made a profound change in his life; some of the joy in his Lake George home had vanished; his wide interests became more demanding. He was needed at Yaddo which, according to Spencer's Will and Katrina's plan, was to be operated as a retreat for artists and writers. In 1914–15, he sold Abenia to his friend, Adolph S. Ochs, publisher of the New York Times, and moved to a small Lake George cottage for the summer. Later, he established an office in Saratoga Springs.

These were the years when Europe was aflame with war, and apprehension was felt that the United States might become involved. Knowing of the horrors of war from bitter experience, Mr. Peabody became a member of the American Peace League which was making every effort to keep America out of the European conflict. He admired Woodrow Wilson's stand against war, became his friend and supporter, and threw his influence into the campaign of 1912 which brought Wilson to the White House. At this time, Mr. Peabody was offered the position of Secretary of the Treasury of the United States. After careful consideration, he refused the post, feeling that he could accomplish more for the country outside a formal position in the Government. Thus, George Foster Peabody surrendered a place in history, which was subsequently filled by William Gibbs McAdoo.

During Wilson's first four years in office, the country was in a state of uneasy neutrality, with definite leanings toward the Allies. Peabody kept up his urgent campaign to preserve peace and supported Wilson's campaign for a second term with the slogan, "He kept us out of war."

Following the re-election of Wilson, the national picture changed and neutrality became armed intervention on the side of the Allies. Peabody now made a hard decision: all his beliefs centered on Peace, which

Fountain at Twin Birches,
formerly Price Manor

Evelley, owned by Charles J. Peabody

he considered a bargain at any price, but he firmly believed that the government must be upheld in its declaration of war. An editorial which appeared in the New York Times captioned "A Pacifist and Yet a Patriot," measured the deep personal conflict between principle and patriotism which he faced; but, once committed, he focused his financial genius on the will to win. He was instrumental in encouraging Liberty Loan Drives at the New York Federal Reserve Bank, and the first issue of $2 billion and the second issue of $3 billion were both oversubscribed nationally. After the war, he became a member of the President's Reconstruction Committee.

He was president of the Men's League for Woman Suffrage, and on August 26, 1920, with Katrina, he celebrated the enactment of Amendment XIX, granting voting rights to women.

One of the most memorable events in George Foster Peabody's eventful life was his marriage to Katrina Trask. Often, since Spencer's death, Peabody had asked her to marry him, but she had consistently refused. Finally, she consented, and they were married at Yaddo in 1921. The following months were a time of great happiness for Peabody. In writing of his wife, he often referred to her as "the Ladye," using the medieval spelling of a more romantic period. His happiness was of short duration, however, as Katrina died less than a year after their marriage.

Without her, there was a vacancy within him that could never be completely filled. In her will she had said,

"No mourning shall be worn for me as the incident of mortal death is but the passing on into a larger sphere of a more abundant life."

He would not follow his Ladye for a while; he still had his own business affairs to conduct, and there were responsibilities inherent in the plans they had made together.

He did not remain entirely comfortless. A few months after Katrina's death, a bright young woman, Mrs. Marjorie Waite, entered his life. She had come as a director for one of his philanthropic enterprises; she stayed to become his adopted daughter. As Mrs. Marjorie Peabody Waite, she brought him companionship and understanding, and her cheerful presence added the light touch which had been missing in his strenuous life. Now his grief was easier to bear, and they proceeded with Katrina's plans for Yaddo as though she were still a living presence among them.

A new project claimed his attention. Work on the Saratoga Commission for the revitalizing of the springs had reawakened memories of a mineral spring at Warm Springs, Georgia. As a boy, he had visited the resort, then famous, and had marveled at the abundance of warm water flowing from Pine Mountain into a natural pool. The old hotel, cottages, and auditorium were in a sad state of disrepair, but the water still flowed as freely as it had a half century before, and in the pool, the water had the buoyancy of the ocean. With the intention of restoring the resort to its former eminence, Mr. Peabody bought the springs and the land surrounding them.

The year was 1924. Franklin Delano Roosevelt, whom Peabody had supported politically, was stricken with polio. Always quick to offer assistance, Peabody wrote to Roosevelt suggesting Warm Springs as therapy for the crippling ailment. Roosevelt investigated and found a run-down resort, but wonderful mineral water naturally heated to 88 degrees. The whirlpool action of the waters brought him some relief, and, in his enthusiasm, he bought the springs from Mr. Peabody. Roosevelt's subsequent election to the presidency cut sharply into the time allotted for treatment, but he returned to Warm Springs whenever circumstances permitted; and the cottage which he built there became world-famous as the "Little White House."

During FDR's New Deal, Mr. Peabody was one of his Brain-Trusters, taking an active part in the Tennessee Valley Authority, the Good Neighbor League involving Mexico and Latin America, and the Farm Program known as the Agricultural Adjustment Act (AAA)—only names now, but then programs of far-reaching importance.

In 1929, the start of the Great Depression, Mr. Peabody became deeply concerned over his vast holdings in Mexico which were bankrupt. Coal mines, railroad properties, and a metal production plant at Fresnillo were involved in this $3 million investment. Additional losses faced him in New York City where an office building which he owned was rapidly losing tenants. This situation was particularly disastrous as he depended on rents from this building for the support of Yaddo.

Since his retirement 23 years previously, he had been using his income and principal for his philanthropic and humanitarian efforts. For his personal use, he was down to several thousand dollars per year, a sum which today is considered below the poverty level.

During his lifetime, he had given generously to educational institutions. Among others, his gifts to the University of Georgia amounted to more than a quarter million. Colorado College, founded by his old friend, General Palmer, had benefited from his generosity by a considerable sum; and in 1911, he had given liberally to Skidmore, a struggling new college in Saratoga Springs and had become a member of the Board of Trustees. In addition to his gifts to educational institutions, he had given freely to churches, Negro organizations, YMCA's, hospitals, museums and libraries. He backed the work of Booker T. Washington, and financed research and costs of a publication of Negro spirituals.

With his income dwindling, he kept Yaddo in operation by judicious management until 1938 when he followed Katrina; as he had requested, his ashes were buried near hers in the Rose Garden on the Estate. Tributes to him as a man and as a benefactor of humanity poured in. Dr. George Washington Carver, Negro educator, said of him:

> "He was a wonderful character. Mr. Peabody was a great friend of the Negro and a great friend of Tuskegee. He had the real Christ Spirit."

The publication, "The Southern Workman," referred to him editorially as a "Lover of Men." The State of Georgia announced the opening of the George Foster Peabody Memorial Highway; establishment of the George

Foster Peabody Memorial Award for Television and Radio followed; and there are people who still remember him with affection. Recently, in the face of a Senior Citizen, the writer saw a more personal memorial as, with a fond smile, she recounted her childhood memories of this great man.

The biography of George Foster Peabody is a true story of success in a developing America. Without compromising his integrity, he acquired a large fortune; during his lifetime, he had the pleasure of giving bountifully, and personally witnessing the results of his philanthropy. He had the gift of forming deep friendships with both great people and little people; and, like a true knight, his adoration of but one lovely Ladye endured all his life.

CHAPTER V

Spencer and Katrina Trask

(Wiawaka—Amitola—Triuna)

In the late 1840's, any of the friends and neighbors of the Trask family in Brooklyn, New York, could have told you that Spencer, the small son of the house, would make his mark in this world. He was quick, precise, and intense, and for all his youth, there was a sureness about him, making one feel that this gifted youngster knew where he was going and just how he was going to get there.

He was born into a family that had been prominent in public affairs for generations, beginning with his Puritan ancestor, Capt. William Trask. It was this Capt. Trask who, in 1628, was wealthy enough to give some of his wealth away, donating land for the site of New England's first school. The school later became Harvard.

Finance and banking were traditional in the Trask family, and there was never any doubt about the profession Spencer would follow. He attended the Polytechnic Institute of Brooklyn, graduated from Princeton in 1866, and for a time worked for his mother's uncle in a financial capacity. In two years, he had formed his own company, Trask and Stone, dealing in stocks and bonds.

At the Reformed Church in Brooklyn, he met George Foster Peabody, a young man who was to share his life as long as life endured. A mutual interest may have brought them together, since Mr. Peabody was chairman of a committee to administer church funds. A different attraction for both existed in the person of lovely Katrina Nichols, who finally chose Spencer. If Spencer knew then of young Mr. Peabody's affection for Katrina, he might have said,

"Poor Foster! He'll get over it."

Foster never did. The lives of all three were intermingled in a curious triangle that was proof against tragedy and loss. The triangle was even more firmly drawn when, in 1875, Peabody accepted a partnership in the Trask Company and thereby became an integral part of the professional and personal life of Spencer and Katrina Trask.

An accurate judge of character, this man who made an unerring choice in selecting George Foster Peabody as his friend and business partner, chose with both heart and mind when he selected Katrina Nichols to be his wife.

As a young girl in the early 1870's, Katrina (Kate) Nichols was lovely with the natural beauty of youth enhanced by the promise of a develop-

47

ing inner beauty. Her eyes were blue, with a contemplative, sometimes far-off gaze; her complexion, protected from the sun, was of a fairness sought by young ladies and their mothers of that period. Her soft brown hair was worn simply, twined into a knot at the back of the neck. She missed being the tall, willowy type by several inches, but compensated for her lack of height by a queenly and graceful carriage.

Born into a well-to-do Brooklyn family, her life was pleasant, made smooth by the social amenities. She undoubtedly took lessons in French and music, was taught to enter a room gracefully and, in general, how to appear to advantage in society. "Lady Katrina," as her friends called her, was schooled in graciousness, but the depth of her compassion was her own.

She possessed a quick intellect and unusual talent for expressing her thoughts in poetry and prose. Although she was by nature gentle and refined, she had a determined will, coupled with the ability to charm her admirers into fulfilling her wishes. Poised, concentrated, delicate, but with an inner strength, she gave the impression of other-worldness, as though she moved in an ethereal realm where none could follow. Katrina, sensitive to the gathering of forces around her, was psychic. Spiritualism was having a rebirth at this time, and anyone with an inkling of the future was looked upon with awe. There was nothing awesome about Katrina. Her gift of prophecy held her hopes and dreams of a better life for a struggling world.

Spencer and Katrina were married in a well-planned, correctly formal wedding on November 12, 1874. Evidently, Mr. Peabody did not attend the wedding, although there is evidence that he received an invitation. Later, all three resumed the interrupted friendship; Mr. Peabody accepted a partnership with Spencer Trask & Company, and thereafter, he was always near, advising, helping, and loving.

Mr. and Mrs. Spencer Trask established their first home in a Brooklyn apartment. Spencer continued to make money; Katrina was an affluent housewife, a good manager of servants, a poised hostess, and an ornament of the social gatherings which the couple attended. In addition, she continued writing the poetry and prose which, as an expression of her talent, released her deepest emotions.

Spencer Trask was already a wealthy young man when the depression of 1873–78 occurred, and although many buinesses failed at that time, the Trask Company continued to prosper. He was energetic, far-seeing, and practical—qualities which enabled him to back Thomas A. Edison with complete faith in the value of his inventions. Trask held the presidency of the New York Edison Company for 20 years; he was also on the executive committee of General Electric. During this time his Company financed the Electric Illuminating Companies that were spreading to the mid-west. Two decades after its founding, the Trask Company was the largest stock-broker in the country with a large part of the business in bonds. Twenty thousand clients were on their books, including both the small investor and such Titans of finance as Harriman, Morgan, and Gould. In the realm of high finance, Spencer Trask amassed a fortune which enabled him to express a love of beauty in art, coupled with a determination to leave the world a better place than he found it.

The Company's business extended throughout the U.S., Mexico, and Europe. The building of railroads figured heavily in their activities; the mining of gold and silver, both in the U.S. and in Mexico, became highly profitable, and the transportation of commodities such as sugar beets was another facet of this ubiquitous company. These objectives could not have been realized without a leader such as Trask, capable of shrewd planning, the ability to outguess a competitor, and daring based on complete self-confidence.

There were rate wars in the railroad companies; competition at the top sifted down to the ranks and erupted into savage fighting among the workers. Often the tycoons were as ruthless, although more urbane and polished in their operations. The times called for cool judgment, insight, vision, and indomitable courage. These qualities were Spencer Trask's innate qualities for a spectacular success. In addition, this man who radiated energy and force and who had the latent power to crush opposition with his fiery, dominant will, was gentle and considerate, with a friendly and winning personality.

Endowed as he was with inexhaustible physical and mental energy, even the ramifications of his far-flung business interests could not satisfy the demands of his ambition, and his creativeness overflowed into broader channels. Loving the arts, he founded the influential National Arts Club and became its president; he was also active in the Art Student's League and the Municipal Art Society. In business, he was founder and president of the Morningside and Broadway Realty Companies, and established a publishing company.

Education of the total person claimed his attention. For years he was treasurer of the New York Kindergarten Society; he founded Teachers' College at Columbia University and, in Saratoga, built and maintained St. Christina's, a vocational school for girls.

The Trasks' first child, Alanson, was born in 1877; the birth of a daughter, Christina, two years later, left Katrina physically depleted. Since the finest clinics, the most skillful physicians were reputed to be in Europe, she went abroad for treatment. Her health improved, but on her return, she found her little son gravely ill; he died soon after.

Restless and grieving, Spencer and Katrina spent part of the year at their Brooklyn home, and part in ultra fashionable Tuxedo Park, New York, where Spencer built a home on the highest hill available. But social life alone could not fill the vacancy in their hearts. The answer to their need came in a 700-acre tract of land near Saratoga Springs. On the property was an old inn, operated as a fishing lodge in the early 1800's by Jacobus Barhydt. Hills, valleys, lakes and springs, first-growth trees and a view of distant mountains offered peace and seclusion, qualities which had so appealed to Jerome Bonaparte, deposed King of Spain, that he had offered Herr Barhydt $20,000 for the property. It is said that the elderly German contemptuously refused the offer with the comment,

"If it's worth that to you, it's worth that to me."[1]

There was another building on the property, a residence built in the 1850's, and although there was no running water or adequate heating, the Trasks knew that the old house could be remodeled into a beautiful villa. With rising enthusiasm, they bought the property.

The new home was called Yaddo, the name given it by their little daughter, a child who had already known the darkness of grief.

"When asked what the name should be," Katrina writes, "she put her head down on the back of the chair in which she was sitting, with her hands over her eyes in concentration for a minute and then, with a radiant expression, cried in her decisive way,

" 'Now I know! Call it Yaddo, Mamma, for it makes poetry; Yaddo-shadow; shadow-Yaddo. It sounds like shadow, but it's not going to be shadow.' "[2]

Three years later, it seemed that the shadows had indeed lifted when a little boy, Spencer, was born to them. With all nature waiting to be explored at Yaddo, summers became bright with adventure. Then, in 1888, Katrina, at the Brooklyn home, fell ill of diphtheria; the two children were also stricken and died a few days apart, and their parents suffered through an agony of grief. Their last child, a daughter named Katrina, born the next year, died in infancy. A book, "Chronicles of 1888," was the reservoir into which Katrina Trask poured her grief, and in the writing of it, she gained strength. Spencer plunged into his business ventures with an almost desperate energy, and together they buried their grief.

In Saratoga Springs, as owner of a vast and beautiful estate, Spencer was a power in the community; loving the area, he planned that Saratoga Springs, surpassing its former glory, would become one of the great health resorts of the world. Working with his great friends, George Foster Peabody and Edward Morse Shepard, he gave unsparingly of his time and energy—serving as chairman of influential committees, seeing legislators, meeting with financiers and scientists, and, in every way, using his great influence for the benefit of his beloved town.

The times foreshadowed the so-called "Gay Nineties"—that period in America when captains of industry, plungers, and gamblers often had more money than they knew what to do with—but still wanted more—and adventurers were on the prowl. Saratoga Springs had become the goal, not only for millionaires, but for those on the ragged fringes of society. To the consternation of the solid citizens of the community, the town was "wide open" and vice of all kinds flourished.

[1]Yaddo: Yesterday and Today: Waite, privately printed, 1933, p. 11.
[2]Ibid., p. 27.

Outraged by the spread of corruption and kindred evils, Spencer Trask mounted a crusade against the sordid conditions that were branding Saratoga Springs the "Monte Carlo of America." He controlled a newspaper, the *Saratoga Union*, in which editorials began appearing, attacking gamblers and their establishments. The results of the newspaper campaign were disappointing to Spencer Trask, the idealist. A majority of the *Union's* readers accused him of threatening their prosperity; newsdealers refused to sell his newspapers; and the owner of the famous race track threatened to close it down—an act which would have been a devastating blow to the economy of Saratoga.

Trask then turned to the church for assistance, but found little help there. Clergymen delivered the opinion that, in general, they saw no difference between gambling with cards, horses, or games of chance, and the risk that the investor took in Mr. Trask's investment corporation. In a desperate attempt to show the citizens where their city was headed, he hired private detectives from New York City. Acting secretly, they were able to collect enough evidence to have the law-violators arrested and imprisoned. They were soon let out on bail, however, and the Grand Jury refused to return an indictment. The crusade for reform had cost $50,000 and the powerful crusader was forced to admit that, in the face of a perverse human element, he was, in this instance, powerless.

Soon afterward, in 1891, Yaddo, the summer home of Katrina and Spencer Trask at Saratoga, burned to the ground. It was a grievous loss to them as parents, for the house had been filled with mementoes and memories of their children. Spencer was dangerously ill with pneumonia when Mr. Peabody brought them the tragic news. Shocked though he must have been, Spencer immediately responded to this new challenge by ordering that the first steps of reconstruction be undertaken.

When Spencer was improved, the couple went reluctantly to visit Yaddo and view the ruins of their home. Of this experience, Katrina writes:

> "It had been a gloomy drive from the station, but as we drove in through the gateway of Yaddo, the sun burst forth in glory; over the causeway and up the road we went with beating pulses. We reached the ruins; we forced ourselves to look!—and lo! the most beautiful rainbow that I have ever seen spanned that charred and blackened mass."[3]

With will, faith, and imagination, the Trasks took this latest disaster as an opportunity to build an edifice more suited to their lofty aims. The granite structure which arose was a copy of Haddon Hall, an historic mansion in England. Suggesting medieval pageantry, knighthood, and the days of chivalry, the new mansion expressed in stone the poetic ideals of Katrina, the romantic.

While the new house was being built, Spencer and Katrina came to

[3]Ibid., p. 31.

Yaddo—Saratoga, home of
Mr. & Mrs. Spencer Trask

Mr. and Mrs. Spencer
Trask and children

Advertisement—Circa 1890

Peace Monument erected by
Katrina Trask on Diamond Island

Three Brothers Island, formerly Triuna, originally Three Brothers Island

their land for a visit, staying at the old Barhydt Tavern. Suddenly, Katrina felt impelled to pick up a book of inspirational verses; on impulse, she opened the book at random and found, as a motto for the New Yaddo,

"The glory of this latter House shall be greater than of the former, and in this place will I give peace."[4]

This motto is carved in the cornerstone of the mansion.

In the great hall at Yaddo is a beautiful fireplace made by Tiffany with a mosaic of Phoenix rising from the ashes; underneath are the words:

Flammis Invicta per Ignem
Yaddo Resurgo et Pace.

The mansion was completed in 1893, and in the beauty of the house and grounds, the Trasks found a measure of happiness, and, ultimately, a purpose for living. They had finally faced the fact that, with no child to inherit this land, all their efforts seemed pointless. Then, one day, while walking under the trees with Spencer, Katrina had a vision. According to her written account, she stopped suddenly, held by an unseen hand; and, as she remained still—awed and wondering—she was flooded by a sense of exaltation, and she knew that Yaddo was destined to be a haven for artists. In her vision, she saw men and women walking among the trees, sitting on the marble benches; and all were at work, creating through the medium of art, of literature, of music. Inspired by the revelation, she spoke to Spencer, describing in detail the activity that she saw, and he responded, deeply moved,

"I, too, see what you see; I, too, hear what you hear."[5]

From that time on they worked with tireless enthusiasm, seeking to make Yaddo a retreat for artists. The garden and walks among the trees became places of beauty and quietness; from the lake on the property, four smaller lakes were created, each one named for one of their deceased children. They called the project "Pine Garde," a name that was later changed to the official "Corporation of Yaddo."

The turn of the century was full of purposeful living for the Trasks and their faithful friend, Mr. Peabody. At Lake George, he had established Abenia as his permanent residence, and the Trasks often visited him. Refreshed by the pine-scented air and inspired by the ever-changing beauty of the lake, they were impressed by the vacation possibilities of the area, not only for the wealthy, but for those with limited incomes. Another humanitarian, Miss Mary Wiltsie Fuller, had similar views. A resident of Troy, New York where her father was a partner in the Fuller & Warren Stove Company, she knew the plight of women who worked in the Troy industries such as the shirt and collar factories where the hours

[4]Ibid., p. 32.
[5]Ibid., p. 35.

were long and the pay was low. Through the Girls' Friendly Society, an Episcopalian organization, Miss Fuller hoped to give working women an opportunity to enjoy low-cost vacations. Katrina was in complete accord with these aims and their only question was where the unique resort would be located.

The answer was found in a 150-acre tract of land at Crosbyside, East Lake George. In 1855, it had been the site of a Young Ladies' Institute; later, the building became the Crosbyside Hotel; in 1901, the hotel burned. The next year, the Trasks bought the property.

Mr. Peabody, too, became interested and, with the Trasks, commissioned Stanford White, the eminent New York architect, to design the buildings for the venture. One of his creations, a stately mansion named "Wakonda," became part of Wiawaka Holiday House, Inc., the complex formed to provide low-cost summer vacations for working women and widows. An old brochure advertising the resort is lyrical in its description and suggests Katrina, the poet:

> "The spirit of Indian tradition and romance still lingers about the east side of the lake, contrasting happily with the modern aspect of the west side, with its fine estates and the village of Lake George—which is within easy walking distance of Wiawaka.*
>
> A stroll of a few minutes will take one into deep, sweet-scented pine woods, or up sunny, fern-carpeted hillsides. And always there is the lake, with the white birches bending from its shores, and the strong blue mountains guarding its peace."

Rates were: Board, $6.00 per week, $1.00 per day, 50¢ per meal—about half the amount charged by comfortable hotels such as Trout Pavillion, and far below that of the luxurious Fort William Henry. Comfort and quiet were promised; "rowboats and croquet grounds" were available; also "baths-houses for those who enjoy fresh water bathing." As director, Miss Fuller brought to the project her dedication and her dreams. To the east of Wiawaka, Spencer built Amitola as a retreat for artists. This was the forerunner of their plans for Yaddo in Saratoga.

But for a few years, Yaddo would be their home and they entertained lavishly. Among their guests were the great and famous, the wealthy and the talented. Concerts and plays were presented in the great hall, and those who attended them knew Katrina would be there to brighten the occasion. She had a flair for the dramatic and, at the most effective moment, would descend the stairs, a vision in floating draperies and dazzling jewels. But as enjoyable as these events were, the social pace soon took its toll, and the pain of Katrina's heart condition returned.

One night, after a tiring round of entertaining, she had retired and was lying weary and sleepless, when she became aware of an angelic presence at the foot of her bed. Wondering but unafraid, she asked:

*Wiawaka—the eternal spirit in women.

Belfry on Triuna Island

Pergola "Yaddo Gardens", Saratoga Springs, N.Y.

"What would you have me do?"

In answer, the angel pointed to the northward and said, "To the Lake; to the Lake."

When she told Spencer of the apparition, he immediately decided that they should go to Lake George. He rented Clay Island, off-shore from Bolton; here there was a spacious house for themselves and household staff. Katrina was carried to the island and there, during the summer months, she regained her strength.

The benefit of the summer's experience was so great that they began looking for a site on the lake as their permanent summer home. Clay Island was out of the question; it was too large and meant the care of another estate. A smaller island would answer the purpose, but for various reasons, none of the islands was suitable. Then Katrina thought of three small rocky islands south of Clay, and urged Spencer to inquire about them. They were called Three Brothers and owned by Mrs. L. H. Myer. Always wanting to give his wife her heart's desire, Spencer visited the proposed site and gave his considered opinion that living on the small islands was an improbable dream. However, Katrina was determined, and with Spencer and Mr. Peabody, she inspected the islands herself, circling them in a pole-propelled boat. What she saw convinced her of the possibilities of these little islands; Spencer remained unconvinced.

According to her plan, the north island would be for the servants and serve as the entrance to the small domain; there a scaled-down Gothic arch and belfry with its ringing bell would welcome guests; the central island beyond the archway would have a long promenade with a colonnaded bridge at each end connecting the islands; sleeping quarters for their guests would be built into a superstructure. The south island would be reserved as their own residence. These islands, she had decided, could also, at some time, be operated for artists as part of the Yaddo plan. They bought the islands.

For this venture, they again commissioned Stanford White to design the buildings. The famous architect was already at work on the plans when, in New York City, he became the victim of a bizarre murder perpetrated by Harry Kendall Thaw. Adjustments were made and the work went on.

In spite of his doubts, Spencer's imagination caught the spark of her enthusiasm and he went to work on the problem of enlarging the islands. The project required a great quantity of stones and rocks of all sizes, and he found an endless supply in long stone fences which had once marked the boundaries of pioneer farms. The following winter, 1906–07, tons of these rocks were taken over the frozen lake and deposited around the islands. In the spring when the ice melted, the rocks, dropping into place, made a solid foundation for the bridges and further construction. The finished structure was a dream-come-true: the bell in the belfry welcomed visitors; a Norman-Gothic keep above the colonnaded bridges enclosed the living quarters. Katrina named her new refuge "Triuna"—three in one: three islands in one; perhaps, three friends—Katrina, Spencer, and Peabody united in purpose.

In the desire to give of their wealth, these three friends were united. The story is told that Mr. Peabody once discussed with Katrina the need of a swimming pool for the University of Georgia.

"How much will it cost?" she asked.

Told that the pool would cost about $3,000, she immediately drew a sapphire ring from her finger,

"Take this ring and sell it," she told him, "There will be enough money to construct the pool."

The depression of 1907 brought ruin to many; even the wealthy curtailed their expenses, but Spencer plunged ahead as though "time was of the essence" of his contract with the Almighty. With George Foster Peabody, he planned the building of the Lake George Club which he saw as a necessity in the social life of the summer colony. The architect was Charles Samuel Peabody, nephew of Mr. Peabody, and a member of Ludlow and Peabody of New York City. On August 14, 1909, the doors of the Club were opened, with Spencer Trask as president.

The Trasks had spent two delightful summers on Triuna Island when, once again, tragedy tested their courage. In the early summer of 1909, Spencer was in Boston on one of his many business trips. Then, as now, Boston was a busy city teeming with traffic: horse-drawn vehicles jammed the streets, trolley cars traversed the city, and an occasional automobile made its way perilously through the maze of vehicles. Spencer had chosen an automobile as his mode of transportation and was riding as a passenger toward his destination. Traffic control was unheard of, and each driver of a vehicle made his own way and took his own chances, except for trolley cars which, by their nature, had right of way.

At a point where the trolley tracks and a street crossing intersected, the accident occurred: the trolley struck the automobile with full force and Spencer was badly injured; in fact, he was so severely injured that one of his eyes had to be removed. Those were anxious days and weeks for Katrina and Mr. Peabody, and that summer was spent, not in the happy activity they had planned, but in a darkened room on Triuna where Spencer awaited several more operations on his eye.

Friends came to see the accident victim. They came to mourn with him, and found that *he* was not mourning, and his gallant spirit buoyed them up. Writing of her husband later, Katrina said, "I have seen him follow through darkness and the shadow of death, blindness, sorrow, financial ruin, grave disappointment, unspeakable desolation of home, and he never failed to show a cheerful spirit."

The summer of 1909 drew to a close and the Trasks left Lake George. In spite of his accident, Spencer continued to divide his time between business and his humanitarian interests, but, more and more, his time was devoted to his chairmanship of the Saratoga Commission. He worked as though he were in a race with time, and there was much to be done.

Christmas, 1909, came. The holiday season was a time of special celebration at Yaddo where, outdoors, children from the area came to slide down hill and skate on the frozen lakes. Indoors, the air was fragrant with pine boughs brought from their own forest; the Yule log burned in the great fireplace, gay Christmas garlands decorated the entire house, chimes rang out a joyous greeting, carols were sung, and a spirit of cheer and good will was an almost-tangible thing.

Christmas morning was an eagerly-awaited time when all the household servants and their families, often numbering several hundred, assembled in the Great Hall to receive the keys to the room where their presents were hidden. Nor was the celebration of Christmas limited to one day—the twelve days of Christmas were observed at Yaddo in the hearty Old English custom.

The festivities continued into the closing days of the year, but this time, Spencer was not part of them. Shutting out the sights and sounds of the Holiday Season, he had spent the entire December day in his study working on reports for the Saratoga Commission. A message from his attorney in New York City, Edward M. Shepard, had increased his sense of urgency, and his work had been steady and concentrated. He now planned to take the reports to Shepard for immediate review; they would then be delivered to the New York State Legislature in time for its first session of the New Year. He knew that the weather had turned bitterly cold, and the thought must have entered his mind: "If only I didn't have to go—tonight." But he brushed the thought aside and went on with his work.

Emerging from his study later, he voiced the thought to his wife. "Do you think I should go to New York tonight?" he asked, less seeking an answer than in bringing an inner conflict into the open.

"Yes," she answered simply. She never regretted her answer, nor felt she should have given any other. Others knew Spencer Trask as a powerful man and a strong executive; with the rapport existing between them, she recognized in him the sensitiveness of a child and a "childlike recoil from suffering and sadness." She realized that the injured area around his eye was vulnerable to the cold, but she also knew that he was determined to go, convinced that the fate of the town he loved was at stake.

He answered his own question, "I must go; it's my duty," he said, and returned to his study to finish his work.

Late that night, with Katrina's wifely admonition, "Do take care of yourself," and his own promise to return soon, he left the warmth and security of his home. Later, Katrina would write:

"Upon that fatal midnight, he went out into the darkness and the bitter cold with unfaltering courage and with the glowing smile upon his lips."

Driven to the station in Saratoga Springs, he boarded the Montreal-New York Express and made his way to his drawing-room at the rear of the last car. Relieved that the reports were finished and hopeful of their acceptance, he dozed. The night wore on. Several hours later, the train traveling along the Hudson River shore was approaching Croton on the Hudson, only a short distance from New York City. Spencer arose; he would soon place the papers in Shepard's hands and his task would be completed. Suddenly there was a horrifying crash, a shrieking, grinding clash of metal on metal, and Spencer's world collapsed. A freight train had plowed into the rear of the passenger train, and Spencer, the only one injured, was near death; he died moments after.

On hearing the tragic news, Katrina was near collapse. Mr. Peabody, who had lost his greatest friend, knowing that the structures they had built together now depended on him, carried on, grief-stricken, attending to all necessary details. Rallying from her grief with strength of will and determination that outran her frail health, Katrina, too, carried on with inflexible purpose.

The grief and sense of loss experienced by those closest to him were repeated in shock waves that reached into the hearts of all who knew him. He was hailed as one of the foremost citizens of New York State, an enthusiastic friend of the communities of Saratoga, Lake George, and Albany. The *Lake George Mirror* expressed the thought, "Lake George has sustained an irreparable loss," and the Saratoga press cried out in despair, "Who can take his place?"

From the thousands of tributes paid to this great man, his widow compiled a Memorial Book which was distributed to those who knew and loved him. His close friend, Edward M. Shepard, wrote of "his vigorous achievements, generous friendship, radiant energy; his undimmed, buoyant youthfulness." He also referred to the tragedies in Spencer's life and his philosophical acceptance of them as "the sharp agony of the loss of his children; his heroism in the face of suffering."

Henry Van Dyke, author and educator, spoke of him as "high-minded and princely; (a person who) lived with his whole being, and kept human—a great achievement in an age of machinery."

Dr. Percy Stickney Grant voiced the thought, "He was an artist and his art was life."

The shock of the death of Spencer Trask was succeeded by disbelief when it was learned that, by New York standards, he was a relatively poor man. Since the depression of 1907, he had carried on his civic and humanitarian interests, neglecting to retrieve his own financial losses. A slip of paper found in his wallet immediately after his death, expressed his philosophy,

"For a man's wealth consisteth not in the abundance of the things he possesseth."

Two years after Spencer's death, Katrina and Yaddo faced a financial crisis. It was then that another vision came to her and she knew what she must do. She would move to the smaller house on the property; Yaddo would be closed for the winter; fewer guests would occupy the mansion during the summer. Everything must be simplified, but the program would continue essentially the same. A great peace settled over her as the way became clear. Resolutely, she steeled herself to return to Triuna for another summer without Spencer.

The summer of 1912 saw another disaster for the Trask holdings—another test for Katrina's frail body and spiritual strength. It had been a typical summer's day on the Lake; waves lapped against Triuna's rocky shore; boats skimmed over the surface of the water, their occupants waving greetings to the Lady of the Island. Evening had come, and the summer breeze became a wind that blew stiffly from the North. Along both shores of the lake, lights blinked on, then off, as peace and darkness settled over the island. The only sound was the splashing of the waves against the Peabody yacht, the Pocahontas, moored at a dock on the north end of the island. Water slapped restlessly against the Trask boats fastened to another dock.

It was 4 o'clock when Miss O'Rourke, Mrs. Trask's maid, was awakened by a sharp explosion and a strange rumble that could only be the spreading of fire. Looking out, she saw that the Pocahontas, the boats, and the docks were engulfed in flames. She immediately roused William King, supervisor, and he marshalled the frightened servants into a bucket brigade. Fortunately, the wind had changed and was now blowing from the south, so there was hope of confining the fire to the north island until help arrived. The fire had now reached the gasoline tanks of the yacht, and explosions sent showers of sparks into the air which fell hissing into the water.

Lights on both sides of the lake blinked on again as residents, aroused by the flames, saw pillars of fire leaping upward from Triuna. The blaze was spectacular: the fire, starting in the ash-pan of the Pocahontas, destroyed two other motor boats, four row boats and, spreading to the gasoline storage and coal bins alongside, consumed both docks. Buildings on the north side of the island were leveled and all the servants' personal property was lost. People from the nearer shore put out in their boats to bring aid; Charles Peabody and Royal Peabody, owners of estates along the Bolton Road, drove immediately to the nearest point of land and waited to evacuate the island's inhabitants.

Mrs. Trask, who had been ill with a severe case of arteriosclerosis, was taken by launch to the mainland, and then to Abenia, the home of George Foster Peabody. She was in pain, but grateful that there had been no loss of life. As soon as she could travel, she would return to Yaddo. Faced with a $35,000 fire loss, she was undefeated, and planned the restoration of the island from her sick-bed at the Saratoga estate—plans which were carried out without her active supervision; she never left Yaddo again. She probably never saw the memorial in Congress Park dedicated in 1914 to Spencer Trask as a benefactor of Saratoga Springs.

The memorial, "The Spirit of Life," was sculpted by Daniel Chester French; the balustrades and fountains surrounding it were the work of Henry Bacon.

During the years, her health had continued to decline and she was almost blind. She continued writing, dictating to Miss Allena Pardee, her companion for many years. She had published two books of poems; her plays, brought out by eminent publishing houses, drew large audiences. Prior to World War I, she wrote movingly on the subject of Peace; her play, "In The Vanguard," published in 1913, won the medal given by the American Peace League for "the most notable effort of an individual in behalf of peace."

Coming into possession of Diamond Island, a large island in Lake George once famous for its diamond-like quartz, she made it a shrine for Peace. Site of many battles, the island was also a place where, it is said, chieftains of warring Indian tribes came to smoke the pipe of peace. Here Katrina built a dock and rest-house, inviting visitors to stop and enjoy the beauty of the island. An obelisk which she erected called the Peace Stone, faces north where invading armies once gathered, and carved on its face are the words:

Peace, here the conqueror of many wars
1666–1777

Carving on the base of the obelisk gives the bloody history of the island during those years of conflict. Plaques to the right and left of the Peace Stone give the biblical prophecy of eventual peace in both French and English.

Now administered by the American Scenic and Preservation Society, Diamond Island provides a picnic area for use by the public.

Sharing her interests, Mr. Peabody remained, as always, her faithful friend and constant admirer; nor could her physical handicaps diminish the fascination which she would always hold for him. Since Spencer's death, he had repeatedly asked her to marry him.

"Now, Foster, I don't want to burden you with an invalid," she would reply, dismissing the subject. But there came a day when, in response to his repeated offer, she accepted his proposal.

The wedding was held in West House on the grounds at Yaddo. This small but exquisite house was alternately called Mansell Alsaada, Arabic for "House of Happiness." The simple ceremony took place on Saturday morning, February 5, 1921, with one niece as the only guest present. Absent friends were represented by quantities of flowers which banked the walls of the room. As they took their vows, they were a striking couple: he, tall and distinguished in his 69th year, and she, delicate and still lovely at 68. A wedding supper for two was served in the Rose Room of the house; all was peaceful; the culmination of years of worship on his part, and for her, a growing reliance on his strength.

Her Will would leave to her new husband the use of West House and five acres of land surrounding it. Yaddo, as she and Spencer had arranged, would be conducted as a retreat for persons engaged in the creative arts. Masterpieces of music and literature were already being produced at Yaddo, and Katrina knew that, with George Foster Peabody heading the Corporation, the flow of talent would continue unchecked.

Christmas, that year, was a time of quiet joy: wreaths and boughs from the estate made the rooms at West House fragrant with a breath of the out-of-doors; the greetings of many friends surrounded them with love; but Katrina's strength was ebbing, and she slipped out of this life January 8, 1922.

The burial took place in the frozen earth of the Rose Garden at Yaddo, and a heavy snow-storm swirled about those who loved her with a deathless devotion.

Their devotion was evident in the fall of that year when the Katrina Trask Memorial Gateway, a gift of the men and women of the Yaddo Estate, was dedicated. Designed to connect the large Broadway Hotels with Congress Park, the gateway is a symbol of love and respect—crystallized in granite.

CHAPTER VI
Edward Morse Shepard

(Erlowest)

Edward Morse Shepard entered a troubled world in Brooklyn on July 23, 1850. His father died when he was six years old, and Abram S. Hewitt, his father's friend, came to the aid of the family in loco parentis. Mr. Hewitt was associated with the Democratic Party, and the Party itself was bossed by Tammany Hall, a group which had become notorious for its corruption. Growing up in a political atmosphere fixed Edward's interest, and, from his earliest days, he recognized Tammany Hall as a moving force.

He went to public school in Brooklyn and in Ohio; later, attending the College of the City of New York, he graduated at the age of 19 with highest honors. In a few years, he had become a successful corporation lawyer in the firm of Shepard, Smith, and Harkness, with offices at 128 Broadway. His holdings in railroads and mining in Mexico and the developing West, were the major sources of his wealth.

Mr. Shepard was small in stature with delicate and sensitive features, a high forehead, and brown eyes that seemed to penetrate to the heart of a problem, or to a person's innermost thoughts. The small mustache which he affected added distinction to his features. Normally, his speaking voice was rather high-pitched and when he was excited, grew shrill and penetrating. He was shy with large groups of people, but shone as a conversationalist in small groups of friends where he felt most comfortable. He was highly respected by those who knew him well and appreciated his keen mentality and his constructive, analytical thoughts on every subject. His closest friends were George Foster Peabody and Mr. and Mrs. Spencer Trask. Drawn together by mutual interests, they remained lifelong friends, meeting each other often in Brooklyn, Saratoga, Lake George, or New York City.

Successful in the legal profession at an early age, Mr. Shepard tried another form of expression and authored two books. His memorial to Richard Dugdale, author of "The Jukes," was published, followed by a study of the life of Martin Van Buren.

In many ways, Mr. Shepard's career paralleled George Foster Peabody's to such an extent that it is possible to assess his career along with that of his great friend. Together they founded the Young Men's Democratic Club in Brooklyn, a group which Mr. Peabody felt did much to insure the election of Grover Cleveland to his first term in the White

House. The two friends also worked for extension of the Civil Service Act in New York State.

Idealism and conservatism were blended in Mr. Shepard's mental endowments. He was the reformer who could see the faults of a system clearly, and he possessed the realistic approach that dictated methods of change. His conservatism, however, was of the type that impelled him to cling to established customs, and he clung to the Democratic Party even though he was revolted by its association with the Tammany Hall crowd. His idealism was severely tried in 1886 when Abram S. Hewitt, backed by Tammany Hall for the office of Mayor of New York City, swept the field, winning over a slate which included newcomer Theodore Roosevelt. A murmur which never quite became a chorus arose, and it was charged that Mr. Hewitt had won the election through the stuffing of ballot boxes by his henchmen. Although both friends were shaken by the disclosure, Mr. Peabody, with firm belief in Mr. Shepard's integrity, continued to urge him toward political office.

The academics of politics interested Shepard far more than the work of the precincts, and he stayed aloof from the handshaking, back-slapping technique. In 1892, his idealism centered on Grover Cleveland who, having successfully filled the office of President of the United States in a previous term, was regarded by many as an outstanding candidate. Trouble broke out in the ranks and a convention was called in Syracuse, New York for the purpose of promoting a rival candidate. Alarmed by the apparent attempt to block Cleveland's nomination, Shepard and Peabody went as delegates to the State Convention and successfully added their weight to eliminating the contender. They then went on to the National Convention in Chicago, determined that their man would win. Following Cleveland's nomination, both men were speakers in his behalf in the New York City area, and had the supreme satisfaction of seeing their candidate returned to office for a second term.

In 1895, Shepard ran for the office of Mayor of Brooklyn on an Independent ticket. Peabody gave him strong support, but Shepard's ticket was defeated.

In 1901, unrest in the political scene amounted to a crisis. The Republican Party had nominated the Honorable Seth Low as candidate for Mayor of New York City. Mr. Low's credentials were impressive: he was a former mayor of Brooklyn and, in 1890, had become President of Columbia University. The Democrats chose Mr. Peabody as their candidate; he refused the honor. The choice then fell on Mr. Shepard who accepted. At this point, Mr. Shepard and Mr. Peabody were in a dilemma: both men had, on occasion, fought the Tammany regime, using the Citizens' Union as their medium, but this time, Shepard realized that he needed Tammany's backing; he also needed Peabody's support. In the conflict between principle and friendship, the latter won, and Mr. Peabody resigned from the Citizens' Union which was definitely anti-Tammany, throwing his support to Shepard in his bid for the mayoralty. His action brought criticism, and the Tribune blasted him with the headline, "Peabody With The Boss." The disturbing implication only spurred Mr. Peabody on to work harder for his candidate, but Mr. Shepard lost the election.

Undaunted, Peabody continued to urge political office on his friend. He knew Shepard's integrity, his sincerity, and, above all, his grasp of the country's problems, qualities which he believed were needed in the fight against corruption. These sterling qualities escaped the average voter who looked for flair, color, and drama in his candidate—superficial qualities which Mr. Shepard did not possess. He was no vote-getter as was demonstrated in 1904, when Mr. Peabody boosted him as candidate for President of the United States; nor was the nomination for Governor of New York State to be his.

"That man couldn't even carry the county," tough-minded political bosses complained as a survey of public opinion confirmed their gloomiest forecasts.

The precincts may have been out of Mr. Shepard's field, but in the Courts of the State of New York, he was highly respected. An indication of his standing in the Democratic Party occurred in 1907. Governor Charles Evans Hughes had worked on the Paige-Merritt bill which would give the Governor the power to remove commissioners for certain reasons; the bill also set qualifications and salaries of commission members.

The leaders of the opposition, believing that a show of strength among Democrats opposing the bill would sway the Governor's position, chose five of their most outstanding party members to present their case, and Mr. Shepard was one of the men chosen. His intellectual grasp of situations, his sincerity and forcefulness were apparent to political leaders, even though the voters consistently cast their votes for his opponent.

Shepard's greatest contributions were not to public office, but to civic and benevolent causes: he was one of the original founders of the Lake George Club; and on the Saratoga Commission, he added his efforts to those of Peabody and Trask. He served as Counsel to the Southern Education Board, a group of practical idealists who were working for better education in the South. All the southern states were under the aegis of this Board, and much was accomplished through group action, each member pooling his influence. The group often met at Abenia, Mr. Peabody's Lake George estate, and many important issues were discussed on the broad porch overlooking the lake.

Often, gazing on Lake George, Mr. Shepard must have thought of his first sight of that beautiful body of water. He was only a boy, and had come by stagecoach to visit at the lake. The beauty of woods, lake, and mountains had so impressed the child that he had vowed, "Someday I'll have a summer place here, too."

He kept that promise to himself later when, a successful and wealthy man, he built the beautiful mansion "Erlowest" on Millionaires' Row. Granite for its construction, it was said, was quarried less than a mile

Erlowest, built by Edward M. Shepard,
owned now by Charles R. Wood

68

One of Paxton "Cottages" at Lake George

Sun Castle, on grounds of former Shepard Estate

from the property. The Queen Anne mansion was classic in design, baroque in decoration, and its stained glass windows broke the sunlight into patterns of color. Considered one of the most beautiful among the many impressive residences on Millionaires' Row, Erlowest stood on a promontory where the view was a vast sweep of lake dotted with islands; mountains loomed on the further shore. Lawns sloped down to the water's edge with flower gardens and ornamental plantings. There were extensive woodlands on the estate, and many shaded walks where branches of tall trees met overhead. Mr. Peabody often came to visit the owner of Erlowest, and they took long strolls on the forest paths, deep in conversation. On chilly days, they could sit before one of Erlowest's 13 fireplaces and continue their discussions.

In the impressive—even baronial—dining hall, Mr. Shepard gave many delightful dinners to groups of friends; he never married, and his gracious hostess was his sister, Mrs. Charles Hewitt. An especially delightful event was the annual farewell dinner which he gave for members of the Southern Education Board at the close of of their conference. The clergy of the Episcopal Church were also entertained here, frequently as house guests.

His devotion to the Episcopal Church was so well known that when he became involved in the famous Crapsey case, parishioners were shocked and bewildered. The Rev. Algernon Crapsey, rector of St. Andrew's Episcopal Church in Rochester, New York, had, in 1904–05, caused considerable consternation by a series of sermons in which he questioned doctrines of the Church, especially the Virgin birth. Summoned to be tried in the Diocesan Court of Western New York on April 17, 1906, the Rev. Mr. Crapsey retained Mr. Shepard as his counsel. Following trial, the decision was announced against the clergyman. Shepard appealed to a higher Church Court; the appeal was denied, and the Rev. Mr. Crapsey was dismissed.

Now Mr. Peabody took up the cause which involved both his Church and his great friend, Attorney Shepard. His feeling about the clergyman's utterances might have been summed up in the well-known phrase, "I do not agree with what you say, but I will fight to the death for your right to say it."

To that end, he wrote hundreds of letters asking that the Rev. Mr. Crapsey be reinstated. His letters were received politely, but the church leaders were adamant. The clergyman was obliged to seek work other than preaching, but for years he kept in touch with the two men who had attempted to assist him.

Mr. Shepard served as vestryman in St. James' Espiscopal Church at Lake George for several terms, earning the esteem and affection of the church dignitaries and the congregation. He gave an organ to the church, and purchased the lot adjoining the church property; he willed this lot to the church so that it would never be crowded in the growth that he knew was sure to come.

In 1910, Mr. Peabody made one more attempt to promote Edward M. Shepard for public office—this time for Senator. There is something pathetic in Mr. Peabody's attempt to place his friend in high political office, and in Mr. Shepard's desire to justify his friend's faith in his political ability. Appreciating Mr. Shepard's greatness of mind and heart, Mr. Peabody tried again and again to make the public understand how much his friend would dignify any political office conferred upon him, but each time, the party bosses withheld their approval. This time, friction developed over the choice of candidates, and Shepard withdrew his name from consideration. Privately, he may not have shared his friend's enthusiasm for political success. With all deference to Mr. Peabody and his vicarious political aims, Mr. Shepard could have said, wearily perhaps,

"Thanks, old friend, for all you've tried to do for me—but it's a little late now, and I'm getting tired."

He died the following year at Erlowest on July 20, 1911. In tribute, Henry W. Hayden, president of the Lake George Association, said of Mr. Shepard,

> "His efforts to advance the uplifting of all men were unceasing and his life and example have furnished us with inspiration ever for higher standards." [1]

Although Mr. Shepard had departed this life, his mansion remained in the news for some years. During World War I, Erlowest became a place of rest and relaxation for wounded soldiers; undoubtedly, Mr. Shepard would have approved of this guest list.

Mr. Shepard's sister, Mrs. Hewitt, continued to make her home on the estate and, in 1922, leased the mansion to Nathan Miller, Governor of New York State, as a summer home. Since there were not enough servants at the Executive Mansion in Albany, some of Mrs. Hewitt's own servants stayed on to augment the Governor's retinue.

There were a niece and nephew who had filled the need for young people at Erlowest. The nephew, Edward Shepard Hewitt, became a prominent architect in New York City. The niece married Russell Leffingwell, senior partner in the J. P. Morgan Company, and known as "one of the ten most (financially) successful men in the United States." With their occupancy, Erlowest was also known as the Leffingwell Estate.

The Shepard-Leffingwell property was purchased by Charles Reeves Wood, President of Charles R. Wood Enterprises, Inc., comprising Storytown, Gaslight Village, Waxlife, Cavalcade of Cars, International Village and other related business ventures. He is also president of the International Ajusement Park Association covering 27 countries. A deluxe motel, Sun Castle, now stands on the former Shepard-Leffingwell premises; the mansion itself has been preserved and still retains its outer beauty and dignity.

---

[1]Memorial, Lake George and Vicinity, Press of Lake George Printing Company, 1929, p. 16.

Mr. Wood, who isn't sure about the number of rooms in his castle of the sun, has lightened and brightened the interior of the mansion in white—ceilings, woodwork and stairways—and has installed soft carpeting throughout. In one room, richly embossed wallpaper glows with brilliant color; in another, a subdued forest green suggests relaxation. On the third story is a nine-hole putting green, where Astroturf on the floors and murals of a golf course on the walls complete the illusion of a spacious outdoor golf course.

Nor is Edward Morse Shepard forgotten. Shortly after his death, his sister, Mrs. Hewitt, and several friends were instrumental in obtaining land in the center of Lake George Village as a memorial to him. The well-loved site is always referred to as "Shepard Memorial Park," and tourists, on learning his full name, often ask:

"Who *was* Edward Morse Shepard?"

In reply, they will probably hear ". . . in politics . . . quiet but influential . . . devoted to church . . . most beautiful home," and always, "He was a great friend of George Foster Peabody's."

CHAPTER VII

The Tuttles

Charles Henry and Helene Wheeler Tuttle

(Rockledge—Halcyon)

Charles Henry Tuttle came into the world in New York City on April 21, 1879. If the good fairies had been presiding at his birth, they could have predicted, honestly, that he would be wealthy, successful in his profession, that he would meet and marry the girl of his dreams and, further, that he would enjoy all these gifts without the price of tragedy that so often accompanies an eminent position in life.

The sum total of these gifts was a happy man: the good things of life came readily to Charles Henry Tuttle; he appreciated them, experienced every moment to the fullest, and never lost his sense of wonder about it all. He lived more than 90 memorable years and, in his 90th year, wrote a book of reminiscenses for his children—a book so full of joie de vivre and happy memories that it is an inspiration to read. On his 91st birthday, he had completed an equally joyful supplement to the first volume.

Among the good things of life which he enjoyed was a place at Lake George where he was an early visitor, coming as an infant to St. James Episcopal Church for christening. His grandfather, the Reverend Isaac Henry Tuttle, DD., founder and occasional summer rector of St. James, winter rector of St. Luke's New York City, officiated at the christening. Grandfather Tuttle cherished the hope that this lusty grandson would be named after him, but he was due for a surprise. The rector's older brother Charles had better reason to believe that the child would be named after *him*.

The christening party had assembled at the baptismal font, the father holding the infant. At the question, "What is this child's name?" the father hesitated, then stammered, "Charles Henry." To the rector's everlasting credit, he concealed his disappointment, retained his composure, and the infant was duly christened.

There was a price-tag on the name "Charles." Uncle had promised to leave his namesake $5,000 in his Will, but when he died a few years later, no Will could be found. Obviously, for Charles, who seemed blessed with phenomenal good fortune, such a situation could only be temporary.

One morning, the Rev. Dr. Tuttle's daughter Mary, a very religious woman, told of a strange dream she had experienced the night before. In the dream, Uncle Charles had come to her, very disturbed because his Will had not been found. He told Mary that they should look in the attic where an old horsehair trunk was stored; the Will would be found under a flap in that trunk. Without a moment's hesitation or disbelief, members of the family rushed to the attic and found the Will, just as the dream had predicted. Evidently, Uncle Charles was a man of his word, both here and hereafter.

Charles Henry Tuttle's association with Lake George came about in the natural course of events. His grandfather, the Rev. Dr. Tuttle, was probably the first annual summer visitor. Coming to Lake George in 1848, he stayed at the old Lake House, now part of Shepard Memorial Park. Later, he bought the Hammond farm, and in 1876, built Rock-ledge, the first mansion on Millionaires' Row. At the same time, he was founding St. James Episcopal Church in Lake George Village.

Toward the end of the 1800's, the Bolton Road, once a trail that had known the tread of moccasined feet, saw a daily parade of sleek horses, elegant carriages, and equally elegant owners. The four o'clock parade became a ritual for the affluent residents of Millionaires' Row as a time to see others and be seen by them. The Rev. Dr. Tuttle's handsome carriage was usually in the parade.

Although the Reverend Doctor's resources could not compete with those of the Millionaires, like them, he had a social conscience; and, with his own money, he developed Roaring Brook as a source of fresh water for the community. With acute foresight, he perceived that, in a relatively short time, all the land bordering the Lake would be solidly built up and the public would have no access to its waters. He, therefore, deeded a strip of land to the Town to be used as a public road leading from the Bolton Road to the shore. Other property owners followed his example, and there now exists, every mile along the Bolton road, a public way to the lake. At the end of nearly every public road is a beach and, as an added advantage, these roads are usable in case of fire.

Summers spent at Rockledge became the usual thing for Charles Henry, but between-seasons was another matter. The boy's father, a law-yer, had died when the child was 3 years old and his mother, unable to af-ford living in New York City, moved to Oak Ridge, New Jersey. She rented rooms in a farmhouse, and there they lived on the modest income provided by royalties from her husband's legal writings.

Charles readily adapted to rural life, as he did to every circumstance. There was the swimming hole in summer, snow-covered hills for coasting in the winter. Penny candy could be bought at the country store, and there were occasional trips in a farmer's wagon to other towns. Brimming over with good health and high spirits, the boy enjoyed the riches of country living, storing away in his innermost being, memories of a life lived simply and happily.

When he was ten years old, he and his mother returned to New York City to live in Doctor Tuttle's home. The position and prestige of his grandfather's family did not prevent the boy from working, however: among other jobs, he sold newspapers on the horse-cars that traversed the city and, in the blizzard of '88, joined with other laborers in shoveling snow.

Pursuing his advantages, he enrolled in Trinity School where the Rev. Dr. Tuttle was a trustee. Graduating with high honors, he went on to Columbia College where he reinforced his habit of success by graduating Phi Beta Kappa. Hope died hard with the Rev. Dr. Tuttle: he would have been pleased if Charles had entered the ministry, but the young man chose the legal profession. Attending Columbia Law School, he passed the bar examination in his junior year. On graduation, he was invited to join the firm of Davies, Stone & Auerbach, becoming that specialist known as a Wall Street lawyer.

Charles Henry Tuttle was already successful when he met the girl of his dreams. With Hélène as his inspiration, he discovered a talent for writing poetry, and his verses compare favorably with the work of better-known poets. They are preserved in his book, "Memorabilia for My Children."

Hélène Wheeler was born on November 12, 1881, into a family situation which today's psychologists would consider ideal for the best development of a child. She had loving parents, several brothers and sisters, aunts and uncles, and grandparents, and they all adored her. Her name, Hélène, given through love, was the name of an upperclassman who was her mother's friend at Vassar. Love fostered her independence; it was a love that guided gently and forged enduring ties of affection within the family without the necessity of physical punishment.

As she grew older, social training put an even higher luster on an already radiant personality. There was dancing school, which she thought rather boring—but the parties were fun. There were manners that became second nature as they were rooted in her innate kindness and consideration for others. To the family first, then to a wider circle, she was a little princess, always the center of a group, generous with her possessions and her affection. Forceful and vital, she had a keen sense of drama which inspired her to write plays and entertainments, directing them with enthusiasm and an inborn flair for artistic effect.

She had an early acquaintance with the medium of Art through an uncle, Theodore Irwin, her mother's brother. Uncle Theodore had built up a remarkable collection of books and paintings which Hélène knew from her earliest years as one of the world's great collections. In his possession was a Gutenberg Old Testament—the first book ever printed. He also owned the "Purple Bible," a tract written about 780 A.D. in uncial (irregular) letters on purple vellum. This treatise dating from the reign of Charlemagne, ruler of the Holy Roman Empire, was presented to Henry VIII by Pope Leo X when the king received the title "Defender of the Faith."

Hélène's father owned a lumber yard; nevertheless, he was interested in finding a substitute for wood paneling. Both parents worked long hours on a mysterious substance combining asbestos and ashes which could be treated to resemble various types of wood. Since the invention showed signs of becoming commercially successful, Mr. Wheeler moved his family to New York City where there was greater opportunity to market his invention.

For a while, Hélène was not happy with the change. She missed her friends, and the familiar area of Oswego. She enrolled at City College, then Barnard. During her second year at Barnard, an unusual opportunity arose: she had the chance to *leave* college.

Uncle Theodore and family were going South for the social season, and had asked the Wheelers to take charge of their daughter Louise for the winter. Uncle Theodore's plan was to rent a house large enough for the augmented family, with the hope that Hélène would have the leisure to devote to his daughter. Hélène was delighted to provide the time, and Uncle Theodore found a large house on West 144th Street with a vine-covered porch. That year proved most satisfying to Hélène. She went everywhere with Louise, going with her to the hearing specialist, the doctor, attending social events with her, accompanying her on daily drives through Central Park, and supervising her schooling.

On her own account, Hélène found that teaching Sunday School at St. Luke's Church was an absorbing venture, and when a fair was proposed, she offered to put on one of the plays her mother had written. Rehearsals for the play went badly; there weren't enough children to take the parts, and those who did report for rehearsals only added to the problem. Seeking advice, Hélène was told to confer with one of the ladies of the church.

Going to the address given, she found that the lady and her husband were playing whist with another lady and gentleman. Brushing aside Hélène's reluctance to break up the game, the hostess insisted that the girl join her friends at tea. A minor event in her life suddenly became one of the utmost significance. She was introduced to Mrs. Croswell Tuttle and her son, Attorney Charles Henry Tuttle, and told them of the plight of her play at St. Luke's. Sparks flashed when the two met, and Hélène went home overjoyed with the success of her mission; but more important was the certainty that something very meaningful had occurred that day. At home, she reported that she had met a wonderful man with red hair. As his reaction, Attorney Tuttle, impressed by a girl who hesitated to break up a game of whist, announced to his mother, "I hope you noticed that young lady because she is going to be your daughter-in-law."

A three-year engagement followed, and in June, 1907, they were married. The large wedding, perfect in the eyes of the bride, was conducted in St. Luke's Church, New York City, and the only flaw was that the Rev. Isaac Tuttle had not lived to perform the ceremony. Following the reception, the couple stepped into a white coach drawn by two white horses. This was window-dressing, and Hélène recounts that they went right through the royal carriage and into an ordinary hack drawn up beside it. They were driven to the pier and boarded the Albany night-boat where the bridal suite awaited them.

The next day, the trolley car took them from Albany to Lake George where Mr. Bly, caretaker of the Tuttle property, met them with a carriage—a signal honor, as most travel, even to roadside homes, was by boat.

At Rockledge, Charles' inheritance from Grandfather Tuttle, Hélène started unpacking their suitcases and rearranging furniture immediately. She knew that the month of June would pass all too quickly; and Rockledge was rented for the rest of the summer. South of Rockledge was the estate Halcyon; both had been built by the Rev. Dr. Tuttle, and off-shore lay Tea Island. All properties except Rockledge had been purchased by Charles Tuttle from Frederick T. Gates, John D. Rockefeller's advisor. In a merry-go-round of property exchange, the parcels had been owned by Grandfather Isaac Tuttle in the first place.

One of Hélène's first contacts with the summer colony came through an invitation from George Foster Peabody inviting the young couple to attend a luncheon at his estate, Abenia. This event necessitated dressing up to an extent not anticipated, and the decision on what to wear became a minor crisis. On the day of the luncheon, Mr. Peabody sent his carriage for them, and as the carriage drew up to the mansion's long porch, Hélène was impressed by the beauty and grandeur of the house and grounds. She was especially entranced by the grace and charm of the host himself who, on hearing that her name was Hélène, greeted her with "What a pretty name."

Abenia had what was probably the first picture window in the area, and it actually framed a picture; a panorama of mountains, lake, and sky. Hélène especially noted the carved dining-room chairs, each one representing a knight of the Round Table. At dinner, she was seated to the right of Spencer Trask, Mr. Peabody's business partner; Mr. Trask's wife, the famous and beautiful Katrina, was ill at Triuna, their island home. Another bride, Mrs. Edward M. Parrott, wife of the rector of St. James, was seated at Mr. Peabody's right. To Hélène with her love of romance, Mr. Peabody became "My Knight of Abenia," because of his courtly and gracious manner.

A few days later, when she was giving a house party at Rockledge, Mr. Peabody sent his steamboat, Pocahontas, for the use of the guests, and the entire party sailed down the lake, with luncheon prepared and served on board.

With this introduction to the elite of Millionaires' Row, Hélène became a member of the colony that flocked to their Lake George mansions each summer. She wrote and produced plays that were presented at Shepard Memorial Park, often featuring, among other notables, Mme. Marcella Sembrich, star of the Metropolitan Opera Company. The list of patrons for these events was impressive, usually headed by Adolph S. Ochs, publisher of the *New York Times*. "I recall that, as a small boy, I took

Rockledge

Rockledge—built by Rev. Dr. Tuttle

*Halcyon, mansion
still used by
Tuttle family*

Charles H. Tuttle at his property, Top-O-The World

part in one of Mrs. Tuttle's plays," admits a dignified County Officer, "I was a butterfly." Hélène also enjoyed the Sunday-evening hymn-sings at the Lake George Club, led by "one of the greatest contraltos the Metropolitan ever had," Louise Homer.

These were star-studded days, when elegance was taken for granted, dress was formal, manners were exquisite, and priceless talent was graciously made available on request.

In this setting, Hélène, the little princess, became a queen.

For Charles and Hélène Tuttle, life was a continuous love-story: to her, he remained always the wonderful young man with red hair; and he never ceased adoring her. She shone in the society of Millionaires' Row, visiting the estates of other residents, attending meetings of The Garden Club of Lake George, and events at the Lake George (Country) Club. The large hotels, Fort William Henry at Lake George Village, and the Sagamore at Bolton Landing, were also resorts where the "in" crowd gathered.

She reveled in the entertainments which she produced; she enjoyed the fun and excitement of party-going and party-giving, and her parties became famous for their originality and for the sumptuous food served.

Four children were born to the Tuttles: three girls and one boy; all were healthy, handsome, intelligent, and a delight to their parents. The social pace continued in New York City where the Tuttles lived during the winter months. Here there were social engagements for Hélène, involvement in schools for the children, and the many interests associated with her husband's profession.

. During the early days of their engagement, Hélène had heard a rumor that disturbing elements were trying to prohibit week-day religious education in the schools. She told Charles; he became interested and, for years, fought for the cause of Released Time for the Religious Education of Schoolchildren. The case was carried all the way to the Supreme Court where the Released Time Program was declared legal in a 6–3 decision.

Attorney Charles H. Tuttle made a name for himself as a Trial Lawyer, then accepted other responsibilities: he was appointed to the Board of Trustees of the College of the City of New York. By 1918, he had entered public life, joining the Republican District Club where he received training in public speaking.

Added responsibility came to him in 1927 when he was appointed United States Attorney for the Southern District of New York. The District included Manhattan, the Bronx, and all Hudson River counties as far north as Albany. All United States law business in this District, criminal and civic, came under his jurisdiction. In this position, he assembled a staff of 50 young lawyers as his assistants. It was a matter of pride to him that all 50 of these men later moved up to positions of distinction.

Appointment of Charles H. Tuttle to responsible positions was made by succeeding governors of New York State, including a position on the State Reorganization Commission under Gov. Alfred E. Smith; later he became a member of the Commission to Revise the New York City Charter. Gov. Dewey appointed him as Counsel to the Commission to Prohibit Racial, National, or Religious Discrimination in Employment. He was also chairman of the Interfaith Commission of Jews, Protestants and Roman Catholics who were concerned over the lack of religious teaching in the schools. Other appointments followed; he was named by Gov. Dewey as Chairman of the Metropolitan Transit Commission. Gov. Harriman made him a member of the State Commission to propose revision of the State Constitution.

A milestone in his political life was his nomination for the office of Governor of New York State in the 1930 election. He was opposed by Franklin D. Roosevelt, and lost the election by a large majority. Two days after losing the election, Mr. Tuttle joined the law firm of Breed, Abbott & Morgan, resuming the practice of law which had been interrupted by his political activities.

A happier aftermath of his loss to Roosevelt was formation of an association of the "Tuttle Boys" who had worked with him in the U.S. Attorney's Office. Thereafter, they met once a year on his birthday and good-naturedly "roasted" the boss. One of the songs, sung to the tune of "Man on the Flying Trapeze," gives an idea of the type of entertainment the Tuttle Boys produced:

> He ran thru the State with the greatest of ease,
> He thought he would win in a walk and a breeze,
> He spoke to the workers and farmers as well,
> And sought Charlie Tuttle to sell.
> Then he urged they discard prohibition
> Oh, with this he should never have dealt.
> For the upstaters made their decision,
> And clamored for Frank Roosevelt. O-O-O
> They drank wet upstate but they all voted dry,
> Just why this should be, Charlie never knew why,
> They wanted their wine and beer under their belt,
> But they voted for Frank Roosevelt.[1]

With a saving sense of humor and considerable aplomb, Charles Tuttle continued as a victor, even in defeat. Other honors came to him: he received from the Greek Orthodox patriarch the Grand Cross of the Knights of the Holy Sepulchre, their highest honor in the Eastern Orthodox Church. He was named a delegate to the National Convention which nominated General Eisenhower for president. Two L.L.D. degrees were conferred upon him: on from Syracuse University, the other from the State Board of Regents and the City of New York.

[1] Memorabilia for My Children: Charles Henry Tuttle (on his 90th birthday), April 21, 1969, Halcyon Press, p. 92.

Medals and plaques awarded to him included: a medal presented by Mayor Wagner naming him "Illustrious Citizen of the City of New York." As President of Brotherhood-in-Action, he received a bronze tablet suitably inscribed; the Alumni Association of Trinity School in New York City gave him a medal as "Outstanding Alumnus." He received the John H. Finley medal from the Alumni Association of the City College of New York for distinguished service to the college and to higher education in the City.

It was after the 1930 election when he learned from his caretaker, Charles H. Bly (nicknamed "B.I.") that a mountaintop was for sale. The 1500 acre tract overlooks Lake George with its islands, bays, and surrounding mountains. On inspection, Mr. Tuttle was so delighted with the spectacular view that he made plans to purchase the property; but what name could suggest the grandeur of that vista?

"Call it 'Top o' the World,' " suggested B.I., and so it became, and still is.

From 1932–39, Mr. Tuttle held the office of First Vice-President of the Lake George Club. He was counsel to the Lake George Association for 40 years, and set up the Charles H. Tuttle citation given annually to a member whose achievements would result in the greatest benefit to Lake George.

Charles and Hélène spent a long and happy life together, and when, at the age of 87, she died, the moment, as described by Charles Tuttle in his "Memorabilia," seemed only a renewal and continuation of their love. As he advanced into his 9th decade of life, there was no mourning for what might have been. Instead, he expressed profound gratitude for what had been, and he faced the future with sublime faith in what was to be.

CHAPTER VIII

Harold Pitcairn

(Green Harbour)

The spirit of adventure was strong in John Pitcairn when, as a young man, he left Scotland to seek his fortune in the United States. The American Civil War was over; people could now resume the business of moving on and establishing homes. Opportunities opened up readily for John Pitcairn, and he found work as a telegraph operator and dispatcher for the Pennsylvania Railroad. It seemed a good place to start: his friend, Andrew Carnegie, had started in a similar manner and, from all accounts, was doing right well. He emulated Carnegie in buying railroad stocks, later investing in oil. He then branched out on his own, founding the Pittsburgh Plate Glass Company, a venture which laid the foundation for his fortune.

John Pitcairn also possessed a strong religious sense and, when he was introduced to the Swedenborgian religion in middle life, he accepted the doctrine whole-heartedly. From that time on, his material plans were touched with spirituality. His wealth grew and he dreamed of founding a dynasty: there would be a settlement devoted to his family and their descendants; at its center would be a great cathedral, and there would be an academy conducted in its shadow.

In the State of Pennsylvania, County of Montgomery, and town of Bryn Athyn, he bought acres of rolling farmland. Here he planned to create his own Garden of Eden where life would approximate perfection, with the Cathedral as its core. Dreamer and mystic though he was, John Pitcairn was realist enough to know that there would be sorrows, even in the most carefully-planned community. But he could not have guessed at the tragedies that would stalk those very descendants whom he strove to protect. He did not live to see the realization of his dream, but as death drew near, he was consoled by the knowledge that the Cathedral was in the early stage of construction.

John Pitcairn left a fortune, of at least $60 million with a possible ceiling of $270 million, to be divided among his three sons, but he left them something else of infinite value: a dash of the pioneering spirit which had once impelled him to cross the ocean in search of a new and more abundant life.

The sons, Raymond, Theodore, and Harold, were also dedicated to the fulfillment of the dream, but with their varying talents, each took a different route to reach his goal. Thus Raymond, a lawyer, assumed the task of completing the Cathedral; Theodore, ordained as a clergyman, went to Africa to preach the doctrine of Emmanuel Swendenborg; Harold, a pioneer in aviation, became involved in the autogiro, forerunner of the helicopter. In some ways, their lives were parallel: each married and had nine children—each lost a son in early childhood. There the similarity stopped.

Raymond, who possessed a deep understanding of architecture and a natural bent toward the details of construction, gathered about him the finest craftsmen and artisans. For years, their shelters clustered around the base of the Cathedral like the guilds of medieval times. When the Cathedral was finally ready for the worshippers, by deliberate design, it was still unfinished. A few subordinate details were left in a rough state so that the edifice would never be finished but always in the process of building, symbolizing God's continuing work on earth. Chiseled in a stone wall was the face of John Pitcairn, patriarch, forever keeping a watchful eye on his domain.

The Gothic Cathedral, world center of the General Church of the New Jerusalem, remains a showplace. A blending of colors in the stained glass windows illumines the altar in a violet glow. The floor rises gradually in height as one approaches the altar, symbolizing the uplift of the spirit. No two features are duplicated, signifying the infinite variety of Deity. Even twin spires have been fashioned with a subtle difference, and no two door knobs are alike.

Raymond Pitcairn was also deeply involved in politics. He never sought elective office, but served the local Council for 50 years. Eyebrows lifted when he backed Franklin Roosevelt in 1932, and he was asked to resign from the prestigious Union League. As the New Deal unfolded, he found his own conservatism outraged and fought Roosevelt's program. He himself was no drinker, but opposed prohibition on the grounds that it violated individual rights. His wealth and political convictions made him a man of influence on the national political scene and, outside of the temporary defection to Roosevelt, he fought liberalism to the last.

Education flourished along with religion at Bryn Athyn. The Academy housed elementary and high school grades; there was an accredited college and a theological seminary. Theodore graduated here and was ordained a minister in the Swedenborgian faith. His ministry took him to street corners in Philadelphia where he preached to curious onlookers. An extension of his religious work reached to Basutoland in South Africa where he worked among the natives for six years, aided by his wife, Marijke, whom he had met on his travels. He returned to Bryn Athyn to become an assistant minister in the Cathedral, and found trouble.

Differences in religious doctrine arose between him, his family, and the clergy, and he left the church, taking his followers with him. The New Church which he built on his own property seemed an affront to Harold, and became a source of contention between them. Raymond refused to become involved, and some family solidarity was maintained in that quarter. Theodore, needing money to carry on his church and his philanthropies, made art history when he auctioned off his art collection at fabulous prices. One painting, a Monet for which he had paid $11,000, brought $1.4 million, a record at that time.

In planning to share part of his wealth, Theodore was following family tradition. All branches of the family have always given generously to causes and organizations. It is said that each family maintains a Foundation covering gifts for charity and the arts. Combined, the Foundation is said to total $21.4 million.

Harold became involved in aviation in its early stages. He obtained a pilot's license signed by Orville Wright, and in World War I, was an air cadet. In 1929, he set a record for the longest solo flight ever made in an autogyro, a machine invented nine years earlier by de la Cievra, a Spaniard. Landing his craft neatly on the White House lawn, Harold accepted a trophy from President Herbert Hoover for achievement in aviation, while cameramen and reporters swarmed over the lawn to catch the historic occasion.

At the outbreak of World War II, Harold Pitcairn turned his aircraft patents over to the Government for use by the armed forces. Subsequently, the Government refused to pay royalties, and Harold brought suit—one of the longest and most expensive lawsuits ever instituted against the Government of the United States. The case was finally decided in favor of the plaintiff some years after his death. Payments are still undecided, but the consensus is that millions are due his heirs.

To the outsider, it must have seemed that life at Bryn Athyn approached the ideal. One man who married into the family attests to this happy state.

"We called outselves the 'Lotus Eaters,' " he muses, recalling unbelievable luxury, princely advantages, and the leisure of his ultra-privileged existence. True, there were no stores or even a post office in the community, and residents had to travel long distances to obtain necessities; but the shopping cars were chauffeur-driven, and the beauty of the owners' estates was impressive. Their very names, Scotch in essence, were romantic: Cairnwood, the estate of the founding father; Cairncrest, Harold Pitcairn's home; and Glencairn, the Gothic structure built for Raymond Pitcairn by the same artisans who constructed the Cathedral.

But there were disturbing rumors that outsiders only half-disbelieved: that the Pitcairns had produced insane or retarded children through intermarriage. There had been intermarriages between first and second cousins, but a scholarly study of the I.Q.'s of Pitcairn descendants revealed that they were generally of superior intelligence.

Disregarding results of the study, the rumor mill continued to grind out bizarre stories about strange children kept hidden in the family dungeons. Sight-seeing groups, touring the Cathedral, have been known to include curiosity seekers, openly searching the basement for the locked closet where the monster children were supposedly kept.

There are special problems native to the very wealthy who also happen to be committed to an established religion, and to the third generation of Pitcairns, being very wealthy was often embarrassing. They were taught to "think poor" and wore well-mended clothes to school. They had guilty feelings about their parents' wealth and, from 1929 through the Depression, went through a pseudo-depression themselves. The parents, determined that their children would know what deprivation meant, allowed them only two presents each on birthdays and Christmas. Until the end of the Depression, the poor little Pitcairns even worried about going hungry, although the family fortune remained intact, and the servants were as numerous as ever.

At times, the Pitcairns left their Garden of Eden and visited resorts in other parts of the country: the Raymond Pitcairn family spent summers in the Catskills; the Harold Pitcairn family chose Lake George in the Adirondacks where they leased Green Harbour, a 42-room mansion, from William T. Carter of Houston, Texas, at a price reputed to be $3,000 for the summer. When Mrs. Pitcairn's birthday came along, Harold Pitcairn bought the property as a $60,000 birthday surprise.

The dwelling was suitable for a family used to the luxury of Cairncrest: of the 42 rooms, 20 were bedrooms, and there were 10 baths. Outbuildings included a boat house, caretakers' and chauffeurs' houses, and a greenhouse for orchids. The mansion rose to three stories, and its chimneys suggested the presence of fireplaces—nine in number. The foyer was inlaid with Italian marble, fashionable at that time, and the location of the estate—on a point jutting into the lake—was ideal, not only for the view, but as a site for an autogyro to land.

The millionaire-aviator had a beacon light placed on the point to guide his aircraft in, and the summer residents, hearing the whirr of the machine above the treetops, would explain to startled visitors,

"That's Harold Pitcairn; he built that contraption he's in—goes straight up in the air." His election as Commodore of the Lake George Club was an example of "type casting." It was a position which he enjoyed for 13 years.

The large family of varying ages blended well with the children of other summer residents, but most often they found each other's company sufficient. Few shared their daring, their love of adventure, and a recklessness that usually resulted in an interesting assortment of cuts, bruises, and broken bones.

All the Pitcairns swam like fishes. They loved speed, and shouted with delight when a stiff wind or a passing steamer raised waves that washed over the boat and drenched them. A few years later, defiance of danger spelled tragedy for John, one of Harold's sons.

Married three years, John and his young wife had set out in a schooner bound for Bermuda. A storm arose and, with the abandon of youth, they were running races on deck, exulting in the salt spray that stung their faces. With rashness native to the Pitcairn name which was now

Green Harbour, formerly owned by the Pitcairns

Green Harbour

hers, the girl, laughing, had refused the safety of a life-line; suddenly a huge wave washed over the side of the schooner, tearing her from the rain-swept deck. Horrified, John saw her for a moment, her face, stricken, as the waves closed over her. Frantically, he sought for her through the night, his lantern a feeble glow in the darkness as the schooner circled the spot where she had vanished.

There was another son, Edward (Ned), ten years younger than John, and older residents along Lake George have reason to remember him. Judging from what is known of him, he was moody and withdrawn, filled with vague fears that nagged his delicately-balanced mind. Perhaps the rumors, the tragedies, the responsibility of belonging to a preeminent family, were too much for him to master; finally, his tenuous hold on reality snapped.

It was September, the end of the tourist season, and a strange restlessness was growing in Edward's mind. His cousin had made an indifferent remark, "Those tourists at the Algonquin are still here; wish they'd go home so we could have the lake all to ourselves."

The careless remark lighted a fire in Edward's susceptible mind—a fire that would smoulder until it erupted into searing flames.

That night, the Algonquin Hotel, a landmark on Lake George, burned to the ground. No one was injured, but much personal property was lost. Onlookers, drawn to the scene by the vaulting flames, watched as the old hotel disappeared in pillars of fire. In the crowd was a young man who lived in the village. Another interested spectator, who stood near him, was Edward Pitcairn.

As the flames roared ever higher, Edward, his spirits soaring in the fury of this grand spectacle, turned to the young man nearby,

"*I* set that fire," he announced with all the pride of a creative artist.

"Then you should tell the State Troopers," was the firm reply.

Again, a suggestion was all Edward needed for motivation. He made his way to the nearest State Trooper.

"I did it. I burned the hotel," he announced proudly. In response to the startled question, "Why did you do it?" he answered honestly enough, "I don't know."

Edward thereafter dropped out of public view, but he is still remembered in Bolton as a highly disturbed individual who just wanted to be left alone.*

A year after the Algonquin fire, Harold Pitcairn died suddenly at his Bryn Athyn home. Officially, it was said that he committed suicide, but some who knew him well refuse to accept the verdict.

As they view the evidence: on the evening of Harold Pitcairn's death, he had attended a birthday party in honor of his brother Raymond's 75th birthday. It had been a lavish party for 450 guests; messages had come from President Eisenhower and Vice-President Nixon. Harold was in a

*Note: In late winter, 1977, the report circulated in the Lake George area that Edward had taken his own life.

particularly jovial mood, and his high spirits were reflected in the speech he gave in behalf of his brother. Shortly afterward, Harold Pitcairn was dead.

As circumstances unfolded, he had returned home after the party and had told his wife he was going upstairs to do some work. He was found later, sprawled face downward over his desk with a bullet in his brain. The obvious deduction was that he had committed suicide. "This is not true," his friends insist.

They say that Harold Pitcairn habitually carried a pistol in the inside pocket of his coat when he conducted his nightly rounds, checking the doors and windows of the mansion; the pistol, ready for instant action, had a hair-trigger. The pocket in which he kept the pistol also contained a notebook in which he wrote down a record of his engagements and future activities; that notebook contained a list of plans projected for the next five days. "It isn't logical" insist these friends, "that a man would list commitments for five days if he intended to end his life."

They theorize that he had either placed the gun on his desk, or that it had fallen from his pocket. In the first instance, an accidental movement of his arm could have caused the hair-trigger to go off; in the second instance, the sudden jar of the fall could have had the same effect. It was evident that the bullet had struck the ceiling, then his hand, and was deflected through an eye.

"He was only 62 and had everything to live for," his friends insist. However, his widow demanded that the inquiry stop, so the self-destruction theory stands.

Perhaps Harold Pitcairn could not have endured still another tragedy that lay ahead. His son, Bruce had become an alcoholic. This was doubly regrettable, since he was an excellent navigator. In spite of his failing, Bruce had found a position as navigator on a cruise ship; then, just before the start of the voyage, his drinking habit tripped him up, and he was replaced by a less skillful navigator.

The pain of regret which tormented him became unbearable when the ship, a few days out on the Atlantic, was wrecked with the loss of several lives. Overcome by remorse, Bruce killed himself.

The Garden of Eden dreamed of by John Pitcairn had produced its knowledge of good and evil. Green Harbour on Lake George passed out of the Pitcairn holdings and into other hands. Today, the Pitcairn clan live at Bryn Athyn as obscurely and unobtrusively as possible, trying to avoid the misfortunes that can beset the very wealty; while, from the wall of the great Cathedral, the face of John Pitcairn, founder of a dynasty, still surveys his empire, undisturbed.

CHAPTER IX

Marcella Sembrich

(The Sembrich Studio)

On February 15, 1858, near Lemberg, Poland, a baby girl was born to a peasant family named Kochanska. They were poor, even by Old World standards, but they had music in their souls and love in their hearts. They welcomed their baby daughter and named her Praxede Marcelline Kochanska, never dreaming that the tiny infant was marked for greatness. The father was a violinist and organist; the mother was also musical, and there was a brother who shared the family talent. Together, the little family took wandering journeys, their old horse drawing the hay-filled wagon where little Marcella slept. These journeys were actually business trips which gave father Kochanska an opportunity to offer his services as a music teacher. In later years, the family formed a quartet with the mother and brother playing violins, the father playing the 'cello, and Marcella at the piano.

Marcella's father did not scorn more practical values, however, and he built their first home, a small cottage with a thatched roof. The modest house sheltered a piano and Marcella started piano lessons at the age of four. When she was six, she began the study of violin, using a small violin her father had made for her. He was also her teacher, and he was a stern taskmaster, insisting on hours of study and practice daily. She loved music, accepted without question the severe practice schedule laid down by her father, and set her sights on perfection. Recreation per se was unheard of in her household, but outdoor work filled that need. She loved the time when she took the family laundry down to the brook. There, while she washed clothes in the stream, she saw the whole world of nature spread out before her, and she reveled in the bright sunshine, the mossy banks of the brook, and its singing waters.

There was no money to buy music, but there were fortunate friends who owned copies of music and would lend them to the less fortunate. Copying the music became little Marcella's task. Nightly, she sat at the table, laboriously copying music, her only light the feeble glow of a candle. As a result, the little girl's eyes were irreparably harmed. In later years, it was said, she could not even see the baton in the hands of the orchestra conductor. But no sacrifice was too great to quench her love for music. The unfolding of her talent was as natural and inexorable as the blossoming of a flower from a bud.

At the age of ten, the young musician was performing in public and thoroughly enjoying the experience. The next year, she was brought to the Conservatory at Lemberg, sponsored by a kindly old villager. At the Conservatory, she majored in violin for which she exhibited outstanding talent, and improved her skill at the piano. From the first, she was fortunate in having good instructors; here, Chopin's best pupil, who was director of the school, became her teacher in harmony.

Even with talent approximating genius, it was necessary to be practical, and she played for children's dancing classes to help pay expenses. As her local fame grew, she was in demand as an entertainer at parties, often playing all night for the social events of the wealthy. Professor Stengel, her instructor in piano. introduced her to the great masterpieces of piano music and fostered her appreciation for the best in musical literature. Probably he was the one who first discovered her vocal talent.

The Lemberg Conservatory, already a thriving center of musical culture, in due time gained greater lustre from Marcella's attendance. In addition, she was a joy to work with; she was gentle, modest, unassuming, and possessed none of the flashes of temper generally accepted as artistic temperament. In her final days at the Conservatory, she gave a concert in both violin and piano; then with the assistance of Professor Stengel, went on to Vienna where her instructors were highly competent in the teaching of violin, piano, and voice.

It was fortunate for the world of music that Marcella was a serious student, or her accomplishments could have been disrupted by social engagements. In addition to outstanding musical talent, she possessed a charming personality which could have ensured her social success; but she declined all invitations, confining herself solely to her studies. That year in Vienna, she faced a crisis and a question that had to be answered: Which avenue of expression should she choose? She could have become a virtuoso on the violin; in addition, her piano-playing equalled that of the great artists of the day, but the year of vocal study had convinced her that she could best express her appreciation of music through singing.

It was Professor Schell who arranged a meeting for her with Franz Liszt, probably the greatest musician of his time. At the interview, she played Liszt's own "Hungarian Rhapsody" with the dash, fervor, and accuracy needed by that demanding work. The gray-beared old gentleman with the bitter smile then asked, "Anything else?" She tuned the violin briefly, then gave him a demonstration of her mastery of that instrument; her technique and expression were flawless. As her final act in the audition, she sang. At the conclusion of the song, delivered with her innate sensitivity and feeling for beauty, Liszt exlaimed in German,

"My little angel. God has given you three pairs of wings with which to fly through the country of music; they are all equal; give up none of them, but sing, sing, for the world—for you have the voice of an angel."

The praise of the great master strengthened Marcella's own belief that she should concentrate on voice. In 1875, accompanied by her mother, she went to Milan for eight months of study with Lamperti. She continued studying piano and violin and learned Italian, a necessity for the singing of great operatic roles.

While in Milan, Marcella, realizing the importance of devoting every moment to her art, continued to remain aloof from social events. She herself designated her type of voice as "dramatic coloratura," a combination of qualities which is a rarity. Through an inborn dramatic sense, she developed her ability to interpret and transmit the meaning of the great composers, a gift which brought her eminence in German lieder as well as in opera.

She was only 19 when she made her operatic debut at Athens where, in an open-air theater, she sang for King George I and his Court. The night sky shimmered with stars and, in the distance, the Acropolis, a page from the architecture of the past, glowed, as another page, this time dedicated to music, was being written. Another enriching experience came to her when she married Professor Guillaume Stengel, her friend and advisor since childhood. His love and loyalty sustained her throughout the greater part of her life.

Following twenty-four performances in Athens, she returned to Vienna for further study in voice and dramatic interpretation. At this time, Marcella chose her mother's maiden name, Sembrich, for her operatic career.

Successful performances followed under contract to the Saxon Royal opera in Dresden. In 1878, granted a leave of absence, she appeared on stages in Milan, Vienna, and Warsaw. On January 1, 1879, she was the youthful soloist at the Brahms Concerto, played by Jacob Joachim, the most famous violinist of the period. The event was staged at the Gewandhaus, the historic and ornate old opera house at Leipzig.

Her fame spread and, when London summoned her, she decided that she should accept the invitation. Music-lovers at Dresden were crushed at losing her and presented her with a large plaque lettered "Stay with us; Stay with us." Marcella was touched, but firm in her decision to leave. It was as though she believed she had an appointment with destiny, an appointment which she must keep.

In May, 1880, she arrived at Covent Garden, London's prestigious opera house where Adelina Patti was just finishing a rehearsal. Marcella had always been an admirer of Patti's. It seems true that, among the greatest artists, there is little jealousy, and the crippling emotion is supplanted by true appreciation of the artist and his work.

The end of a long rehearsal with Patti was no time for another singer to appear and try the patience of the conductor and his orchestra. All the musicians were tired from the previous session, but since Marcella had come a long distance, she was granted an audition. Weariness in her listeners disappeared as she began to sing. Here was another great, a different, voice. She was received with enthusiasm and given a five-year contract.

Marcella was summoned to the musical capitals of Europe: Madrid,

Lisbon, Warsaw, St. Petersburg, and Paris. In St. Petersburg and Moscow, she appeared with the American-born singer, Lillian Nordica, one of the great singers of the day. In that part of Poland then dominated by Russia, she sang Chopin's songs in Polish and was wildly acclaimed by her countrymen. Called to St. Petersburg, she sang for Czar Nicholas II at the Winter Palace. During her recital, the Czar asked for a certain song composed by Chopin. One does not refuse when the Czar commands, but Marcella could and did, explaining,

"Your Majesty, I sing this song only in Polish, and your Chief of Police has decreed that I may not sing it again." The Czar smiled,

"But I would like to hear it," he insisted, and this time, the royal will prevailed.

At the conclusion of the song, the Czar said, "I am deeply moved, and I shall not forget Poland." He presented the young singer with a diamond bracelet, one of the many priceless mementoes which were bestowed upon her during her career.

In the fall of 1883, an event of supreme importance in the world of opera occurred: the Metropolitan Opera House opened in New York City. The "Met" had not arrived without fierce battles between its supporters and a group of musicians, music-lovers, financial interests, and journalists who owed allegiance to the Academy of Music already established at Union Square. The new opera house was destined to rank with La Scala, Covent Garden, and the great opera houses of the capitals of Europe, and appearance at the Metropolitan would signify that an opera singer had arrived at the apex of his or her career. The first opera, "Faust," was a triumph, starring Christine Nilsson, reigning favorite of the American public, with Sofia Scalchi and Italo Campanini.

Henry E. Abbey, director, had chosen Marcella Sembrich, already a world figure, to sing on the second night of the opening in "Lucia di Lammermoor." In theatrical circles, the second night of an opening is the hardest spot in which a performer can appear; the first night's performance has established a precedent; the second night's offering will be judged by that standard. The opening of the Metropolitan was made more dramatic by a rival opera company vying for public favor at the Academy of Music, but the old Academy was doomed by the wealth, power, and prestige of the Met.

Marcella Sembrich, well aware of the dangers implied in the timing of her New York debut, was undisturbed. She accepted this challenge with characteristic self-confidence, and her performance established her among the great operatic singers of all time. Following her first appearance, Henry E. Krehbiel wrote of her singing:

> "It united some of the highest elements of art which can be found only in one richly endowed with deep musical feeling and ripe artistic intelligence . . ."

Another reviewer stated,

Birthplace of Madame Sembrich near Lemberg, Poland

Marcella Sembrich, as student

ANTON RUBINSTEIN
1829 – 1894

Marcella Sembrich

Program—Sembrich—Rubenstein

Interior—Marcella Sembrich's Studio

"Sembrich's voice has that unique quality which is the vocal equivalent of originality in literature and art."

And, from the *New York Times:*

"No singer ever won the recognition of a New York audience more easily than Mme. Sembrich did. The very first note she uttered seemed to establish her in the favor of her hearers . . . The new favorite's tones are clear and brilliant and she encompasses without seeming effort the highest notes in the music . . . her execution is absolutely faultless . . ."

Adelina Patti and other shining luminaries of opera were Marcella's friends. Among them was Christine Nilsson, and together they took Sunday morning walks through Central Park. During the 1883–84 season, Marcella made 55 appearances in leading cities throughout the United States. At a special performance staged at the Metropolitan as a benefit for Henry E. Abbey, Director, she thrilled the audience with her versatility. Announcement had been made that she would appear as violinist, pianist, and vocalist, and the audience who knew her only as a superb opera singer, was prepared for moderate accomplishment in the first two mediums; they were due for a revelation.

She picked up her violin and played, and her listeners became aware that here was a violin virtuoso; they responded with amazement and applause. But the piano—surely she could not play that as brilliantly; she did, and tumultuous applause followed. When she sang a passage from "La Somnambula," the audience could not contain their enthusiastic response, and the dignified opera house rang with "Bravas." Everyone present knew that they had witnessed a nearly-unbelievable performance. Sembrich would seldom consent to appear as a triple artist. Only for an occasion benefit performance would she employ all three mediums.

At the close of the '83–84 season, she returned to Europe where she shone with the greatest stars in all European capitals. Her genius was of an all-embracing character: the superlative voice, expressing the depth of her emotions, and the dramatic values which she infused into a performance, cast a spell over her audiences. She sang with an artistry that seemed effortless, as though she had found a core of truth and beauty within herself to share freely with the world.

Among her friends was Kitty Wetmore, an American woman living in Europe, who became Marcella's companion on her concert tours. Mrs. Wetmore also joined the opera star in her favorite pastime—mountain climbing. Photographs of the period show Marcella in the costume then thought suitable for lady mountain-climbers: large hat tied securely with a scarf to prevent its being blown down the mountainside; long-sleeved white blouse, and a long skirt made without regard for the freedom of the mountain-climber's sturdy limbs. Stout boots were a concession to the rigors of the activity, and the staff was a necessity.

In 1897, she returned to the Metropolitan. There was no opera that year, and she appeared in recitals. At that time, her repertoire included the three slelections considered to be the most difficult in opera singing: "Ah, non giunge," from *La Somnambula;* "Costa Diva" from Bellini's *Norma,* and "Martern Aller Arten" from Mozart's *Il Seraglio.*

The following year, Marcella became a regular member of the Metropolitan Opera Company and her life, with that of her husband, Professor Stengel, fell into a rhythm of Spring in Europe, Autumn in America. On stage, her artistry lifted Grand Opera to new heights, but she is credited with other achievements: with all America enthused over Wagner, she kept Italian opera alive, concentrating on its artistic value; she became one of the first artists recorded on the new "talking machine." This was a sacrificial experience as the cylinder produced was scratchy and crude. (Later recordings on improved equipment have preserved her glorious voice for modern listeners.) She made theatrical history when, at a recital in Carnegie Hall, she received one of the first ovations ever given to a performer by a New York audience—that spontaneous outpouring of love and admiration given to an artist when the entire audience rises as one body in tribute. Marcella's generosity to her follow performers was legendary. When an opera, "Manru," written by Ignace Paderewski, received a cool reception, it was she who coaxed her compatriot to the stage for recognition.

She formed close personal and professional ties with Mme. Louise Homer, and in recital, presented one of Sidney Homer's songs, a setting of Robert Louis Stevenson's "Sing Me a Song of The Lad That Is Gone." On tour with Louise in the light opera, "Martha," she sang in the largest cities of the U.S. Her singing of "The Last Rose of Summer," an old Irish tune included in the opera, was warmly received and became a favorite recording.

The fall season of 1903 brought changes to the Metropolitan: the interior of the Opera House had been re-decorated by two designers associated with Stanford White, architect. Draperies and upholstery in a deep, warm red cast a glow over the theater; gold leaf used throughout added glitter to the brilliance of the jewels worn by patrons. The opening performance was Verdi's *Rigoletto* with Sembrich, Antonio Scotti, Louise Homer, and the new sensation, Enrico Caruso.

Another change was disturbing to the opera personnel. Maurice Grau, who as director had welcomed so many of the great ones to the Metropolitan, had left; in his place was a new director, Heinrich Conreid. Performers were concerned, knowing that he lacked a musical background. His regime was severe, and the singers felt that he considered their art secondary to his own business success.

For several years, there was dissension between performers and management; then a new theater, The Manhattan Opera House, built by Oscar Hammerstein, arose to threaten box office receipts at the Metropolitan. The situation was relieved by the resignation of Conreid and the hiring of Gatti-Gasazza of La Scala as director. His credentials were impeccable, his manner authoritative, and the furore subsided.

In 1906, Marcella was on a nation-wide tour with the Metropolitan Opera Company. They were in San Francisco when, on the morning of April 18, a severe earthquake occurred, and in the holocaust that followed, musicians with the troupe lost many valuable instruments. In quick response, Mme. Sembrich immediately started planning a benefit to replace those instruments. She postponed her annual trip to Europe to follow through on the plan, and after a recital at Carnegie Hall, presented the musicians with $10,000.

On February 25, 1909, Marcella Sembrich gave her last performance at the Metropolitan where she had sung for 25 years. The program included scenes from three of her most successful operas: she appeared as Norina in *Don Pasquale,* Act I; as Rosina in *The Barber of Seville,* Act II, and as Violetta in *La Traviata,* Act I.

Brilliant stars of opera joined Louise Homer and Emma Eames in planning a tribute to Mme. Sembrich. For this sentimental occasion, Marcella sang her final role before the curtain. Meanwhile, a throne had been placed on stage to which she was escorted by Director Gatti-Gasazza. Gifts included an ornate mirror from the chorus; a loving cup from members of the orchestra; a silver bowl, suitably inscribed, from the Board of Directors. A pearl necklace and chain set with diamonds, purchased by funds raised by popular subscription, was presented to her by the Honorable Seth Low, former mayor of New York, who closed his remarks by saying,

"Think not so much of the gift of the lovers as the love of the givers."

Near the end of the ceremony, Marcella played and sang the Polish song which always ended her recitals. It was the same song which she had dared to sing for Czar Nicholas years before.

In a final tribute, a shower of rose petals covered everyone on the stage.

A few days later, she was guest of honor at a dinner given by members of the Opera Company at the Hotel Astor. With Paderewski seated at her right, the star received many glowing tributes, and, from her fellow-performers, a surprise: to the tune of the "Merry Widow" waltz, one person began singing the titles of several operas in which Marcella had appeared. Each singer joined in at appropriate intervals until the whole room was vibrating with harmony produced by the greatest opera singers of the day.

Marcella made a farewell operatic tour in 1909–10; then with her husband, left America for Nice, France, with the hope that his health would benefit. With the outbreak of World War I in 1914, they again sailed for America, and for the next few years, spent winters in New York City. Summers were spent at Lake Placid in the Adirondacks, where Marcella maintained a studio. Following the death of her husband, in 1917, she accepted Directorship in the Vocal Departments of both the Juilliard

Here in the woods where Silence reigns
  More eloquent than Sound,
The place I stand on 'neath the trees
  Seems somehow, holy ground.

The birds withhold their carolling
  The breeze abandons play:
And Heaven in this atmosphere
  Seems not so far away!

Martha Martin

Marcella Sembrich's Studio, Bolton Landing

Graduate School in New York City and the Curtis Institute of Music in Philadelphia. In 1921, she came to Bolton Landing to make her home, establishing a studio three years later.

Her devoted students followed Mme. Sembrich to the Lake George Studio where they received musical training almost as rigorous as her own had been. She insisted on extensive memorizing, and at one of her evening recitals this proved to be a saving grace. Her students were singing the quartet from *Rigoletto;* the pianist was probably Frank LaForge, her accompanist for many years. In the midst of the recital, a sudden storm blew in from the north; the electricity went off and the room was in complete darkness; but, uninterrupted, the performance went on. The participants sang as accurately and expressively as though they were reading the music, and the accompanist distinguished himself further by not missing a note. Such was Mme. Sembrich's drive for perfection.

Her musicales were important events among the summer residents, partly for the opportunity of hearing promising young singers, and, partly for the experience of seeing one of the great figures in the world of music. Mme. Sembrich, still adored and honored, was already legendary. She was small in stature, but had Presence—that indefinable quality of charm and distinction that makes even a small person appear larger than life. Always elegantly and formally dressed and coiffed, she usually appeared in a richly embossed gown with a jeweled velvet choker around her neck and, as a final touch, silk gloves.

Artists—those still struggling for success, and those who were world famous, came to visit her at her studio; and she gave them advice and counsel from her own experience. Above all, she was honest and realistic and, while she gave every encouragement to a serious student, she emphasized the rigors of a singing career as she had known it, the hard work essential to achieve effortless production, the sacrifice of home and family, and the inevitable clash with highly individualized members of an artistic profession. She herself had sacrificed much to her career, but rewards had come back to her in life-long adoration from friends and public.

Devotees of her art still make pilgrimages to the Marcella Sembrich Memorial Studio which was opened to the public in 1937. As one turns from the main route following an unpaved road to the studio, the noise of traffic ebbs, and time slips back to another era, which Georg Behr, the devoted caretaker, and George Cornwell, the curator, have succeeded in preserving. Here, in the studio beneath the pines, is the grand piano which knew her flawless touch; here are tributes from friends—the great ones who valued her achievement and her friendship. Here are costumes which she wore in famous opera roles, and articles which she used: a fan, gloves, printed programs . . .

Outside the studio, a rustic path follows the contours of the shore, far above the lake. Loving the out-of-doors, Mme. Sembrich must have taken this walk often along the winding way, through silent woods, to a small summer-house overlooking the lake. Here the lake is broad, the further shore distant, and, on soft summer days, its waters are serene and sparkling.

Within the studio and the woods surrounding it, one may feel the enduring presence to be found in a shrine—an aura of greatness. This is hallowed ground devoted to art and to a brilliant artist. Go reverently.

CHAPTER X

Louise Homer,
Opera Star

Sidney Homer,
Composer

(Homeland)

Louise Dilworth Beatty began her memorable life at Shadyside, a suburb of Pittsburg, on April 30, 1871. Her father was a clergyman, her mother a homemaker in the true sense of the word. Louise whose personal and professional life radiated joyousness, was born into a home of sorrow. A month before her arrival, the youngest child of the Beatty's had come down with a fever and sore throat that was afflicting the three older Beatty children. The three oldest recovered, but the youngest, a girl, died. The mother was inconsolable in her grief with a remorse that excluded the new arrival from her attention. Louise, consequently, survived without much mothering and, instead, became everybody's baby. Gregarious by nature, this arrangement was probably just the climate she would have chosen. Three more children were born to the Beattys, and Louise thus became the middle child. Generally an equivocal position, this meant to Louise strong family ties, but later, a sense of independence and freedom not usual in girls and women of that day.

They were a musical family; the two older girls took piano lessons and taught Louise. Their father bought a triangle for her and she was added to the ensemble. She took her addition to the family music circle very seriously, concentrating on the music and waiting for the precise moment when, with a little mallet, she made the triangle ring with a bell-like sound. During these happy times, she could not have known of her father's ill health—the tuberculosis which would shorten his life-span.

Fortunately, Louise and her brothers and sisters were born in robust health. Their stamina was intensified when, in response to a call from a church in St. Paul, Minnesota, their father moved them into a more rugged climate. Their new home was a big, rambling house built for summer and unsuited to winter, but to the children it was a glorious adventure. Because the house was cold, Mrs. Beatty bundled them into warm clothing and sent them out in the snow; but as they grew stronger, their father became weaker and died a few years later. His struggle to live had given the older children time to grow up and they were now ready to assist the rest of the family. There was insurance and, adding to their small income, an aunt and uncle came to live with them.

As his greatest bequest, the Rev. Mr. Beatty had left to his children a sure foundation in the Christian faith. Louise, in particular, could quote long passages from the Bible and did so when, on joining the church, she was questioned by the elders. She was beginning to sing publicly and enjoyed the experience, although her untrained voice sometimes seemed unmanageable to her. She also joined a chorus, a feature of an Exposition planned by the City of Minnesota under the direction of Theodore Thomas, a famed conductor. Since there was no hall big enough for both performers and the expected audience, the enterprising city fathers had directed the building of a huge hall with a tower at one end and inside, bleachers for the chorus of a thousand children.

On the evening of the performance, everything seemed to be going smoothly when a severe storm burst upon the city. The tower, struck by lightning, crashed, felling electric wires. The entire hall was in darkness, filled with people who fought and scrambled to find the exits, screaming for their children. Many were killed in the pandemonium, but Louise, carried along by the crowd, somehow escaped. The Exposition Hall, built for music, soon became a mass of charred timbers, twisted wires, and shattered glass; but, in startling contrast, a new building, also dedicated to music, had arisen in New York City: the Metropolitan Opera House, built to stand for decades, awaited those who could meet its high standards and its inherited tradition.

Soon after, Mrs. Beatty sold the Minnesota house, and the family moved back to Pennsylvania, living for a while with Mrs. Beatty's sister. The house was small, filled to overflowing with the Beattys, and the many aunts, uncles, and cousins who came to visit. One day, Mrs. Beatty, determined and desperate, took a trolley car "to the end of the line." Here, she hoped to find space and relative peace. At West Chester, she found the house she wanted; it was big enough for her growing family, and she bought it at once. There were many large, empty houses in the town, evidence of the wealthy who had once lived there but had moved on to a better economic climate. Quakers, a sober, black-garbed people, still lived in the quiet little town but, as Louise noticed, there were few children. The Beatty group filled this lack to some extent, and Louise attended school; here her vocal abilities brought her the leading role in a cantata. She loved practicing for the role and, in her enthusiasm, learned the other parts, too. On the night of the performance, the director was in despair: the male lead could not come.

"I can sing both parts," Louise offered, and she did. All went well, although some listeners who knew the score must have been startled at hearing a questioning female voice answered by the same voice. The cantata was a triumph for Louise, and the director urged Mrs. Beatty to give her daughter singing lessons. Further training was impossible at that time, but the girl decided that, after high school, she would go to work and pay for her own lessons.

The question was: what kind of work should she do? The choices open were factory work, store clerk, or teaching, and she had no specialized training for anything. The answer came unexpectedly. The family fortunes had improved to the extent that her sister, who had taken teacher training, had rented a cottage at Indian Deep. She invited those of her family who could come, and Louise and her mother were among the fortunate ones who made the trip. The occasion proved to be very important to Louise, for she heard her mother talking to one of the visitors, a young lady who said she was a "lady typewriter." She had attended the Lingle College of Shorthand and Typewriting in Philadelphia for three months and was now entitled to command the princely sum of $9 per week.

All Louise needed was the suggestion—the incentive was already there. She took off for Philadelphia where she stayed with an aunt, and enrolled in the Lingle Business College. At the end of three months, she could type the required 125 words per minute and took a position with a lawyer at $3 per week. Then, as a further step in her career, she went to Bonar's Music Store looking for a paying position in a church choir. Mr. Bonar, organist at the Spruce Street Presbyterian Church, suggested that she sing on trial. The trial developed into a regular assignment of two services each Sunday at $3 per week. Although her office salary was soon raised to $4, she left to work for a Steel Company which paid $12. She was now advancing in the business world, and following the custom of the day, bought a fancy hat to wear while working at her typewriter.

To be nearer to her center of activities, she moved into the home of her aunt's friend, paying $8 a month. The rental of a piano was $15, and she started looking for a voice teacher. Mr. Bonar recommended Miss Whinney, and the lady graciously accepted the challenge of guiding an untrained voice which seem too low and too heavy. Louise's lessons were a delight to her and she worked hard, but strangely, she made little progress.

Concerned relatives played a large part in Louise's life, and her next move was dictated by receipt of a newspaper clipping from a cousin. The item listed the requirements for a position at William Penn Charter School, paying $800 per year, with daily hours from 8:30 to 2:00 p.m. and a long summer vacation. She applied and was accepted. A raise to $900 soon followed; her church contract now paid her $300, and she was on her way to financial success. At church, she arranged with the Rev. Mr. James Paxton to take down his sermons in shorthand; he and his wife became her close friends, and they remained devoted to her throughout their lives.

Meanwhile, it had come to the attention of Mr. Jones, her employer, that her work at the School, while satisfactory, was only of secondary interest. Toward him, she was crisp and businesslike; every day, once she was satisfied that the work on her desk was finished, she was off to her first love, music, and to this affront was now added another interest: Mr. Calhoun, her fiancé. Louise was stunned when Mr. Jones asked for her resignation, accusing her of lack of loyalty to Penn State Schools. The other girls in the office rallied to her support, but she refused their help, feeling that they must not risk their own positions.

The set-back was only temporary. Another relative of Louise's, an uncle, suggested that she open a Public Stenographer office in his building. She plunged into this activity with enthusiasm, made the service a success, and after a while, had the satisfaction of adding the Penn Charter School to her list of clients.

The following spring, she closed her office, resigned from the church choir and prepared for her eventual marriage to the eminently desirable John Calhoun. It must have been with some misgiving that the prospective bridegroom asked his fiancée to meet his mother. The meeting was inevitable and decisive. Louise was stunned to find in Mrs. Calhoun not the kindness and openness of her own mother, but a cold, unbending pride. To the Southern lady, bearing a famous old name, the wounds of the Civil War were still unhealed, and she made it plain to Louise that a Northern daughter-in-law was unacceptable. Dismayed, Louise broke the engagement, and went to visit sister Bess in Arlington, Massachusetts.

She reopened her public stenography office in Philadelphia. The year was 1893, a time of depresssion for many, but for Louise, who had taken up court stenography, the depression did not exist. Soon she was making $200 a month—an unheard-of sum for a girl—and was able to help her family.

What more did she want? She wanted the fulfillment of that musical genius within her that cried out for expression. Responding to an inner prodding, she again closed her office and again resigned from her church. A vacation at Lake George with the Paxton family whose several "cottages" clustered along the shore, was a memorable experience, and she swam, cruised, and climbed Prospect Mountain with other summer visitors.

Seeking advice on her voice problem, she learned the names of two vocal teachers, one in Chicago, and one in Boston; on impulse, she chose the latter. Then she was off to stay with sister Bess in Arlington again. She was twenty-two years old and successful in business, but she still could not use her voice to her satisfaction.

In Boston, she auditioned for George Chadwick at the New England Conservatory and registered as a student; she also auditioned for the St. Cecelia Choral Society and was accepted as a member; now she found that among these accomplished musicians she felt her own ignorance. Now she wanted to learn "all about music." Bess knew of Sidney Homer, a young man considered to be the best harmony teacher in Boston, and accompanied her to Mr. Homer's studio. Here Louise met a man not yet 30, tall, rather angular, with the sensitive face of a poet. He was drawn to this serious young student, and agreed to give her a series of forty-minute lessons at $2.00 per session. Louise agreed, although she was a little aghast at the price; she had expected to pay 25¢. Now her days would be filled with music: vocal lessons with Mr. Whitney at the Conservatory where she was learning the Italian Method; a paid position with a church, and harmony lessons with Mr. Homer. In Boston, she took a small, unheated room at $8 a week; it was near the Common and within a short radius of all her activities.

Seeking the fullest expression of his talent, Sidney Homer had opened his Boston studio at the time and place for a meeting with Louise Beatty. From the moment of that first meeting, their lives would be enriched, each by the other, and their talents would deepen and strengthen.

In childhood, Sidney had learned lessons of patience, sympathy, and compassion. His mother was a deaf-mute, a condition caused by an attack of scarlet fever at the age of three; her own mother had died soon after, and the first words the child might have said were never uttered. She was educated at the New York Institute for the deaf that stood on the site of the future St. Patrick's Cathedral in New York City. Learning sign language, the universal means of communication, she graduated from the Institute after seven years of study. Shen then went to live with an aunt in Waltham, Massachusetts.

One day, two ladies brought a young gentleman to see her; he was George Homer of an old Boston family. He, also, was a deaf-mute, and the young man and woman immediately began a lively conversation in sign language. Eventually, they were married and had three children with normal faculties: a boy, who died at the age of three, a sister, Georgiana, and Sidney. Relatives taught the children to talk and, in addition, Sidney learned sign language from his parents. Mr. and Mrs. Homer were a happy couple: far from feeling shut off from the world, they were very much a part of it. Mr. Homer worked for the government for many years as a dependable public employee; Mrs. Homer loved life, color, and the vibrations of sound; and Sidney often recalled how she took them all over Boston to see parades, museums, and notable people. She even succeeded in getting them a close view of a great fire which occurred in the city.

She loved music and expressed her sense of rhythm in dancing, thrilled to the Boston Symphony, sensitive to its vibrations, read omnivorously and intensely, and took piano lessons. Sidney, intellectual and artistic, followed her example, and often said that he had done his most significant studying at home.

When the boy was three, the family bought a home in Boston, and his father retired from government service. He could now be at home all day, sharing the lives of his wife and growing family.

Sidney went to grammar school, then to Boston Latin School for a year, and spent another year at Andover Academy. Contrasted with the excitement of learning at home, these studies seemed dull, the teachers unenthused. Outside activities filled the void: he heard Dwight L. Moody speak, and was caught up in oratory. He developed a love for the stage and, when Edwin Booth came to Boston, saw every performance. But he was restless and undecided, wondering what role in life he would play.

Europe, the treasury of culture and art, beckoned; his father agreed and, at the age of 16, Sidney sailed for London. Here he sensed adventure in every moment. A $500 annuity from an uncle's estate enabled him to live in a residential club. The members took him sightseeing, and he gloried in the historic and literary sites of London. One of his acquaintances was the music critic of the London Daily News, and on one memorable day, he played the entire *Messiah* for Sidney; and, on seeing the boy's rapturous response, insisted that he should go to Germany to study music. Sidney realized that he was getting a late start on a life-long study, but so strongly was he attracted to music that he set his sights on Leipzig as the best place for him to start.

At Leipzig, Sidney rented a room from a businessman. The family taught him German, and in three months, he was a fluent speaker in the language. He met a group of American boys, all music students who asked him to join their social club. They solemnly agreed that it was too late for him to start a music career, but allowed him to share their musical experiences. As music students, they were able to attend orchestra rehearsals at the Gewandhaus, and graciously smuggled their new friend into the place of enchantment. After a while, secrecy was unnecessary: Sidney was recognized as the serious music student he was, and allowed to attend rehearsals on his own account. And then, inevitably, as it was to occur periodically for some time to come—his funds dwindled dangerously. Fortunately, his landlady gave him breakfast; he was able to buy a dinner at a restaurant for 17¢.

There was a Wagner Festival at the Leipzig Opera and Sidney attended, thereby opening a new world, a world that for him touched the depths of emotion, the highest in art. Encouraged by his family, he struggled on. Luxury, even comfort, was beyond his means, but he found a room, five flights up in an old hotel where $15 a month included breakfast—and he had a piano. He found a teacher, Carl Hauser, and worked all day at the piano, perfecting his technique and exploring the intricacies of harmony. He heard his first song recital, a Schubert evening at the Gewandhaus, and was moved to the depths of his being, hoping that someday he, too, would add to the world's repertoire of great songs. The exalted idea took possession of him and one day, looking out of his window into the crowded streets, he fell to his knees asking God to let him serve humanity in some way; yet he claimed to be an agnostic.

And then, in the intensity of his ambition and the lack of ordinary comforts, he came down with shingles: incidentally, an ailment visited on

Louise Homer

*Louise and
Sidney Homer*

Homeland, Louise and Sidney Homer

the great Bismarck. In the doctor's opinion, the seventeen-year-old boy's nervous system was unequal to the strain of music study and he returned home, outwardly defeated, but inwardly still dedicated to the fulfillment of his hopes and dreams.

Well, then, since music was lost to him, he would be a writer. In the silence of the Boston Library, he tried writing. Perhaps architecture was his calling: he read books on the subject and studied the magnificent old buildings of Boston; but these diversions only took him back to music. At the age of 19, he met George Chadwick, composer, studied with him, and the flame of ambition grew brighter. He took organ lessons to assist him in entering the Royal Music School at Munich and went deeply into harmony and composition. His confidence returned; he would go back to Germany; this time his mother, father, and sister would go with him, staying only long enough to see him launched on his career.

Another set-back occurred when he came down with rheumatic fever, an ailment whose effects were then barely understood. He took the "cure" at Wiesbaden and passed the entrance examination at Munich where two blissful years of hard work awaited him.

At the end of that time he returned to the Boston area to find changes in the family structure: his sister had married a composer and conductor in New Bedford; his father had developed heart trouble. Sidney formed a class in harmony that kept him near his family; then his father died.

In the fall of 1889, he took two studio rooms in the old Hotel Pelham near Boston Common and advertised for pupils. The results of his work and study in Germany soon became evident. A German pianist living in Boston was advised by a teacher in Munich to send his pupils to Sidney for lessons in harmony. His classes became large and successful, and he branched out into groups studying symphonies and the musical dramas of Wagner. His success grew; life was full; he was using his talents and serving humanity in the way he knew best; his family, always a loved responsibility, had built a home in Arlington. And then one day, something happened to dwarf his other successes and to blend with his musical talent and ideals: a Miss Beatty who wanted to know "all about music" stepped into his life.

Miss Beatty and Mr. Homer began to see quite a lot of each other: she attended his classes in the Beethoven Symphonies, free; he went to the church where she sang and accompanied her home on the trolley, and he suddenly decided he would take his meals at her boarding house. Both went for long walks after dinner and she learned that Mr. Homer was an agnostic (her mother would be troubled about that); for him, her lively spirits awoke a light response, previously unsuspected. Together they attended a recital given by Lillian Nordica. She had never heard opera, and, when Maurice Grau brought the Metropolitan Company to Boston, they heard the great stars Nellie Melba, Jean de Reszke, Emma Eames, and Emma Calvé.

Opportunities unfolded. Louise was asked to sing a leading part in the oratorio *Elijah* given by the Mozart Society and she became engaged to Mr. Homer, wondering how she could explain his agnostic stance to her mother. That hurdle was cleared when Sidney wrote a letter to her mother which softened her objections to some extent, and a visit to the Beatty family completed his success with them all. Since both Louise and Sidney had little money, the Beattys expected a long engagement. After all, a man had to be able to support a wife, and a girl had to have accumulated an extensive trousseau before a marriage could take place. The young couple, who had different ideas, managed to find a way around the financial impasse. Louise borrowed $150 from the bank for her trousseau; Mr. Homer was still able to rely on the small yearly income from his late uncle's estate, and they were married by Dr. Paxton in Bess' home on January 9, 1895.

After a brief honeymoon near Boston, the couple moved into the same house where Louise had first lived, but now they rented the whole upper floor with a room on the floor below for Sidney's studio. "At Homes" replaced the traditional wedding reception, and they were host and hostess to friends and family including Sidney's famous cousin, Winslow Homer, the artist, and another cousin, Augusta, married to the eminent sculptor, Augustus Saint-Gaudens. Life for both settled into a peaceful routine with Sidney's classes in harmony and music appreciation, and Louise's vocal lessons and engagements to sing at recitals and weddings. The little girl born to them heightened their joy, and with a girl hired to watch the baby, Louise was free to pursue her musical interests which brought her $1200 per year on her church contract alone.

Louise was not completely happy: dimly, she realized that something was missing from the daily routine; although her singing pleased her listeners, she knew that she was not progressing as she should. She confided her frustration to Sidney and after considering the problem, he conceived a bold plan.

His years in Europe had been a valuable experience and he had always intended to return. Why not pool their resources and go to Europe where Louise could have the best teachers, and he could spend his own time writing art songs? At first, Louise was horrified at the suggestion that they leave friends and family and the opportunities at hand and strike out on their own. It seemed a desperate gamble, but finally, won over by his enthusiasm, she agreed. They borrowed $2500 from a relative; Sidney again had his annuity from his uncle's estate, and they were off for the next great adventure.

In Paris, they rented an unfurnished apartment which they proceeded to furnish with second-hand pieces, some of their own movable treasures brought from home—and packing boxes. Nearby, Sidney rented a one-room studio with a piano, and they found a 15-year-old girl to care for the baby. Louise enrolled with M. Bouhy, whose voice students graced stages all over the world; Sidney found instructors for her in

French, diction, and dramatic presence—the stylized gestures used in opera. They were ecstatic, sure that this move had been made in the right direction.

But Sidney, who attended her lessons with her and listened carefully, became aware that, under M. Bouhy's technique, the brilliant quality was disappearing from her voice. After much discussion, they left M. Bouhy—a difficult move, since his reputation was world-wide—and selected Signor Juliani as voice teacher. This was another mistake, and the results soon became evident in the noticeably forced production of Louise's voice.

They found their new friends, the Koenigs, sympathetic and eager to help. M. Koenig was a coach for singers in the Paris Opera and, although he was not a teacher, he had suggested that he could be of some assistance to Louise at this critical time in her musical life. With the realization that their money was nearly gone, they turned to M. Koenig as their last hope. After a few lessons with this non-teacher, it seemed that, where the former techniques had diminished her voice, M. Koenig's method of relaxation and release was the one approach she needed. For the first time, her voice reached its natural richness and depth; her range extended, and she found that she was singing coloratura passages, something she had believed to be beyond the range of a contralto.

That year (1897), the Metropolitan Opera House in New York City was closed for the first time since its opening in 1883, giving Maurice Grau, director of the Opera Company, an opportunity to visit France. M. Koenig seized upon Mr. Grau's visit as a chance for Louise to audition for this influential man. The audition, a curious affair, took place in a nearly empty hall, and while Louise sang, Mr. Grau looked out the window. At the end of the audition, he remarked that the Metropolitan did not take beginners; she should get experience, and then return to him.

Now her letters home became full of the excitement they were experiencing. She had an engagement at Vichy; her contract was for 10 weeks, 8 appearances a week, with a salary of $800–$10 per engagement, and she had to provide her own costumes. A similar arrangement at Angers followed. Then came the opportunity to sing at London's Covent Garden. Louise had never attempted singing *Aïda* in Italian and Die Walkure in German as her contract specified, but she "crammed" for two weeks, and her appearance was a triumph. An engagement at La Monnaie with the Brussels Opera Company followed. La Monnaie was second only to the Paris Opera Company. One of her most socially brilliant appearances was before royalty at Buckingham Palace. Queen Victoria, who was limiting her public appearances, did not attend, and was represented by the Prince and Princess of Wales.

An offer came from Maurice Grau of the Metropolitan. She would receive $800 per month covering 10 performances each month. Judged by the salaries of today's top-flight stars, $80 for an operatic performance seems small indeed. It was only with the development of recordings that stars in the entertainment world were able to command large salaries. The Metropolitan contract was for three years, and there would be no concert privileges. The terms limited her appearances, but the "Met" was the Mecca for artists, and Louise signed the contract, happy to be going home.

Arriving in America, Louise and Sidney found how movable Americans had become: an Opera Train was scheduled to make a cross-country pilgrimage with performances in Los Angeles and San Francisco, where Louise would make her debut in *Aïda.* They went first to West Chester, Pennsylvania, where there was a family reunion; this was an opportunity for little Louise, who seemed like a French child, to become re-acquainted with her relatives. Then they went to North Newton, Massachusetts, to visit sister Bess and other relatives. From then on, adventure beckoned.

The adventure was not for Sidney. In North Newton, he became ill and was taken to the hospital. Louise, anxious, was ready to give up the Opera Tour, but Sidney insisted that she go on without him. She refused, and sent M. Grau a telegram stating that she could not take the Opera Train; his return wire suggested that she come directly to San Francisco. Sidney's persistent fever grew worse as he argued that everything they had worked for was at stake; she must go on without him. After a few days, with assurance from the doctor that Sidney was no worse, Louise consented to go on alone. For her, enduring anxiety and loneliness, the journey was heart-breaking. The miles which carried her further away from her dearest friend were agonizing.

On her arrival in San Francisco she found a telegram assuring her that Sidney was better. Then she could appear on the stage, radiant, assured, and as always giving her best to the performance. The newspaper reviews of her American debut were tributes. One wrote:

"It will be a wonder if Louise Homer does not become a very great prima donna contralto."

Another review said of her, "Remember the name; it is going to spell something big in the years ahead."

Following her San Francisco debut there was a ten-day pause, and Louise was entertained by the great and wealthy families of San Francisco who provided her with every conceivable form of luxury. At the close of the schedule, she left San Francisco on the Opera Train with its letters "Metropolitan Opera House" a foot high. A memorable experience occurred in Minneapolis: here she appeared in the same Exposition Hall that had almost claimed her life as a child.

She arrived in New York on December 17, and all her pent-up longings drove her to prepare a Christmas celebration for Sidney and their little girl. She rented an apartment, bought a tree and trimmed it, took the night train to Boston, and made plans to move her family to New

York. On December 22, she made her Metropolitan debut in AÏDA. It probably seemed to her of equal importance that her family was together for Christmas Day and that Louise, Jr. had her Christmas tree.

Great expansion in the world of music was occurring. After years of lawsuits with the Edison Company over patents, the Victor Talking Machine Company was in a position to record for posterity the great voices of the period. Their competitor, the Columbia Company, had tried to record Mme. Sembrich's voice with little success; now Victor, with technical improvements, was signing up great performers in opera. Louise was one of the first to sign a contract, and, on September 12, 1903, in a small room at Carnegie Hall, made the first recording. The recording process was complicated, and she had to regulate her distance from the recording device constantly, but the result was a success. With the dissemination of music through recordings, the salaries of entertainers in all fields began to move up—a far cry from the days of the early minstrels who, literally, sang for their supper.

Louise and Sidney went to call on Mme. Nellie Melba, a justly famous opera star whose glamor embraced items from perfume to Melba toast and Pêche Melba. She was very kind to her visitors, talking long and earnestly of the pitfalls that could trip the unwary in the highly competitive field of opera. Both Louise and Sidney were dismayed; petty jealousy was foreign to their natures. Later, they would learn at first hand what the great lady had meant. At the end of their visit, Mme. Melba gave the young singer a sincere compliment. "My dear," she said, "you have the most beautiful voice in the world."

The afterglow of the visit inspired Sidney to contact the house of Schirmer, Music Publishers. They spent an entire morning with Gustave Schirmer, son of the President of the Company, and Louise sang a group of Sidney's songs set to Tennyson's lyrics. The resulting contract with performing rights and royalties was evidence that Sidney was well on his way to recognition.

The organization of Maurice Grau had been dissolved, and in his place as manager had come Heinrich Conreid who ruled with a heavy hand. Trusting the management, Louise had signed a contract which failed to protect her interests. Now she saw some of her greatest roles taken from her and given to Edythe Walker. She took the parts assigned to her with considerable misgiving: apparently the new manager was bent on reducing her status in the company. News writers alerted the public to the rivalry which was presumed to exist between the two artists; but on Louise's part, at least, there was only hurt and a loss of confidence in the management.

This was a situation which could not endure very long, and one morning, Conreid found to his consternation that his star could not perform that evening. It was a crisis: the house was sold out. Faced with disaster and nearly in tears, he sought Louise and asked her to sing the lead in Wagner's *Das Rhinegold;* it was a part she had never sung.

Trouper that she was, she accepted the assignment and, with an accompanist, practiced the role all that day; they were still rehearsing when the last touches were being made to the costume she was wearing.

Then—one last quick run-through with the accompanist—the patrons were arriving—the curtain would soon rise—and she could not remember a word or a note. They tried again and again, and slowly, the role came back to her. True to tradition, the show went on; she gave her best, and the evening was saved. After the performance, she regained her former roles, and her status was never in question again. Conreid died a year later in the Austrian Tyrol, and Louise was one of the singers at his funeral conducted on the Metropolitan stage.

Even a disaster in her professional life could not have conquered Louise Homer. One of the most fortunate women, she had great beauty unmarred by self-consciousness, and a personality radiant with warmth and generosity. Her husband was devoted to her as a person and as an artist, willing to sacrifice anything, if necessary, to ensure the use of her great talent. Six children were born to them, and this remarkable couple succeeded in giving them a normal, happy home life while pursuing their own musical careers.

A serious threat to Louise's health occurred while she was on tour with the Opera Company in 1906. She and Sidney were staying at the Palace Hotel in San Francisco, an elegant building built to stand for decades. On the morning of April 18, the great earthquake occurred, followed by a consuming fire which drove them and the rest of the population, from one doomed building to another, until that building, too, caught on fire. Finally, like awakening from a nightmare, they reached Oakland and, in time, were on the Opera Train heading east. All opera personnel were safely on the train; they had lost most of their possessions, but they were buoyant with relief. As the train sped on, Louise, usually in perfect health, became more and more ill. Finally realizing the seriousness of the situation, Sidney wired ahead for an ambulance to meet the train in Chicago, and Louise was taken to the hospital. Of the whole company, she, always in radiant health, was the only one who had collapsed under the strain of the holocaust. No one knew, and the mores of the day forbade telling, that Louise was pregnant; she had had a miscarriage.

But she recovered, and went on to crowd every moment of every day with glorious, successful living. Royalties for recordings mounted; salaries rose to unbelievable heights; Sidney's songs were hailed as remarkable compositions, and Louise Homer, "the greatest contralto the Metropolitan ever had," was secure both in the affections of her public and in the hearts of her family.

The Homers spent summers at Lake George, renting "Rockledge," the house owned by Charles H. Tuttle, New York Attorney; but with a family of six children, ranging from Louise, Jr. a young lady, to Hester, the baby, they felt the need for more room. The problem was solved by purchasing from W. K. Bixby of St. Louis, a hundred acres of land with a mile of shore-front. The price, according to Sidney, was only a fourth of its value, and they set about, joyfully, on this great adventure with the intention of incorporating into "Homeland" their needs and even their extravagances. Edward Shepard Hewitt, nephew of Attorney Edward Morse Shepard, benefactor of Lake George Village, was the architect of their dream mansion. In 1916, an epidemic of the dreaded polio (infantile paralysis) broke out, and the children were kept at Lake George in isolation as it was generally believed that polio attacked only children. The Wellesley graduate who came to live with them kept them up to grade level.

The war years took their toll: Sidney was hospitalized and Louise took the hospital room next to his in order to be near him. Daughter Louise, blessed with a beautiful voice, preparing to sing for the soldiers in Europe, became very ill from typhoid preventives. Louise's contract with the Metropolitan had expired and she had not renewed it, due to a dispute over terms. The next offer from that organization was more favorable, stipulating 10 performances at $900 each, and a lessening of restrictions.

During the years of bitter conflict, German opera was cancelled; the Leider beloved by singers was banished, and German singers sailed for the Fatherland. Joffre, Field Marshal of France, visited the United States to gain American support and was met by Mme. Homer at the newly created statue of Lafayette in Prospect Park, Brooklyn; both spoke in French. Later, in a gala celebration at the Metropolitan, the visitor was given a tribute from the citizens of New York; Louise led the singing of the Star Spangled Banner with a fervor that sent a thrill through the audience. Many notables were present, including Charles Evans Hughes, Chief Justice of the Supreme Court, who was introduced by Governor Whitman.

A tour of Texas had been scheduled, but Sidney became ill with a recurrent attack of rheumatism and, since with her, Sidney always came first, she cancelled the tour and went with him to a sanitarium in the Berkshires. At Lake George, the twins, Anne and Katherine, were graduating, and despairing calls came from school to please, please come and watch the commencement dances. Louise decided on a quick trip; Sidney decided to go, too; so to the twins, graduation was a success. They stopped around to see the new house, and the construction was so absorbing that they stayed not one day, but several weeks. When Sidney finally reported to the sanitarium, he was so much improved that the doctors discharged him immediately.

Their home was now ready and they moved in. Several ideas that were strictly their own had been incorporated in the house: five sleeping porches, five studios, later complete with five grand pianos for all the musical Homers.

There were delightful neighbors on so-called "Millionaires' Row." Next door, but widely spaced as all the mansions were, lived Mr. and Mrs.

Maurice Hoopes of Glens Falls. Mrs. Hoopes was a member of the Finch Pruyn family of Glens Falls, long associated with the making of paper; Mr. Hoopes was a Quaker from Mrs. Homer's own hometown, West Chester, Pennsylvania, and the couple often strolled across the lawn to enjoy, with loving dignity, the high jinks of the Homer children. A few miles north lived Chief Justice Charles Evans Hughes who had so narrowly missed being President of the United States. His daughter, Elizabeth, played with the twins. Adolph S. Ochs, publisher of the New York Times, was another summer resident and the children were often invited there. They were in awe of the vast baronial hall of Abenia with its stately statues, but not at all in awe of their host who could so easily become one of them.

President Wilson had prohibited the use of gasoline except for dire emergencies, and transportation, except for those who owned horses, became a thing of the past. Community singing to improve the citizens' morale was springing up everywhere, and, on establishing their home at Lake George, Louise began hymn-sings. She had made religion a great part of her life since childhood, and the hymn-sings were her contribution to the war effort of the community.

The great and famous as well as old residents joined in the Sunday singing: the pupils of Leopold Auer, violinist who had fled from the revolution in Russia, came to the patriotic gathering. Professor Auer's most famous pupil, Efrem Zimbalist, and his wife, the Met's lyric soprano, Alma Gluck, who lived in Lake George Village, also came. Often a hundred and fifty people would be gathered in the huge living rooms at Homeland, coming by rowboat, horse and carriage, and on foot. When the crowd became larger, the hymn-sings were moved to the Lake George Club, and with Peace, the automobile once again replaced the horse.

Samuel Barber, Louise's nephew, was another visitor at Homeland. His interest in music had surfaced at the age of two and expanded into a successful career in the composition of symphonies. Ultimately, he won the Grand Prix de Rome, and the Pulitzer Prize.* He was often accompanied on his visits by a fellow student from the Curtis Institute of Music in Philadelphia, Gian Carlo Menotti, whose operas have achieved a brilliant success.

In a large family, little ceremonies, repeated over and over, take on group significance: such a ceremony occurred at noon on each summer day when the excursion boat, Mohican, passed "Homeland." All rushed out to wave table napkins, and the captain, with an amplified explanation to the excursionists, had the whistle blown in reply. The dining room table at Homelands often accommodated as many as 22 persons at one time, and on one memorable occasion, while the family and their friends were at the table, they heard a beautiful soprano voice singing an

Note: In 1966, the "Met on moving to its new home in Lincoln Center, chose Samuel Barber's opera, Anthony and Cleopatra for a gala opening. It was the world premiere for this work.

operatic air in the hallway. That could only be—yes, it was: all rushed to greet Mme. Marcella Sembrich who had come to Lake George where the new studio on the lake awaited her students.

Since leaving the Metropolitan, Louise had taken concert tours, had appeared in recitals, and made recordings. Fees for performances now ranged from $1,500 to $2,000. In 1925, she was guest singer with the Chicago Civic Opera, then went on to San Francisco where she sang at the ground-breaking for the San Francisco Opera House; 50,000 attended.

The children had always absorbed the interest of their parents, and now that they were growing up, it became harder than ever to leave them. All children were exceptionally talented in music or literature, and their parents made every effort to bring them into contact with influences that would expand their talents. There were college, trips abroad and, above all, a rare family solidarity. Their daughter Louise gave concerts and recorded duets with her famous mother; daughter Kay became her mother's capable accompanist at recitals; daughter Anne wrote and published stories in magazines and, years later, wrote a remarkable book, "Louise Homer and the Golden Age of Opera"; Sidney, Jr., chose to establish a business dealing in bonds; Joy wrote a book and lectured on her Asian travels,—and Hester married at 18.

The sons-in-law and daughter-in-law were warmly welcomed: Louise married Ernest Van Rensselaer Stires who, later as a clergyman, followed in the footsteps of his famous father, Bishop of Long Island; he performed the wedding ceremony for Hester, who married Robert Henry at St. James' Episcopal Church, Lake George, and for Anne who married Robert Warner at Homeland. Kay married Douglas Fryer, eminent psychologist, and the ceremony was conducted by Dr. Paxton, long-time friend of the Homers'.

Nine years after Louise left the Metropolitan, she returned for a special engagement, singing one of her most famous roles, that of Amneris in AIDA. There was speculation throughout the audience thronging the Opera House: Had she retained her beauty? Had her voice become flawed? When she appeared on the stage in the regal garments of the daughter of the King of Egypt, their questions were answered: she was as beautiful and as youthful-appearing as ever. The cultured crowd broke into wild cheering with cries of "Brava" and "Welcome back"; stamping of feet from the more unrestrained, continuous clapping, and many nostalgic tears greeted the singer.

An ovation given at a star's first appearance on stage can create difficulties: Shall she acknowledge the tribute and break the continuity of the story unfolding on the stage, or shall she disregard it completely? Louise Homer did neither: she stood perfectly still in profile to the audience as waves of love poured over her and surrounded her; there was no change in her role as Amneris. As the tumult rose, she raised her hand, a gesture in deference to the god Ra combining gratitude to the audience, and the welcoming furore gradually subsided. The reviews of her return to the Metropolitan exulted that the years had brought only greater maturity and depth to her flawless voice.

With this spectacular triumph behind them, and the children pursuing their own careers and interests, it seemed a good time for the Homers to steal away on a trip of their own. Since childhood, Louise had longed to see the Holy Land, and they departed on an ocean liner with all the anticipation of two children. The Holy Land was all that Louise had hoped for, but in the rubble of centuries lay a menace that neither had thought of: dust. In this tropical climate, the dust infiltrated Sidney's lungs and he became ill with double pneumonia, then double pleurisy. Returning from the voyage to visit his doctor in New York, he was dismayed to learn that he must go to a warmer climate.

From that time on, their schedule became Palm Beach in the winter, Homeland in the summer, with Louise's engagements adjusted to meet the demands of his health. He finished his book, "My Wife and I," a sparkling account of their life together, on the sands of Palm Beach.

Seven years after publication of the book, their daughter Joy, married and the mother of a baby, died. This was the first rift in the family, but the depth of their loss was not allowed to dim the brightness of their lives nor their love for one another.

Meanwhile, the strain of long-distance traveling to keep concert engagements was becoming more difficult to Louise, and she decided to give up that part of her singing career. They opened studios, both at Palm Beach and Lake George for the teaching of voice and harmony; their friends, Mr. and Mrs. Maurice Hoopes, patrons of the arts, established two scholarships for students with promising voices, and they were embarked on another satisfying career. Louise revived the hymn-sings which had proven so successful at Lake George, and they were held first at their home, then at the Everglades Club in Palm Beach.

In 1941, a situation had to be faced: with income diminished, Homeland must be sold. Taking what must have been a heart-breaking trip to Lake George, they cleared out of the mansion all the mementoes, the memories of departed years, and closed the door on the past.

They spent their 40th wedding anniversary at Palm Beach where they were hailed as "one of the community's best-loved couples." Their Golden Wedding Anniversary occurred at Winter Park. In 1947, still planning for the future, they hoped to rent a home in Vermont near daughter Anne and her newly-born twins. Louise never saw the twins; she died in Winter Park of a heart attack. There was a memorial service in Rollins College Chapel, and she was buried in the Bolton Rural Cemetery, near Homeland.

Sidney was devastated, but he still had a reason for living: his compositions needed revising and, hiring a secretary, he set about the task. The work was long and painstaking, but on a certain day, the revisions were finally completed to his satisfaction; at the close of that day, he said to his secretary, "Good-night; I'll see you next Tuesday." For him, next Tuesday never came; he died in his sleep at the age of 87.

During their lifetime great honors were paid to the Homers: Louise was awarded a Master of Arts degree from Tufts University in 1923, and from Smith College in 1931. Russell Sage College bestowed upon her the degree of Doctor of Music. From Miami University, Ohio, came a Doctor of Letters degree, and Doctor of Music from Middlebury College. The League of Women Voters selected her as one of 12 most eminent women in America; she represented the category "Music." The explorer of the Far North, Donald MacMillan, named a section of mountainous country "Louise Homer Land" in her honor.

Sidney was awarded an honorary doctorate by Rollins College, and Doctor of Music by Curtis Institute. A special edition of his collected songs were published by Schirmer and called "The first collection ever made of the works of a living composer." Both he and Louise have been accorded a place in the Biographical Dictionary of Musicians published by the University Society, and in other publications. A unique distinction was conferred upon Sidney Homer when his cousin, by marriage, Saint Gaudens, was commissioned to construct a statue of Phillips Brooks. The sculptor planned that a shadowy figure, indicating the Christ, should be in the background of his work, and as a model for the Christ-like forehead, chose Sidney Homer's brow. So, in Boston, there now stands a statue beside Trinity Church whose Brow was inspired by Sidney Homer's serene countenance.

The life story of Louise and Sidney Homer is the chronicle of two talented and highly individual people who managed to create the almost-impossible; a happy marriage, a family, and two outstanding careers. Sidney, creative and sensitive, was his wife's constant companion and loving critic when he could be with her; the guardian and protector of the family ties when he could not. This lovely woman, one of the greatest singers of all time, could have happily made a career of caring for husband and children, so intense was her devotion to them; instead, time after time, she had to leave them, wrenching herself away mentally, if not physically, to give of her art to a waiting public. Once on stage, she could pour out her talent with supreme concentration and a serenity born of the knowledge that the life at home was in Sidney's capable hands.

In an era when equality of the sexes was still to be established, theirs was an equality fostered by confidence and love. In tribute to her husband, Louise often said that she could never have filled her dual role without him. To Sidney, his wife was a constant inspiration. At their first meeting, she had kindled a fire within him that would never be extinguished. Their own love story has a beauty and sincerity unmatched by any opera she ever sang, or by any song he ever composed.

CHAPTER XI

The Doctors Jacobi

(Juniper Hill)

Miss Mary Corinna Putnam knew exactly what she wanted from life and, what was just as important, what she did not want. In itself, this was a rare achievement in the 1860's when the field of activity for young ladies was definitely limited.

From the age of six, this daughter of George Palmer Putnam, publisher, was a writer, but writing was only of secondary importance in her life-plan; her first interest was in the medical profession. In this she was encouraged by her parents who believed that there was a place for women in medicine beyond obstetrics. George and Victorine Putnam fostered their daughter's natural spirit of independence and let her "have her head" like a spirited filly that knows its destination. The Civil War had broken out, and the time was right for an embryo doctor. Mary nursed the wounded in Northern hospitals, and even traveled from New York City to New Orleans to care for her wounded brother.

"How can the Putnams allow that girl to travel about in wartime?" asked the neighbors, "It isn't safe."

Safety was not uppermost in Mary Putnam's mind. She was preoccupied with thoughts of doing whatever she must do in order to become a doctor; but even in those days, a medical education was expensive. Although the large Putnam family lived comfortably, there was not much extra money in the household. George Putnam's publishing business had failed in 1857, and sporadic publishing ventures since then had not been entirely profitable. His interest in literature and art continued in spite of losses, and he had become actively engaged in founding the Metropolitan Museum of Art in New York City.

Mary attended the City's first public high school. Learning was easy for her, as was writing, and she sold her first story to the *Atlantic Monthly* at the age of 17. Payment for the story was substantial and would help pay her expenses toward a career in medicine. In 1861, she entered the New York College of Pharmacy and was graduated in 1863.

Opportunities existed even then for women of courage and dedication, and in the fall of 1863, Mary entered the Female Medical College in Philadelphia. There was the expected harassment from male medical students, covert hostility from the public, and disdain from young ladies who considered a woman doctor to be someone unfeeling and unfeminine. Didn't Dr. Mary E. Walker, Civil War surgeon, wear men's clothes and smoke big, black cigars? No, thank you, they said.

It was unlikely that Mary would ever fit Dr. Walker's pattern. She was small, barely five feet tall, with glossy brown hair and expressive brown eyes that betrayed a depth of feeling. In the years of her early womanhood, she would become engaged twice and, deciding each time that she had made the wrong choice, would break the engagement. When the right man came along, she would know that he was the one she needed to complement her life.

The year in Philadelphia had been rewarding, and she returned home to work in the New England Hospital. That lasted a month and she left, now sure that research, not nursing, was definitely her field. During her years of training she had become aware that the best doctors and surgeons were European trained, and she set her sights on the École de Medicine in Paris. But where was so much money coming from?

The problem was partially solved that summer when she took a position tutoring a young man for his West Point entrance examinations. She became deeply interested, worked hard with her student, and was gratified when he was accepted into military college. That fall, with the money she had earned, she sailed for Paris. Arriving in that romantic city, she found a small room in the Latin Quarter, and proceeded to enjoy the sights and sounds of Paris. She was delighted when she was given permission to follow two notable French doctors as they made their hospital visits. She went sight-seeing, awed as the edifices she had read about became real in her experience. She made close and enduring friendships and in-between-times, wrote articles for publication in American magazines. She depended on the sale of these articles to defray her expenses, and her plan—that one talent should serve the other—proved workable.

Articles flowed from her pen destined for the New York Evening Post; other articles went to the Medical Record. Travel articles came next in which she told of the quaint, often bizarre features of the Latin Quarter as seen through her eyes. She borrowed books from the École and absorbed their contents with the knowledge that, once she was accepted into the École, her American credits would be converted to a B.S. degree. Finally, the opportunity came; she received permission to take the qualifying examination for entrance into the world-famous school.

The examination was oral, taken before a large crowd in the Grand Ampitheater of the College. Mary had chosen the three doctors who she thought would be the least adamant toward a woman in the medical profession. The three examiners were seated at a long table as she took her place before them, oblivious of the crowd. She was secure in the knowledge she had acquired, sure that she was equal to any situation. To her, brimming with confidennce, the questions seemed easy, and she answered them with a sureness born of intensive preparation. Then the examination was over; the examiners retired while she awaited their verdict, thinking, "But it was so easy." Of course something could go wrong—and she wanted so much to realize her particular ambition—to make her parents and brothers and sisters proud of her achievements.

The three examiners had rendered a decision: they were striding toward her in all the splendor of their educational trappings. One, the spokesman, came up to her, smiling. Mary waited, tense, for their judgment.

Now came the traditional, "Do you wish to know the verdict?" Mary nodded assent, then the pronouncement, "You have done well; very well indeed."

She was in! The first woman in the foremost medical school in the whole world! Her parents would be pleased; Mary was ecstatic; in that one moment she knew the present joy of fulfillment, and the promise that greater opportunities lay ahead for her to achieve success. On hearing the joyful news, her parents *were* pleased and probably a little awed at the accomplishment of their offspring. As a token, they sent her money for a dress. Mary didn't want a dress; she wanted something else very much more. She bought a microscope.

And then, suddenly it seemed, Paris, the City of Light, became in 1870, a city of darkness and fear. There was war with Prussia and the enemy encircled the city. Mary continued her studies and worked on her thesis, De la Graisse Neutre et de les Acides Gras,* to the accompaniment of bursting shells and increasing hardship.

The École closed; coal grew scarce; gas was turned off; everyone was on short rations and suffered with the cold. Mary continued to write to her family in America. Sometimes the letters went safely by baloon; at other times, the balloon was shot down. Testifying to America's strong position in the world, Bismarck, chancellor of Prussia, permitted letters from the American legation to go unmolested, and Mary's letters were among them. The shelling of the city continued and Mary, with hordes of other Parisians, slept in the Pantheon. Meat vanished from the shops; soon there were no domestic pets left, and rats became choice edibles. Finally, Paris surrendered. "Sold out," the people muttered as their sacrifices now seemed all in vain. Anarchy took over and Civil War erupted, while the Prussians waited outside the city, knowing that they could enter as conquerors at any propitious moment.

Mary persisted under difficulties and when the École reopened, her thesis was ready. Again she came before a group of the faculty and, at that time, defended her thesis. Her quick and ready answers drew applause from the crowd and her degree was granted with the highest grade possible. A medal would be awarded to her for excellence.

The years in Paris had been exciting and productive of results; Mary had become fluent in French—she even thought in French—but she was eager to go home and, in the fall of 1871, she returned to her homeland. She found many changes: her parents' 11th child had been born, dying

*Note: "Of the Neutral Fat and the Fatty Acids."

soon after birth. Three years had wrought great changes in the lives of her brothers and sisters, with marriages, children, business, and professions. Her father's project, the Metropolitan Museum of Art, was flourishing, and he was its Honorary Secretary. The Putnams were living at 328 East 15th Street, and there Mary established an office. Patients could now come with greater ease; horse-cars had become the new mode of transportation in the city.

Mary was anxious to share the precious knowledge she had obtained through her studies in Paris, and when the opportunity came to teach at the Women's Medical College in the New York Infirmary, she was eager to begin. The students were just as eager to have this famous woman as their instructor, for they had heard of her success in a man's world. Unfortunately, the first session was a disappointment both to Mary and to her students. She complained that the students were unresponsive and uninterested; they countered with charges that her lectures were over their heads. It took all the diplomacy of the Drs. Blackwell, women directors of the Infirmary, to bridge the gap between instructor and students; but Mary, with patience and humility learned from her experiences abroad, was surprisingly cooperative.

And then, three months after her return home, another important event occurred in Mary's expanding world; she was accepted as a member of the New York County Medical Society. She could not know that a doctor whom she would meet there would enrich and focus the direction of her life.

Abraham Jacobi was born in Westphalia, a province of Prussia, on May 6, 1830. His home was crude with a fireplace in the center and a hole in the roof to let out the smoke. The hut had small windows, but it was a matter of pride to the Jacobi family that the glass in them was real. The educational outlook for a boy born under such adverse conditions was unpromising: the Universities were excellent; preparation for them—the primary schools—was poor. There was shrewd reasoning behind this discrepancy; Germany wanted highly trained leaders, but preferred that the masses be kept less literate. Jacobi had an additional problem; as a Jewish child, he would encounter a great deal of anti-Semitism. He was a sickly boy with an illness that was probably rickets, but somehow, he managed to survive. Brought up on an insufficient diet and lacking fresh air, this undersized child would one day insist on the need for proper living conditions for all children. His father was harsh and stern with little patience for anything beyond the daily struggle for existence; his mother, looking past the dismal present, made sacrifices to put him through the Gymnasium (High School). From there, he went on to attend the University of Greifswold in Pomerania.

From the first, Abraham Jacobi was a fighter. He fought to live, and he struggled against beliefs that were dooming people to sub-standard lives. Schelling's "Natural Philosophy"—the doctrine of the oneness of all substance, had dominated medical thinking for 40 years, but here and there, interest beyond the theory was reviving, and great medical discoveries were taking place.

Doctors often took a dim view of their own calling. It was generally believed that a good diagnostician could not treat the disease itself. It was the old struggle between science and art, they said. Impatient with the slowness of his progress, Jacobi went to Gottingen to study with Virchow who was making startling discoveries in the field of health and medicine. Virchow, a doctor who dared to raise his voice for reform, declared that starvation and poverty with resulting epidemics must be reversed. His heresy cost him his position. At the University of Bonn, Jacobi found to his delight that professors were proceeding from symptoms of diseases to their causes with the dictum, "Never let anything interfere with the life and welfare of a patient."

Revolt was growing in Germany, a rebellion born of the misery of the many and spurred on by the promise of hope offered by a few compassionate leaders. In 1848, the uprising reached a crisis, but the movement was too weak to sustain itself, and the revolution was crushed. Dr. Ernst Krackowizer, later one of Jacobi's greatest friends, fled to escape hanging. He reached Europe, and nine years later, came to America.

Another friend entered Jacobi's life in a clandestine manner. At Bonn, a man named Schimmelpfennig* came to him in great distress. Hungry and weak from his ordeal with the authorities, he asked Jacobi to act as go-between in behalf of Professor Gottfried Kinkel, a leading revolutionary who had been imprisoned. Jacobi agreed. A meeting was then arranged and, as planned, Jacobi met a stranger—a tall, curly-haired man who gave him "certain information." No names were exchanged, but the secrecy of the situation drew a curtain of privacy around the two conspirators. They talked freely of the revolution that had failed, and of America where a great experiment in human freedom was going on.

Later, when Jacobi heard that Professor Kinkel had been rescued from the fortress of Spandau through the daring of a man named Carl Schurz, he knew that Schurz was his fellow-conspirator. They would meet again in America and become devoted friends.

Jacobi went on to Schleswig-Holstein. Less a politician than a humanitarian, he hoped to serve as an army surgeon. Alas for his good intentions: at Berlin, he was arrested along with Karl Marx and several of his followers. Sentenced, he spent 18 months in prisons at Berlin, Cologne, and Bielefeld, charged with lese majesty. At Minden, where his mother visited him, he was given an additional six months prison sentence.

"You did what you thought was right, and that you must always do," she told him. He never forgot her words.

After spending two years in prison, he was given his freedom. Warned by a friendly jailer that the authorities planned to rearrest him, he left Germany, reaching the United States in October, 1853.

At their secret meeting two years before, Schurz had suggested that,

---

*Later, Brig. General Schimmelpfennig of the Union Army in the American Civil War.

Dr. Mary Jacobi

Dr. Abraham Jacobi

Ruins of Dr. Jacobi's home day after fire

Dr. Abraham Jacobi and grandchild

since there was a large German population in New York City, it would be advantageous for Jacobi to go there. Once in the city, he rented rooms and immediately began taking patients. His fees were 25¢ for an office call, 50¢ for a house call. Confinements brought $5.00. Dr. Jacobi had found freedom in America and a modicum of success, but he could not close his eyes to the burning question of slavery. He became an Abolitionist, seeing in slavery a parallel with the hopeless poor of his own country.

His native German and knowledge of English were of value, and he was asked to select and translate European magazine articles for the *New York Journal of Medicine*. Many of these articles dealt with the diseases of infants and children which were in line with his own interest. His considered advice which repetition developed into a slogan, was "Boil the milk," and where his advice was followed, infant mortality decreased noticeably. Within a year after his arrival in America, he was writing his own articles on child care. His first textbook, "A Treatise on Midwifery and Diseases of Women and Children," was published but attracted few readers. The entire printing was sold for $68 as waste paper. At this period in his career, his life was circumscribed by work in the clinics and in his professorship at the Medical College. Although he received many invitations to social events, he accepted none of them.

In the early 70's, an incident occurred which could have wrecked the career of a lesser person; he was accused of striking a woman patient and, worse, of cruelty to children. As a result of this charge, he lost his volunteer position at the Nursery and Child's Hospital.

Jacobi, always a fighter for principle, refused to drop the matter. He forced the issue, and the "witness" testified that she had seen the doctor *almost* strike a woman patient. Jacobi testified that he had never struck a patient; that he had been angered by a mother whose baby was suffocating. He had begged and pleaded that she allow him to perform a tracheotomy on the child to save its life; the mother refused, and the child died. As for "cruelty" to children: this accusation stemmed from Jacobi's refusal to permit visitors to give candy to the children in his charge. He was exonerated and the unhappy affair took nothing from his reputation as the country's leading pediatrician. Ironically, he had served the Nursery and Child's Hospital for ten years without pay.

On December 4, 1871, it was his pleasant duty as president of the New York County Medical Society, to welcome 12 new members into that prestigious organization. One of the new members, Mary Palmer Putnam, he had nominated himself. He had no prejudice against women in medicine, and she seemed well-qualified. In fact, his welcoming speech to the new members centered around women's place in the profession, along with congratulations to Mary on her outstanding achievements at the École in Paris.

She gave rapt attention to his address which included a resumé of his work with infants and children. At the close of the meeting, she spoke to him, offering some ideas of her own. In order to continue the discussion, he accompanied her home that evening—and many evenings thereafter. By mid-summer, they were engaged.

The wedding took place July 22, 1873, in City Hall where a civil ceremony was performed. Mary's father had died recently and, with the family in mourning, a church wedding was out of the question. Furthermore, such a ceremony would have seemed hypocrisy to Jacobi who claimed to be an atheist.

The nine-month engagement period had given him time to design a house in the city for Mary which she termed a mansion. A second home awaited them: in 1867, he had come to Lake George, purchasing Hiawatha, an island; the cottage on that island would shelter them during their honeymoon.

Immediately after the marriage ceremony, the couple left for Lake George on a northbound train. Such a trip, involving several different methods of transportation, would have seemed arduous to many, but to Mary, always keenly interested in everything around her, it was a delight.

After a train ride of several hours along the Hudson River, they arrived at historic Fort Edward where they changed trains taking the spur to Glens Falls. From the top of the stage which ran between the railroad station and the hotel, Mary looked in vain for a glimpse of the cave on the Hudson River made famous by the writings of James Fenimore Cooper. From Glens Falls, a plank road led north for ten miles through the "dark and bloody ground" of the French and Indian War.

Arriving at the village of Lake George, they stopped briefly at the impressive Fort William Henry Hotel with its long view of the beautiful lake, then took the paddle-wheeler, the Minne-ha-ha, ten miles further down the lake to Bolton Landing. They made the last lap of the journey to their island in Huddle Bay by rowboat.

Mary's appreciation of the cottage was all that Abraham had hoped for. He had designed it himself and had instructed the builder to place the house as close to the water as possible, so that the sound of waves lapping the shore, rhythmic and soothing, was always audible. There was a grove of trees at one end of the island where they enjoyed picnics like children, later setting up a table where they worked on their studies and papers "like the middle-aged people we are," Mary thought somewhat ruefully. They would return to the island whenever possible, but the summer of 1875, two years later, was the most eventful.

Their first child had died soon after birth, and now Mary was pregnant again. Both she and Abraham were happy at the prospect of becoming parents, although he worried more about her than she did about herself. She had always been strong and, during pregnancy, continued to see patients and carry on her work as usual. She insisted on going to Lake George that summer, and they enjoyed their working vacation on the island as much as ever.

Abraham had arranged for a doctor in Bolton Landing to attend Mary, but as the time drew near, he became apprehensive.

"Don't worry," Mary told her husband, "I'll let you know in time."

She had every intention of keeping her word, but events failed to work out that way.

Realizing that the time had come for decisive action, Abraham had pulled the rowboat off shore ready to leave when he heard an infant's cry. Mary, the practical and independent, had managed everything all by herself.

The infant was a boy, and they named him Ernst after Dr. Krackowizer, Abraham's dear friend. Back in the city, their home became a place in which their roots went deeper because of little Ernst. To Abraham, especially, having a child of his own made his work even more meaningful. A little girl, Marjorie, arrived a few years later, and Abraham felt a completeness he had never known before. Professionally, the fame of the Drs. Jacobi had spread, and they were often referred to as "The First Family of Medicine."

"How fortunate those children are," people said, "in having parents who know all about bringing them up."

During these years, the doctors studied, wrote, taught, and in every way extended their influence. A new edition of Abraham Jacobi's "Infant Diet" appeared. Originally a medical treatise, it was adopted by Mary to public use, proving so successful that, for a number of years, annual editions were printed. Abraham became president of the New York State Medical Society; Mary was president of the Association for the Advancement of Medical Education for Women. Every summer they relaxed and renewed their energies at Lake George, but always they were working, producing, and caring for the children who needed their help.

In the summer of 1883, unexpectedly, both Jacobi children came down with a severe illness which was diagnosed as diptheria. Dazed, Abraham wondered how this was possible. True, he had attended cases of diptheria recently, but faithful to his own teaching, he had always made it a practice to wash thoroughly—it was said he even washed his beard—before coming into the presence of his children.

Anxious, fever-filled days passed; then, on June 10, nearing his eighth birthday, Ernst died, the mystery of how he became ill still unsolved. Then the truth was discovered: a German nursemaid who cared for the children, proved to be a carrier of the dread disease. She had come down with a sore throat but, through fear of losing her position, had told no one. Jacobi was helplessly furious, but his only action was to give the woman a pension and send her back to Germany. Out of his suffering came a monument to his son: at the end of Hiawatha Island, the grieving father had a five-ton block of granite erected as an enduring memorial to Ernst's bright but short life. The inscription reads:

Ernst Jacobi, born on Hiawatha Island, August 3, 1875; died in New York, June 10, 1883.

Abraham Jacobi never recovered from the death of his son. He worked as usual, took responsibilities and discharged them magnifi-

Built by Dr. Jacobi for his daughter Marjorie McAneny

Memorial to Ernst Jacobi—Ernest McAneny—grandson of Drs. Jacobi

cently, but he became more silent and withdrawn. His monograph, "Diptheria Spread by Adults," came from the heart of an anguished father. Only Schurz, the jovial could, on rare occasions, rouse him from his depression. Abraham tortured himself needlessly with regrets over his son's death, pondering the unanswerable "Why . . .?" and "If only . . ." But the world remembered only his remarkable successes.

Heavy-hearted, sharing her husband's grief and enduring her own, Mary continued to contribute to the world's medical knowledge. She delivered a paper on Pathology and Infantile Paralysis before the New York County Medical Society. This, and forty other papers on various medical subjects which she presented, received wide attention, and have since become classics. She became interested in the cause of women in politics and wrote "Common Sense Applied to Woman Suffrage." Her husband approved of the suffrage movement, believing, as he did, in the equality of all persons, but Schurz disapproved on principle, probably still influenced by the German adage which restricted Women's interests to Children, Church, and Kitchen.

Mary wrote philosophically on the Value of Life, giving as life's greatest aim "The development of all faculties to the greatest extent to which the individual is capable, and the satisfaction of all desires to their utmost capacity." She helped found the Consumers' League, and the League for Political Education. She was also chairman of the Section of Neurology of the Academy of Medicine and produced "Essays on Hysteria and Brain Tumors." Both she and Abraham were founders of the Pediatrics Division of Mt. Sinai Hospital.

For a while, summers at Lake George were lost to them; Abraham could not bear to go back to the island where Ernst had been an inquisitive, carefree little boy. In 1889, Carl Schurz and his family began spending summers at the Sagamore Hotel and persuaded Jacobi to accompany them. From these sojourns came the doctor's desire to build on mainland property which he had purchased in 1875 and here, about a mile north of Bolton Landing, he built two cottages: one, sometimes called Juniper Hill, for his own family and one for Schurz, bringing the two friends within shouting distance of each other. They were inseparable, both in New York and at Lake George. Here in a densely-wooded section was their Schwartzwald. Later, Dr. Jacobi built a third cottage for his daughter, Marjorie.

But each summer, on August 3, Ernst's birthday, Abraham disappeared, returning much later, deeply depressed, and Mary knew that he had been to the island mourning the loss of their son.

A joy of their later years was the marriage of their daughter, Marjorie, to George McAneny who first appeared as a guest at Schurz' summer home. McAneny became a secretary to the National Civil Service Reform Association, a movement initiated by Schurz and supported by Jacobi.

In 1896, Abraham Jacobi was elected to the presidency of the Associ-

ation of American Physicians; the organization also nominated him honorary president of the International Medical Congress to be held in Paris.
The dual honors were the occasion of a testimonial dinner given in his
honor and attended by many notables in New York City. A poem by Weir
Mitchell lauding the famous physician was read; Dr. William Hanna
Thomson spoke on "Dr. Jacobi, the Physician"; William Osler's contribution was to "Jacobi, the Scientist"; the subject taken by Carl Schurz was
"Jacobi, the Citizen." He stressed Jacobi's great courage which he had
known intimately for many years. Seth Low, President of Columbia University, spoke of Jacobi's contribution to medical education.

The Association also presented the guest of honor with a bound volume containing 53 treatises written by the greatest medical scientists in
eleven countries. Deeply moved, Jacobi responded, outlining his deep
devotion to the cause of medicine and to America.

Another great honor which came to him was the offer of a profes-
sorship at the University of Berlin. The honor was especially signigicant
and a tribute to his great accomplishments. The University was considered the greatest in the world and, of personal significance to Jacobi, it
was in Germany that he had spent two years in prison. He refused to consider the offer; he had found freedom and a broad field of action in
America which he could not relinquish.

There was much more work to be done: he was an advocate of the
newly-discovered antitoxin; he was an active participant in the Society for
the prevention of Tuberculosis; he gave strong support to Nathan Straus'
free milk stations where depots placed at various points, distributed milk
either free or at low cost to residents of the city.

It was a life that still had its good moments, warm with service to
others, but great changes were inevitable. In April, 1906, Abraham's
great friend, Carl Schurz, became gravely ill. During this, his last illness,
Schurz realized a strange circumstance; he and Jacobi had always ad-
dressed each other in formal German, never using the familiar terms
when speaking to each other. A lessening of formality was long overdue,
he decided, and for the last 24 hours of his life, the two friends chatted
away as though they had known each other nearly all their lives, as indeed they had.

Mary Jacobi, who had always possessed radiant health, was now ter-
minally ill, but she kept in touch with events. "The greatest blow has
fallen," she said when she heard of Schurz' death, knowing that Jacobi's
deep friendship with Schurz surpassed any other existing relationship.

As her own life drew to a close, the heroic stature of this great
woman became increasingly evident. For some time, she had known that
she had a brain tumor. Analyzing her condition, she wrote to a friend of
the progress of her own ailment, and its probable duration. The treatise
was published later as "Meningeal Tumor Compressing the Cerebellum,"
and is considered one of her best clinical works. She died on June 10,
1906—the same day on which Ernst had left them.

A Memorial Service was held in the Great Hall of the Academy of Medicine with many eminent physicians and nearly every woman doctor in the New York area in attendance. Testimonials were given on the pioneering work of Mary Jacobi in medicine and child care, and on her influence as a person. Special mention was made of her nobility of character and her innate ability to draw out the best in her associates. During the service, announcement was made that, in her memory, the Mary Putnam Jacobi Fellowship for women doing post-graduate work in medicine had been established. Mary would have appreciated that.

Somehow, life had to go on for Abraham Jacobi. There were compensations; he had his work, and there were friends who believed in him. There were grandchildren, and there was his home on Lake George where he helped organize the Lake George Association, served as chairman of the first committee to check the pollution of the waters, and chaired the first committee on the general public health of the area. There was Dr. Willy Meyer, son of his former brother-in-law, whom he had persuaded to come to the United States from Germany. He would be a brilliant surgeon as Jacobi had known, contributing great service to America.

His associates continued to honor Dr. Abraham Jacobi: a testimonial banquet had been given for him at the age of 70; greater honor would be paid him on his 80th birthday. This, and additional honors still lay ahead: in the immediate future, he would be elected President of the American Medical Association; the next year, when introduced to the House of Delegates at the National Convention in Chicago, he would be given an ovation. And, for his remaining years, there was the lake which he loved, sometimes with a light breeze ruffling its placid surface—But the waters of Lake George are not always placid and weather conditions can change suddenly and unexpectedly.

One September night in 1918, after Jacobi had retired to his downstairs bedroom, he smelled smoke; then wisps of smoke started coming around the edges of the door. He knew then that the house was on fire; possibly the wind had blown sparks out of the fireplace. The cook had already discovered the fire; he could hear her cries for help as she raced to the nearby home of his daughter and family. He knew that the fire would spread rapidly and he must get out; it would be fatal to open the bedroom door. There was only one way, the window. He tried desperately to open it, but it was swollen shut from dampness. Quickly, he pulled down the shade to protect his hand and smashed the glass. Then he let himself out, clinging to the window-ledge for a moment before he dropped to the ground. Because the house was built on a rocky ledge on uneven ground, he fell about 8 feet.

He was dazed by the fall and for a few minutes lay where he had fallen, and there they found him: his daughter, her husband, and children, all rushing over from the house adjoining his, panic-stricken when they found him leaning against the blazing wall of the house, angry flames reaching out over his head.

He was not badly hurt. A small bone in his foot had been broken but, in other ways, his loss could not be estimated. There had been valuable letters, irreplaceable books, historic documents in the house now being devoured by flames. The first hand-written section of his autobiography was going up in smoke, and he knew that there would not be time to replace it. Saddest of all, the flames had taken the little treasures that Ernst had loved.

Jacobi's friends in the medical profession were encouraged to know that he had survived the shock of the fire, and might be able to attend the dinner planned for his 90th birthday. This event, they promised, would eclipse all other observances. The following summer, when Jacobi returned to Lake George, he stayed in the house formerly occupied by Carl Schurz. He saw a few patients, the last one on July 6, when a neighbor, William K. Bixby, brought his granddaughter for an examination. The child was seriously ill, and Jacobi spent an hour with her, prescribing medicine and how it was to be administered. For many years, it is said, the local druggist had the prescription—the doctor's last—framed and hanging on his office wall.

Jacobi tired easily now, and his doctors, Dr. Huber and Dr. Willy Meyer, realized that he would not celebrate his 90th birthday on earth. On July 10, 1919, he passed out of this life, and the newspapers reported that his work was finished.

Finished? His was a work begun and it would continue in other hands with supplements and additions to the main theme; the welfare of infants and young children. Some of the views that he held, so startling in his lifetime, are being heard today—and they do not startle. He believed in controlling the size of the family and heartily endorsed a book published at that time, "Fewer and Better Babies," by Dr. William J. Robinson. He opposed prohibition, not on psychological or moral grounds, but in the belief that alcohol is a medicine and should be treated as such. He believed that no doctor should ever tell a patient that he or she faced death; and that a doctor should never terminate the life of an incurable, for his mission is a never-ending struggle to save life.

Their work is not finished; it is continued: wherever a baby, healthy, well-fed, and contented, nestles in loving arms, the influence of Mary and Abraham, the Doctors Jacobi, is present, still guiding, protecting, and, above all, caring.

Note to Reader: Less than a mile north of Bolton Landing stands a boulder near the stone bench erected in memory of Carl Schurz. The boulder bears a plaque reading:

"In memory of Abraham Jacobi, a pioneer, occupied the First Chair of Pediatrics in America. The scholarly and broadmined physician, once president of the American Medical Association who loved these woods and waters about his summer home."

Erected by friends and colleagues . . . American Pediatric Society June 13, 1936.

CHAPTER XII

Carl Schurz

Carl Schurz was born on March 2, 1829, at Liblar Near Köln (Cologne) on the Rhine River, 325 miles southwest of Berlin. From his earliest years, he seemed destined for an adventurous life lived before the public, using his talents to the fullest and taking every opportunity to fulfill his destiny. Symbolic of romance, he began his life in a castle, but this time there was no evidence of grandeur: his father was a schoolmaster; his mother was the daughter of a tenant farmer who rented part of the old castle as a home. Carl's mental abilities soon convinced his parents that he should be well educated, and he attended the schools that were available, finally entering the University of Bonn. Here, as a youth dedicated to the principles of human liberty and brimming over with idealism, he came under the influence of an ardent reformer, Professor Gottfried Kinkel.

The Revolutionary movement of 1848 broke over Germany, and Carl became one of its most enthusiastic champions. On one occasion, at a meeting of like-minded men, he was asked to speak. Without notes, he rose to his feet and, as his hearers later testified, his fiery words poured out in a torrent, seemingly without his volition. Many other young men shared his revolutionary zeal, among them, a young man named Abraham Jacobi. They met, and thus began a lifelong friendship for these two young men. Years later, in America, they would continue that friendship: Dr. Jacobi as one of the most famous physicians in the country; Carl Schurz as an eminent scholar, writer, and military leader. Both would be residents of Millionaires' Row on Lake George, and both would bequeath great legacies to the American people gleaned from the development of their special talents.

Now, in 1849, the heavy hand of government descended on the revolutionaries and Carl was obliged to make his escape. With the courage that was always part of his adventurous nature, he escaped by way of a sewer, which in itself presented the danger of drowning. Making his way to another province of Germany, he learned that Kinkel had been imprisoned and sentenced, not to death, as treason demanded, but to a life sentence. This, to a freedom-loving man, Carl knew, would be worse than death. He determined to free his beloved professor.

Under an assumed name, and with a forged passport granting the bearer permission to leave the country, he went back to the place where he had narrowly escaped arrest himself. Enlisting the aid of other revolutionaries who had absolute trust in him, he rescued Kinkel and, with the Kinkel family, escaped to France. Here he found that his fame as the hero who had rescued Kinkel had preceded him, and that his presence was an embarrassment to the government of France. London offered a haven to the refugees and, in England, Carl found that he could meet expenses by giving lessons in music and German. He neglected to learn English—one of the few opportunities for learning he ever missed—as the language seemed unmusical to his German-trained ear. During his several years in England, he met and married a lovely young German-born girl, and both planned that, when the revolution succeeded in their homeland, they would return there.

These hopes were dashed with the collapse of the revolutionary movement in France, a setback which they realized would spread to the Fatherland. Now Carl knew that the great hope of the world for independence was in the United States, and the young man of 21 and his even younger wife sailed for the New World with its promise of freedom. They arrived in New York City, then went to Pennsylvania where there were many German-speaking people. This time Carl realized he must learn to speak English. He did this by reading books, newspapers, even advertisements and, in a few years, he had mastered English as he had mastered French. For a while, he delivered his speeches in German, addressing German-Americans, not quite daring to trust his newly acquired English; but as he gained public attention, his field widened and in a short time he had become one of the most prominent orators of the day.

Now he began to make the acquaintance of people of influence and distinction. Such was his charm of manner and the vitality of his personality that he invariably drew about him the most outstanding personalities of that time and formed fast friendships with them. Visiting Boston, he met the most famous authors of the day: Longfellow, Emerson, Lowell, Agassiz, Holmes, Field; he sought out Whittier whom he greatly admired. Deciding to visit relatives in Illinois, he journeyed there and found that section of the country embroiled in the question of slavery. He also visited Wisconsin and found that state so much to his liking that he purchased property. Making his home there, he was admitted to the bar in Milwaukee in 1859.

He had become deeply identified with the question of slavery which was repugnant to his democratic nature. Visiting Washington, D.C., he heard the opposing forces debating the issue; he met Jefferson Davis, Secretary of War, and outstanding leaders in government: Douglas, Seward, Sumner, and Chase.

He was asked to speak on the question of slavery in Chicago; he delivered the speech in English; it was printed in full in the newspapers, and he was on his way to political recognition. A later engagement took him to Quincy, Illinois, where the Lincoln-Douglas debates were scheduled. Then he met Abraham Lincoln.

The meeting came about when Schurz was traveling by train to Quincy with a member of the Republican State Committee. Suddenly, there was a great commotion and men jumped to their feet to greet the

Prof. Gottfried Kinkel—Carl Schurz

*Brigadier General
Carl Schurz*

Built by Dr. Jacobi for Carl Schurz

Carl Schurz at Lake George

TO THE HAPPY MEMORY OF
·1829· CARL SCHURZ ·1906·
SOLDIER · STATESMAN · SCHOLAR · PATRIOT
FOR FOURTEEN SUMMERS 1892-1905 HE ACHIEVED AND
RESTED IN THESE PRECINCTS WHOSE BEAUTY WAS HIS
NEVER ENDING JOY · ERECTED SEPTEMBER 1925 ·

Bench—Memorial to Carl Schurz, North of Bolton Landing

Dr. Abraham Jacobi and grandchildren

Carl Schurz
1829–1906

man who had just entered the car. According to Schurz' account, he was very tall, and stooped as though to come nearer to his constituents. His face at that time was cleanshaven, and the furrows in his face were deep, lighted by kind but melancholy eyes. He wore the stove-pipe hat usually associated with him in his pictures, carried a shawl in place of an overcoat, a bulging umbrella, and a black satchel. Schurz and Lincoln were introduced and sat down together, talking in the most informal and friendly manner. They exchanged political views; Lincoln told several of his witty and pointed stories, and thus began an association, even friendship, that proved to be of deep significance for both men. When Lincoln was nominated for the presidency, Schurz' standing was such that he was chosen as one of the members of the committee that went to Springfield to notify the candidate. He was one of seven men chosen to direct Lincoln's campaign, and spoke for him in the Northwest in both German and English.

After Lincoln's election, Schurz was appointed minister to Spain with instructions from the president to watch public sentiment closely and to communicate with him personally. At the Spanish Court, Schurz found a life of ease and luxury—a pattern which did not suit him at all. From his post, he followed the course of the American Civil War and used his leisure time to study the great military campaigns of history. News from the battlefront was disturbing and he was particularly distressed when he received news of the Northern defeat at the battle of Bull Run. With a consuming desire to be where the action was, he applied for leave of absence from his post. After agonizing delays, permission was finally granted, and he returned to America, eager for an assignment in the struggle, in which the question of slavery was, to him, the dominant issue.

At a conference with the President, Schurz told him of his desire to serve the country in the military forces. Lincoln agreed on his qualifications and sent his name to Congress recommending that Carl Schurz be placed in charge of a brigade.

Schurz was not without military experience: as a young man in Europe, he had had military training at Zurich where he studied military tactics, winning the commendation of officers on the staff. Nevertheless, there were officers in the Northern Army whose life had been devoted to the military and who resented having this German-born civilian elevated over them. The resulting friction could have been disastrous, but Schurz knew that he could not let their resentment impair his usefulness. Resolutely, he put the matter out of his mind and directed his men in exemplary fashion. His troops saw service in the great battles of the Civil War: Second Manassas, Chancelorsville, Gettysburg, Chattanooga, and he was with Sherman on his march to the sea. He reported personally to Lincoln on the conduct of the campaign, and received letters from the Chief Executive in return. In recognition of his services, he was promoted to Major General.

By April, 1865, the War was drawing to a close. Terms of surrender were to be discussed. Then, clouding any joy which the men might have felt over their victory, word came of the assassination of Abraham Lincoln. To Schurz, it meant the loss not only of a great man, but of a personal friend. A deep, grim melancholy settled over the troops as they sat about the campfires discussing the tragedy. He had been "Father Abraham" to them, an over-soul who cared for them.

When Reconstruction set in, Schurz was dismayed by the attitude taken by many Northern leaders. He was appointed by President Johnson to travel through the South, assessing the plight of the Negroes and Whites who were struggling to repair the devastation of war. Schurz' reports were ignored. Later, he quarrelled with Grant over the harsh treatment meted out to the South. He hated injustice and, throughout his life, strove against oppression wherever he found it.

He moved against a corporation stealing timber and minerals; he fought against crooked agents who were defrauding the Indians; he opposed the State's taking over public lands; he fought against the Army's exceeding its authority. He became nationally famous as a political writer, and a reformer in Civil Service administration. His voice was heard in Congress when he served as Senator from Missouri. As Secretary of the Interior under President Hayes, he became one of the first conservationists; his was the loudest voice raised to protest the plunder of our natural resources, and his writings of a hundred years ago, guide today's conservationists.

In New York City, he became a writer for the New York Tribune; he founded the New York Evening Post and served as its Editor. As a champion of social justice, his newspapers supported Grover Cleveland, and fought the tyranny of Tammany Hall. He opposed the action of the United States government in extending sovereignty over other peoples; he continued to fight unjust treatment of the Negro, and he advocated cooperation with other nations.

His interests included music, literature, and universal education, and he was known for his remarkable mastery of English. He wrote a two-volume work on Henry Clay; his own three-volume biography (unfinished) gives a graphic account to the times in which he lived, and his short biography of Abraham Lincoln has become a classic. He was a world citizen, but first of all an American, and although he felt a fatherly affection for the groups of German-Americans who adored him, he himself was never a hyphenated American.

Whenever he was in New York, he saw his dear friend, Dr. Abraham Jacobi, and they continued the friendship which had begun when both were young men in Germany. Schurz' first New York residence was in East 64th Street; later, he moved to East 91st Street, next door to his friend, Andrew Carnegie. This address he considered his permanent home, and New York City claimed him as their own. Here he contributed to the life of the City and could always be found in gatherings of men whose influence was of high caliber.

In 1892, he became a summer resident at Lake George, occupying the summer home which his friend, Jacobi, had built for him. The landscaping of the grounds which surrounded the residence was planned by his daughter, Marianne, first president of the Garden Club of Lake George.

The last years of Schurz' life were spent in alternate climates. Attempting to escape the bronchial troubles which plagued him, he spent summers at Lake George, brisk weather in New York City, and the coldest months in Augusta, Georgia.

In April, 1906, he returned from the South with his usual intense interest in everything about him, but symptoms of a deep-seated illness became evident. This, coupled with the results of a previous fall and grief over the death of his 25-year-old son, was more than Schurz' once-powerful frame could bear. He departed this life on May 14, 1906, cheerful to the end, and perhaps eager to pursue some further adventure in discovering what lay beyond. It was characteristic of the man that he should leave instructions concerning the work that he had to leave unfinished, expressing regret that he could not complete it himself.

The City of New York has honored this great man. Carl Schurz Park lies between 82nd and 89th Streets and between East End Avenue and the East River. Gracie Mansion, residence of the Mayor of New York, is located within the park.

The Carl Schurz Monument is located at 116th Street and Morningside Drive, Manhattan, near Columbia University. This is a portrait statue of the man who contributed so much to his adopted country. Overlooking the community of Harlem, it is a fitting place for one who believed so deeply in the brotherhood of all men. An organization formed soon after his death, the Carl Schurz Memorial Society, still awards scholarships in his name.

The earthly remains of Carl Schurz are buried in Sleepy Hollow Cemetery at North Tarrytown, New York. The cemetery, adjacent to the historic old Dutch Church, is also the burial place of Washington Irving and other famous people who have added luster to the American scene.

On the Bolton Road, a fraction of a mile north of the former Jacobi property, is Schurz-Jacobi Memorial Park. In this clearing edging the road is a concrete bench where Schurz used to sit and gaze at the lake, with the inscription:

> ". . . Carl Schurz, soldier, statesman, patriot. For 14 summers, 1892–1906, he achieved and rested in these precincts, whose beauty was his never-ending joy."

CHAPTER XIII

Count Mankowski
and the
Gold Challenge Cup Races

In a democratic society, nobility and rank shine with a certain luster. This was even more true in the early years of the century than it is now, when glamor is an over-the-counter commodity. So inevitably, in the society of Millionaires' Row, Count and Countess Casimer S. Mankowski occupied a unique position. There was an aura of romance surrounding "Count" or any other title, and when Count Mankowski demonstrated those qualities deemed essential in a nobleman, i.e., dash, spirit, and a flair for the dramatic, he became all that a true democrat hopes to find in a nobleman. He was a bona fide Polish nobleman, and the Countess was the traditional American girl from the mid-West elevated to the nobility by marriage. Her family's fortune was derived from the success of Bixby's shoe-polish which her father had invented and marketed. Although the family name was Bixby, they were not directly related to the family of William Keeney Bixby, already established on the shore of Lake George.

The Count and his Countess lived on an estate just above the Village of Bolton Landing, complete with mansion, servants' quarters, boat-house, and garage. The boat-house was the Count's own domain where his restless nature found release in the noise and excitement of fast boats. The Countess was a shadowy figure who seemed plagued with ailments which kept her from an active social life—ailments pinpointed as rheumatism and pleurisy. How great a part the couple played in the life of the summer colony is undetermined, but it was well known by residents that the titled couple resided at Tallwoods, a place to be pointed out to visitors.

The Polish Count drove a small racing boat, "The Gem," and when he had experienced the thrill of winning a few local races, he decided to enlarge his field and bring glory to Lake George and to himself. Money seems to have been the least of his worries: the American-born Countess, a native of California, was probably one of the great number of American women who had traded wealth for a title and considered the exchange a bargain.

With excitement, tempered with cool determination, the Count began to implement his plans. He ordered a 40-foot boat with two engines built at Detroit. He went over specifications and made trips to Detroit to check on the progress of the craft that he hoped would carry him to victory and bring the Gold Cup Races to Lake George. Fifteen thousand dollars went into the building of the boat which he called the "Ankle Deep." Throughout the winter and spring of 1911–12, the craft was under construction. At the earliest possible date, Casimir S. Mankowski, owner and operator, entered his boat, the "Ankle Deep" in the prestigious Gold Challenge Cup Races held at the Thousand Islands. The races were scheduled for July 31, August 2nd and 3rd.

Summer came and the Count drove the little "Gem" through the waters of Lake George at high speed, hoping that any day, the new boat would arrive from Detroit. By mid-July, the boat was still not ready for release. Worried, the Count sent urgent telegrams, and received soothing replies that the boat would be finished in plenty of time. The Count's final wire demanded that the boat be shipped at least a week before the races so that he might become used to handling it. From the builders came the suggestion that the Count go on to Alexandria Bay, the site of the races; the boat would be delivered there "in plenty of time."

With enthusiasm already dampened, the Count and his mechanic went to Clayton on the St. Lawrence to await delivery of the boat—and waited impatiently. On July 31, a half-hour before the start of the races, the Ankle Deep arrived with the builders' encouragement, "Fine boat; nothing to worry about."

But the Count knew that there was plenty to worry about. He had never sat behind the wheel of the craft before, and his mechanic was unfamiliar with the working of the engine. Undoubtedly, there was some tinkering to be done, and the craft still had to be driven ten miles to the starting point of the race. The show had to go on.

With mechanics and helpers rushing nervously about, the Count in desperation telephoned headquarters trying to get a half-hour's postponement of the race. With his plea unanswered, the harried Count started the engine, his mechanic jumped aboard, and the boat leaped ahead, covering the distance in record time. At the starting point they found sympathy; the race was held back for half an hour in order to make the necessary adjustments, and the race was on.

As the speed boats roared into the contest, the Count found that he needed all his optimism, determination, and courage to compete with the experienced racing drivers. Unfamiliar with his boat, he could still see that she was making good headway and might overtake the boat in the lead. Suddenly, the Ankle Deep was caught in the wash from the boat just ahead and, to the horror of the spectators, the boat foundered and went down. Both men were good swimmers, and the danger to them was minimal, but the set-back, the severe disappointment, the near-despair, were almost unsurmountable.

But the dauntless Count refused to admit defeat. He had faith in the Ankle Deep; he believed that his own unfamiliarity with the craft had contributed to the disaster, and he resolutely looked forward to next year's races at the Thousand Islands. During the winter of 1912–13, the Ankle Deep was overhauled at the shop in Detroit. Any weak points were strengthened; her balance was improved, and it was noted that she kept an even keel even when being driven at the speed of 40 miles an hour.

Interest and enthusiasm in the Gold Challenge Cup Races at the Thousand Islands again ran high the following summer; the drama of a defeated contestant again trying for the highest honors caught the imagination of everyone with the slightest interest in speed-boat racing. In Lake George, excitement was intense; newspapers ran editorials stressing the effect which a victory would have on the economy and prestige of the resort area.

Along with their bright hopes, residents had cause for anxiety; the Count was besieged with offers, even demands, from the Motor Boat Club of America to enter the Ankle Deep in the races in England as a challenger for the International Harmsworth Trophy. In a letter to the Count, Commodore Melville pleaded and implored the now-famous Count to enter his boat as the American challenger. She was the only boat who could represent America with any assurance of winning, he wrote. Trying to enlist the Countess in his plans, the Commodore sent her a telegram telling of the royal welcome planned for the owner of the Ankle Deep, and emphasizing the social prestige that would accrue to the winner of the race. Unfortunately, the Gold Challenge Cup Races and the race for the International Harmsworth Trophy were scheduled for the same date, and the Count was obliged to make a choice. Reporters crowded about him; would he go to England? Would he go to the Thousand Islands?

The Count stood firm on his first decision. He would not change his plans, nor would he let Lake George down; he would race at the Thousand Islands for the glory of his beloved Lake George. Count Mankowski was the Man of the Hour; every resident in the area loved and admired him, hailing him as a hero who could not fail. From the shop in Detroit, the Ankle Deep was shipped directly to the Thousand Islands.

On the first day of the race, the excitement at Lake George was only matched by the rising tide of excitement at Alexandria Bay. Published reports on the other craft entered gave the Ankle Deep an edge over her opponents, and she was designated the most powerful contender. Her 16 cylinder Sterling engine could develop, 3,000 hp driving the boat at nearly 50 miles an hour.

The starting gun was fired at 4 p.m. on the first day of the race, and all boats shot over the starting line—that is, all but one. To the consternation of the spectators, the Ankle Deep was lagging. Later, it was said that she did not get the starting signal. But when she, too, shot over the starting line, any disappointment was forgotten. Skillfully driving his craft, the Count easily overtook the lead boats, passed them, and roared on to victory, covering the 30 miles of the course in 45 min. 55 sec. Whistles sounded, horns blared, and spectators cheered at the victory of the Ankle Deep. The next day, the Count and his invincible boat won again, and it was a foregone conclusion that she would take the race on the third day.

So sure were the judges of the final outcome, at a dinner that evening, the Gold Cup was given into the hands of T. E. Krumbholz, leader of the Lake George group, who referred to the old saying, "Many a slip 'twixt the cup and the lip." But there was no slip, and the Ankle Deep also took the third race. Of all the plaudits which the Count received, the most gratifying was a telegram from Commodore Melville informing him that the English races had been postponed to September so that the Count might enter the great Ankle Deep. Fame, both local and international had come to the Count from a victory made even greater by a previous defeat. He made plans to enter the English races.

Prepared for any emergency, the Count took with him to England $2,000 worth of spare parts for the Ankle Deep, but had no need of anything other than a screwdriver and a monkeywrench. The boat made a remarkable showing, and the consensus was that she could have won, except for a broken propeller-shaft. There was some disappointment at home, but it was overshadowed by the Count's choice of Lake George as the site of next summer's American Power Boat Associations' Gold Cup Races.

"Think what this will mean," exulted the local newspapers. "Having the race in Lake George will bring thousands here from all over the world; we must be ready to accommodate them." Editorially, it was stated that the coming races constituted the biggest event of the century.

Before plans for the coming year had gotten well underway, a cloud loomed on the bright horizon at Lake George: in Southern waters, a boat called the Hydro-bullet was making history, and it was learned that her owner was planning on coming to Lake George to wrest the trophy from the local Association. Immediately, several wealthy and influential men formed a syndicate to forestall any circumstance that threatened Lake George with the loss of the Gold Cup. Then they hit upon an ingenious plan:

They would build a boat of their own. Presumably, this boat would be able to outdistance the Ankle Deep, but only if it became necessary. The proposed racing craft would be a back-up boat. In short, if anything happened to the Ankle Deep—which, judging from past experience was possible—then the syndicate's boat would put on all speed and take the race. Members of the syndicate canvassed the field of speed-boat builders and decided on the firm of VanBlerck in Detroit to build the "Hawkeye," named from a character in James Fenimore Cooper's "Last of the Mohicans."

Construction of the boat was followed carefully by the syndicate; the engineer, Henry Pole, who would know the boat intimately by the time it was finished, was at Detroit constantly supervising the fine points of its building. Her pilot had also been chosen; Fred G. Peabody, son of F. F. Peabody of the Troy firm of Cluett and Peabody, and a resident of Millionaires' Row, would drive the craft to victory—but only if it proved necessary. Many times, it was emphasized by the syndicate that the boat would not compete with the Ankle Deep, but would cruise along in readiness to take the lead should the Gold Cup seem to be slipping out of their grasp.

One wonders what thoughts passed through the mind of Count Mankowski on learning that a boat was being built "not to surpass the Ankle Deep but ready to take over in case of disaster."

"I have the fastest boat in the world," he had claimed after his 1913 triumphs. He could hardly have been blamed if he had taken the action of the syndicate as less dictated by civic pride than by a lack of confidence in him and his boat.

The problem of the Hydro-Bullet's appearance was soon solved simply by telling the owner that there would be no financial awards among the gentlemen and ladies who, as true sportsmen and women, were taking no money for their accomplishments. The owner of the Hydro-Bullet thereupon withdrew his entry and headed for some other race where the rewards were less noble and more practical.

There was still another threat to the peace of mind of the promoters of the race: Glen Curtiss of Hammondsport, New York, had built a 12-foot boat with an airplane engine capable of running a mile a minute. An addition built on the back of the boat and extending another 12 feet into the water, carried the shaft and propeller. All admitted that the boat was a freak, but unfortunately, its strange specifications were within the requirements of the race. Lake Georgians breathed a sigh of relief on learning that Mr. Curtiss could not spare the time to race his boat.

The National Gold Cup Races were to be run under the auspices of the Lake George Regatta Association. In addition to the Gold Challenge Cup which the winner's Boat Club was allowed to hold for a year, another trophy was promised; for a thousand dollars, the Association had purchased a second Gold Cup to be awarded to the winner of a special one-mile race. This race would be held mornings; the Gold Cup Races would be run afternoons. It was not anticipated that any of the notable contenders would enter the shorter race.

Amid all the excitement generated that year on the forth-coming races, a tragedy occurred: on Easter Sunday, 1914, the Sagamore Hotel, a focal point in all the arrangements, burned to the ground. With the race course laid out in Bolton Bay, the great hotel would have been at the very center of festivities. Adjustments had to be made quickly, and the planning committee made them: although the hotel was gone, observers would be allowed on the grounds, but no automobiles were permitted; visitors must respect the privacy of those who still had cottages on Green Island.

Great were the expectations and preparations: the 6-nautical-mile course off Green Island was in the form of an ellipse; the steamer Horicon would be moored in the center of the ellipse where passengers would have a good view of the race from all sides. Since the best view could be had from the site of the former Sagamore Hotel, a grandstand was set up and special boxes erected. The latter were designated as a "token of appreciation to those who had done so much for the Association," at $100 each. A roster of those who took boxes was a summing up of the sporting elite of Millionaires' Row and included:

> Commodore Harrison B. Moore, William F. Bixby, F. W. Rockwell, Mrs. E. F. Slausen, Maruice Hoopes, L. N. Spier, F. F. Peabody, T. E. Krumbholz, manager of the former Sagamore Hotel; LeGrand C. Cramer, Dr. Willy Meyer, George C. Van Tuyl, William Mitchell, W. F. Roberts, A. L. Judson, Mrs. W. E. Reis, David Williams, George O. Knapp, and Count Mankowski.

Among the State inspectors was a name which would mean much to Lake George in the future—George Reis.

The races were scheduled for Wednesday, Thursday, and Friday, July 30 and 31, and August 1. For several days, people streamed into the resort area. They came by train, by private automobiles, public conveyances, and locally, by trolley car and taxi. Excitement was in the air as people talked of the thrilling spectacles they were about to witness. But during the day, the sky darkened and a gale blew in from the northwest, turning the placid waters of the lake into an angry sea.

There was quick consultation among the sponsors of the race and the owners of the contesting boats. Should the race go on as planned? In reality, a heavy sea meant nothing to the Ankle Deep, built to withstand any weather, but to the other craft it could mean disaster. Refusing to take the advantage for the Ankle Deep, Count Mankowski, as defender of the Cup, made the decision that the race would be postponed until the following day. The crowds now shivering in the wind were disappointed, disgusted, and weary as they left the site of the postponed races, but they would return tomorrow.

The following day was one of those blue and gold days that reflect its loveliness in the mirror-like surface of a calm lake. The sky was unclouded, a circumstance not favorable to the Ankle Deep. The crowds returned; the 30-piece band played, and anticipation was keen. The clock moved toward the late-afternoon starting time. All vantage points were filled to overflowing with observers; wherever permitted, automobiles jammed the streets.

At 5:10 p.m., the starting gun was fired, and thereafter, each minute a black and white ball was dropped, notifying the racers of each passing minute. The boats were coming toward the starting line; two minutes to go, and other boats advanced; one ball dropped—one more to go.

"Where is the Ankle Deep?" asked the anxious crowd. As the last ball dropped, Ira Hand, timer, counted "Five, four, three, two, fire!" The last boats crossed the line, and the race was on.

Suddenly, from the sheltered side of Crown Island, shot the Ankle Deep, and the crowd cheered as the speedy craft took its place belatedly in the race. Many thought that the race was timed and did not realize that the defending boat had lost a precious minute in starting the race. The

Ankle Deep, owned by Count Casimir S. Mankowski of Lake George, winner of the Gold Cup in 1913 at the Thousand Islands. Speed 50 miles per hour

Count Casimir Mankowski brought Gold Cup Races to Lake George

Hawkeye—back-up boat for Ankle Deep

boats tore around the race course; five laps constituted one race. The Ankle Deep clocked 9:23 on the first lap, reflecting the loss of time in starting; her last lap was 8:43. The Count, at the wheel, was straining the engine to its utmost when, with a jolt, the craft stopped; her propeller shaft was broken. There was a wail of anguish as Lake Georgians saw their brightest hope dimmed; but those who knew of the back-up boat, the Hawkeye, built for just such an emergency, looked for their second hope. The Hawkeye had made a good showing in the first two laps, but gradually slowed and was the last entry to finish the race.

Two boats owned by Mrs. Paula H. Blackton representing the Motor Boat Club of America, were the acknowledged stars of the show. Her boat, the Baby Reliance, made the second lap in 7:59, a new world's record which was lowered the next day by the Blackton-owned boat, Baby Speed Demon II.

Chagrin over his poor start of the previous day sent the Count into the one-mile race held the next morning. This time, the Ankle Deep was at the starting line, and at the command, "Fire!" leaped forward, going into full speed within a few feet of the start; but she still had the Baby Speed Demon II to contend with, and the Baby was gaining—had passed the Ankle Deep, and roared to a finish at the hitherto unheard-of speed of 7:39 for the 6 nautical miles at a rate of 50.49 miles per hr. Where was the hoped-for winner, the Hawkeye? Her driver had mistaken the signals and, since he thought the race had been postponed, failed to start.

As crowds gathered to watch the Gold Cup races that afternoon, the question was discussed, "Why had the Ankle Deep been a late-starter in yesterday's race?" Someone recalled that, at the 1913 race at the Thousand Islands, the Ankle Deep did not get the starting signal and made a late start, but an exciting finish. Was the Count over-confident, believing that the late start would ensure a more thrilling finish for the Ankle Deep? There was no answer to this puzzling question; but there were other aspects to consider. Those with odds on the outcome were now figuring whether the Ankle Deep had any chance for victory. Pointwise, there was a slender chance, and they waited and hoped. The Hawkeye had only 3 points and was completely out of consideration. But all speculation ceased as Ira Hand once more shouted, "Fire!"

All eyes were on the top contenders: the Ankle Deep and the Baby Speed Demon II. Both started with a flourish: the Ankle Deep, thrusting into the race, gained speed with each lap until, on the fourth turn around the course, her time was clocked at 8:39. The boat was responding nobly, surpassing its previous record when, on the fifth lap, the propeller shaft snapped and the boat listed sharply, taking on water. The Count, fearing that the boat would go down, gripped the wheel, and its return snap threw him into the water. The engine stalled, and the famed boat now lay idle and helpless.

It was ten minutes before anyone realized what had happened. Meanwhile, the Count swam back and boarded her, and the ill-fated craft was towed home. The Hawkeye broke a magnetochain and left the race; so now, the contest was between the Speed Demon and the closest contender, the Buffalo Yacht Club's Enquirer. It was obvious which boat would win; the Demon was two miles ahead of the Enquirer at the finish line.

The clamor of victory drowned out the disappointment of many. Ironically, the guests in the Count's box: the Countess, Miss Evelyn Parkinson of Saratoga, and Mrs. Worthley of New York, had excellent seats—from which to view the Count's misfortune.

Count Mankowski's supporters were stunned by this latest debacle. Grasping at straws, they wondered if Mrs. Blackton would bring the Gold Cup back to Lake George next year. As the contests closed, there was still the Regatta Ball to be enjoyed by many, and endured by a few, with the Count among the latter. Sporting tradition demanded that he mask his disappointment immediately and rejoice with the winner. With cultivated graciousness, he did just that.

The Regatta Ball was held at the Fort William Henry Hotel; flags and banners decorated the foyer and ballroom; banks of flowers were everywhere, and music was provided alternately by the hotel orchestra and by Noller's 30-piece band from Troy. The Association had found it impossible to reach all who were entitled to attend the ball, so a blanket invitation had been extended. The hotel was now crowded with people who had come to celebrate a victory.

At 10 o'clock, the awards were presented to Mrs. Blackton. As the winner of both the Gold Cup Race and the special short-course contest, she received the Gold Challenge Cup and the new thousand dollar trophy donated by the Lake George Association. Among groups of people, there was talk of the events of the last few days, of the tragic loss to Lake George, and the slim chance of re-capturing the Gold Cup next year.

There was one more race held that year, and the Count entered the Ankle Deep in a speed-boat contest on the Niagara River. During this race the boat caught fire and was partially destroyed. This was the final blow; the engine was sold and the remains of the hull sent to Tallwoods where, a romantic report circulated, the boat would be set up on the lawn and filled with flowers. A reporter who called to check on the truth of the story was promptly set in his place by the Countess.

"How can you accuse us of such abominable taste?" she demanded, "The Ankle Deep to be filled with flowers and placed on the lawn!" The Count smiled politely, but his expression was enigmatic. Later, the reporter would remember that mirthless smile.

There was little surprise when announcement was made that the 1915 Gold Challenge Cup Races would be held at Manhassett Bay, Long Island. No one had really believed that Mrs. Blackton, defender of the Gold Cup, would bring the races back to Lake George.

More surprising was the fact that, during the winter of 1914–15, the

Count was readying an entrant for the Long Island race. With the Ankle Deep gone, he set about rebuilding a replacement, the Ankle Deep Too. The new boat was only 12 feet long, but the Count had built all his hopes into this new craft. The Hawkeye, pride of the syndicate, was also put in top condition, and Lake Georgians tried to believe again that one of the two boats would be a winner.

Determined that, this time, nothing would be left to chance, the Count took a model of his new boat to Washington where it was powered, set in the water, and its defects analyzed. Changes had to be made, and it was evident that the Ankle Deep Too would not be ready to start the race. Since she was the challenger, the officials reluctantly postponed the event for two weeks. Meanwhile, during the trial runs, the new craft went to the bottom not once, but twice, necessitating further repairs. She was not alone in her difficulties: during the trials, the Hawkeye caught on fire and required a complete overhauling.

News accounts of the 1915 Gold Challenge Cup Races at Long Island are unenthusiastic and brief. The races, postponed on behalf of the Ankle Deep Too, to August 14, had begun without her as she was not ready; nor was she ready on the 16th. Pointwise, it was noted that whatever else the Count did with the Ankle Deep Too, she now had no chance of winning. The Hawkeye, built as a buffer against disaster, failed to start at all.

Here the account stops abruptly, for the Count disappeared, and rumors circulated; he had, it seemed, made a sudden decision to return to Poland and fight for the liberation of his country. Later, another rumor saddened his friends and supporters; the Countess, it was said, had received a telephone call informing her that her husband, fighting bravely in Poland, had been killed by the Bolsheviks.

A few people who knew the couple and their domestic situation were skeptical. "The Count didn't go to Poland," they scoffed. "He went to Hollywood to get away from home. The movie stars showered him with attention and he loved it. He was quite an adventurer, you know."

In addition, a Lake George resident with excellent memory, recalls that, some time later, he and his father met the Count at Madison Square Garden where a motor-boat show was in progress. Shortly after, they learned that the Count had died of pneumonia. And when Tallwoods was sold, it was noted that the papers bore only one signature—that of the Countess.

A motel, the Contessa, now stands on the property.

CHAPTER XIV

George Reis

and the

Gold Challenge Cup Race

The American Power Boat Association's Gold Cup Race continued its yearly run, but not at Lake George. People in the resort area forgot their hopes for motor-boat supremacy, and went about their business—mainly, the tourist business. Then, nearly twenty years after Count Mankowski's gallant attempt to bring glory to Lake George, along came George Reis.

The future champion was born to wealth in Newcastle, Pennsylvania, in 1889, where his father, W. E. Reis, was founder of The Shenango Valley Steel Company. With his parents, he spent summers from 1901 to 1914 at the Sagamore Hotel learning to love the Lake George area. He was a young man when, in 1914, Count Mankowski had succeeded in his efforts to bring the Gold Challenge Cup Race to Lake George, and he served as State Inspector on that occasion. When the Count lost the race, and the bright hopes of those who witnessed the debacle were dashed, George Reis was there. Perhaps then was born his own determination to bring victory to Lake George. Meanwhile, he was turning his talents in other directions. California had become his place of residence, and there he helped found the Pasadena Playhouse which became a stage for his flair for the dramatic arts. He continued this interest at Lake George where he joined the Bolton Players and, at Bolton Landing, built a home on the lake-shore where the house itself was built over the boat-house. In 1925, he bought a speed-boat and found a new interest: the boat, El Lagarto—the Lizard—was destined for fame.

For several years, he surmounted the inevitable losses and disappointments in the racing game, but there came a day in 1933 at Detroit when, in the American Power Boat Association's Gold Cup Race, El Lagarto led the pack, and he knew the sweetness of victory. As winner, Reis also had the supreme satisfaction of choosing, for the site of the 1934 Gold Challenge Cup Race, his own Lake George. A new generation had grown up since Count Mankowski's involvement with motor-boat history, and time had dulled the sharpness of defeat, so the general public was ready for a hero who would bring them the fruits of victory. Their confidence was justified: George Reis, with his "Wall-Street-broker" mechanic, Richard Anderson Bowers, came home a victor in both the 1934 and 1935 Races at Lake George, and again as winner, he chose Lake George as the setting for the running of the 1936 Race—the 33rd in the history of the great classic.

The great day drew near and plans were again made to accommodate the racing enthusiasts who would swell the normal resident population of Lake George Village and the village of Bolton Landing.

"There was never so much excitement around Lake George before," the younger generation exulted. But the older generation remembered a dashing Count Mankowski and his "Ankle Deep," 22 years before; they recalled how he and his famous boat had gone down to defeat just when victory seemed certain, and they hardly dared hope for another triumph. Even with two victories already won, there was still the possibility that something could go wrong.

George Reis himself, in his interviews with *Mirror* reporters, did little to dispel the uneasiness that persisted. He was working every spare moment on El Lagarto, doing everything possible to ensure that the motor was as perfect as human skill could make it, and constantly testing her engine in innumerable runs down the lake. But while he and his mechanic worked, Reis himself dwelt on the possibility of failure.

"Newer hydroplanes with smaller, lighter hulls and equal power will beat her out," he prophesied, all the while working on her engine with precision instruments, and always testing, testing. There had been changes made in the 1936 requirements for racing boats; the permitted weight of a hull, 1,400 lbs, was half the weight of the previous year's standards. "The old Lizard stripped of every excess ounce, now weighs 3,400 lbs. If we take out another screw, she'll fall apart," was the owner's gloomy prediction.

In general, the public was inclined to accept Mr. Reis' disparaging remarks as a rather becoming modesty. It was well known that in previous years, the sturdy, dependable El Lagarto had won over lighter and faster craft and they still had faith in the aging boat as defender of the Gold Cup. In addition, El Lagarto now had a new 725 cubic inch engine, an adaptation which Reis had worked on for the past year and a half. What could go wrong? Lake Georgians asked. The answer, of course, was "Anything."

Unlike races held 20 years before which lasted three days, this race would be run in one day, with no second chance to retrieve losses. The course was a 90-mile grind on powerful but delicate engines, and speed was of the essence. The Notre Dame, challenger from the Detroit Yacht Club, held a previous record of 70.08 miles per hour, but the defender, El Lagarto, had hit 72.72 miles per hour, and with her new engine, she should go even faster. So they discussed, hoped, and believed. On Friday evening, July 24, Reis took El Lagarto out on the lake for a final trial run, and lake shore residents heard the roar of her "souped-up" motor as she ploughed a great trough with a wall of foam surging in her wake. Tomorrow at Lake George, records could be broken, said loyal supporters. With another victory, Reis would be a four-time winner of an exciting Race, and the Lake George Association could hold the Gold Cup for another year.

On Saturday, July 25, 1936, ten thousand spectators gathered along the shores of Bolton Bay; the owners of several large estates opened their grounds to the crowds, and out on the lake, 400 boats stationed outside the perimeter of the 6 nautical mile racing course, held a thousand more observers.

The day was perfect; the crowds, in holiday mood, were anticipating victory for the Lake George entry. Many had purchased the official Gold Cup Program, a 9x12 folder, printed in gold and black with pictures and information on the contestants. Entrants listed were: Notre Dame, Delphine VIII, and Impshi of the Detroit Yacht Club; The Hotsy Totsy III from the South Bend Yacht Club (Indiana); El Torbellino, Long Beach, California; J. D. Two from Miami; Florida, El Lagarto, Lake George Club; and Miss Canada II, from the Canadian National Exhibition. It was not generally known that, since the program had been printed, three entries listed had withdrawn because of difficulties at their home berths.

In Kaye Don, racing driver from England, the crowd generally agreed that George Reis would have a worthy opponent. Those who followed motor boat racing knew Kaye Don as the driver of Miss England II, the craft that held the speed record. They also knew that he had once taken a heat from a Gar Wood entry in a race for the International Harmsworth Trophy. Don's record was impressive, and a race between giants of the racing world was eagerly anticipated.

One o'clock came: a roar of approval greeted Kaye Don and his mechanic as they drew up to the starting line, accompanied by surprise when they saw that he was driving Impshi from Detroit instead of the expected Notre Dame; then George Reis and Bowers appeared, Reis driving El Lagarto; and the latter was clearly the favorite.

In the excitement of the moment, everything was forgotten except the presence of two great racing drivers who were facing a gruelling competition; then the obvious question was asked, "Where are the others?" There was no answer; and now attention focused on the remaining contenders, El Lagarto and Impshi.

The two boats were poised for the start, the drivers alert. On the count, one-two-three, Fire! both leaped into the race. El Lagarto had beaten his opponent over the starting line and excitement rose as the crowd, tense, saw that the Reis craft was holding the lead around the backstretch. Was the Detroit entry gaining on the leader? No one would ever know, for suddenly, El Lagarto stopped on the far side of the course, and Kay Don in Impshi, roared past to claim the lead.

People stared at each other seeking answers; what had happened? They watched, hope fading, some in tears, as the Lizard picked up enough energy to start, and slowly, slowly moved back to the boat-house. There was little interest in a so-called race which was already won by Impshi. Kaye Don, sportsman that he was, hardly enjoyed his lone ride

Dick Bowers—George Reis

George Reis, mechanic Dick Bowers and El Lagarto

Former home of George Reis

George Reis,
Gold Cup Winner

around the course without competition; nor did he treat the spectators to a useless show of speed, cruising around the first heat at 46 + miles per hour, the second at 43 +, and the third at 47 +. Meanwhile, "back at the boat-house," three other racing drivers stared gloomily at engines that would not start. Someone brought a report back to Bolton Bay on El Lagarto's disaster, and the news filtered through the crowd; one of the connecting-rod bearings in the new engine had burned out. There was a stunned silence, then the wailing post-mortem "if only—if only the bearing had given out on her trial run the night before; it could have been replaced.

In spite of the disaster, history had already been made and only the last chapter was missing. George Reis had taken the Gold Cup three years in succession, winning in '33, '34, and '35. He had brought the famous trophy back to Lake George as Count Mankowski had yearned to do a generation before, and one failure took little from the luster of the great racing craft, which, on retirement would have added the President's Cup—won three times—and the National Sweepstakes—won twice—to its list of victories.

George Reis willed El Lagarto to the Blue Mountain Lake Museum where it may still be seen. Another stipulation in his Will directed that his body be cremated and its ashes scattered over the waters of Lake George where he and his gallant boat had covered so many joyous miles together.

SALUTE TO CHAMPIONS
(by Everett B. Morris)

Poet, actor, motorboat king,
Mayor of his town and everything;
Composer whose rollicking, sprightly song
Is sung from Bolton to old Hong Kong;
Speedboat hero whose ancient crate
Has blasted records, confounded Fate.

Faster than fire in a flaming canebrake
Tougher than her reptile namesake,
Quicker than a frightened rabbit,
A boat that has the winning habit.

George Reis, El Lagarto, unbeatable pair,
Benignly blinking in the spotlight's glare.

CHAPTER XV

The Bixbys

Lillian Tuttle and William Keeney Bixby

On August 25, 1856, a baby girl, Lillian, was born to the Sidney Tuttles at their North Bolton home on Lake George, New York. She came of sturdy pioneering stock: over the years, her father and grandfather had bought up tracts of land, cutting the trees and plowing the rocky ground until, from this "bleak and inhospitable" land they had found the basic fertility of the soil. Sometime before 1811, Sidney had built the homestead on Federal Hill. Lillian's mother was his second wife, and there were children from both marriages. Everyone in the family worked on the farm, and in later years, Lillian remembered crossing her father's fields on her way to school; the fields were stony, and as she walked, she picked up stones to add to a fence of piled-up stones, one of many boundaries on the farm.

When she was six years old, her father died, followed by her younger sister. A tintype of Lillian taken when she was about ten, shows the face of a sober little girl who has already known sorrow. She was a pretty child with a broad, intelligent forehead, expressive dark eyes, and a full, generous mouth with firm control suggested by the downward lines of the upper lip. Even in a photograph, her poise is evident, showing calm acceptance of the life about her. In later years, her son Ralph wrote of her patience and understanding, her humility, and a strength of character that made her superior to any circumstance.

By the mid-1850's, the Township of Bolton had been carved out of the wilderness, and its clearly defined lines bordered the western shore of Lake George. Directly to the south lay the Township of Caldwell, and along the head of the lake, extending further south was the Township of Queensbury. The latter was the province of another illustrious family, the Harrises, and although the two families were not related, there was a bond between them. In 1772, the Crown had deeded to John Lawrence, Henry Boel, and Stephen Tuttle, 2,000 acres of land. This tract was later purchased by Moses Harris, Jr., famed patriot and spy of the Revolution, and called Harrisena. His exploits are recalled on a monument erected in the Harrisena Churchyard by John J. Harris, his grandson, with reference to Washington, Schuyler, and Burgoyne.

In 1844, the wife of John J. Harris died in childbirth, and the motherless baby boy was taken immediately to Mrs. Sidney Tuttle in North Bolton who had just lost a new-born infant. In the Tuttle home, the new baby, Johnny, was gladly accepted as one of the family; twelve years later,

Lillian arrived. In the intervening years, Mr. Harris had built a small but graceful stone church on his property using stone brought from Canada; he also built a quaintly beautiful brick house, with a cut stone entrance; both are still in use. It was ironic that the first service held at the church in 1869 was the builder's own funeral.

Mr. Harris left his brick home and the surrounding land to Johnny. The young man was ready to accept the new responsibilities at Harrisena, and asked Mrs. Tuttle to come and keep house for him. She accepted; the Tuttle home in North Bolton was occupied temporarily by a neighbor, and Mrs. Tuttle with her daughters Florence and fifteen-year-old Lillian moved into the Harris home. Here Lillian spent one of the memorable years of an eventful life, recording the happenings of each day in a diary which extends from January 1, 1871, to the following December 31. It proved to be an exciting year; there were more people in Harrisena than there were at North Bolton, and Lillian loved people.

She went to school and church, helped her mother with the housework, and every day, she called on neighbors and friends, or the friends and neighbors called on the Tuttles. The young people especially were attracted to the Harris home with its lively occupants, and there were sessions of popping corn, sleigh-rides, strolls through the church cemetery, evenings spent playing "Pochesi," reading *The Ledger,* or hymn singing. Life was full for Lillian Tuttle whether she was at North Bolton or at Harrisena: there was sugaring time in early spring with the hot maple syrup poured on snow to harden; berrying came in the summer, and chestnuts were gathered in the fall—all work that, when done in the company of others, became fun.

In 1872, she attended the Academy, a private school in Glens Falls. After she left school, there were several years of service to friends and family. A half-brother, Sidney, had left home before she was born, and had gone northward to Pottersville where he opened a general store. Evidently she spent some time with Sidney and his wife Thirza, for they were close friends. She taught school for a year or two following the occupation then thought eminently suitable for women—and also taught by her own example. There was much to be done in the day-to-day chores of existence: there were responsibilities at home on Federal Hill, occasional visits at Johnny's home in Harrisena and trips to The Falls (Glens), along with socializing in the rural community.

At Pottersville, Sidney helped organize a troop of cavalry and was made an officer, but the pioneering spirit was urging him on, and with his wife he went to Virginia where he again went into business operating a general store. One of his most poignant memories was his presence in the Ford Theater the night Abraham Lincoln was shot when, with the rest of the horror-stricken audience, he saw the murderer leap from the President's box and disappear. From Virginia, Sidney went on to Kansas City, Missouri, and finally wound up in Texas, this time as station-master for a railroad company.

When, in February, 1879, his wife Thirza died, it was inevitable that

he should send for his half sister Lillian to come to Texas and keep house
for him. She was probably not averse to travel, and never one to resist a
cry for help; so, leaving everything in order on Federal Hill, she started
for the State that lay farthest from home; that it was accessible at all was
due to the existence of the Railroad.

In 1879, a long journey enlisted a number of conveyances. From the
very nature of the clothing worn, Lillian's packages and boxes must have
been bulky and, in addition, she was carrying a bag of chestnuts which
Sidney had especially asked for. Piecing together the methods of travel
then in existence, she probably traveled by horse and carriage down to
the village of Caldwell where the Lake George Stage stopped at the Fort
William Henry Hotel. A nine-mile drive south on the plank road took her
to the Rockwell Hotel at Glens Falls for the delivery and taking-on of passengers; then on to the Railroad Station at Fort Edward where she
boarded a train for New York City. The trip south to Texas was long and
dusty. Up ahead in the engine compartment, men worked constantly,
loading wood into the steam boiler that powered the engine. Black smoke
poured from the funnel, and the smoke and flying particles of charcoal
blew into the cars and over the travelers. No discomfort bothered Lillian
very much; patiently she accepted the hardships as a necessary part of a
long but interesting journey. Of course she made friends on the trip; solitude was not in her nature.

The train finally reached Palestine, Texas, then the station where she
would meet Sidney, and she alighted with the conductor's admonition
"Watch your step, Please." She was carrying the bag of chestnuts and
watching her step at the same time when, suddenly, the bag broke and
the chestnuts spilled on the ground. She was struggling to pick them up
when she heard a man's voice asking, "May I help you, Miss?" She looked
up and found that the owner of the voice was already retrieving some of
the wayward chestnuts without permission.

She accepted his help in her friendly manner, and laughed a little
over the ridiculous situation. In the banter over the chestnuts, the two
young people discovered a mutual interest. She found that the stranger's
name was William Keeney Bixby, that he had come from Adrian,
Michigan to work on the Railroad, and that Sidney Tuttle, her half-
brother, was his boss.

In a developing America, opportunities were plentiful and a young
man determined to seek his fortune usually found it. In looking for work,
Mr. Bixby had aimed high and had written to Jefferson Davis, under
whom his father had served in the Mexican war, asking advice of the late
President of the Southern Confederacy. The Ex-President had achieved
considerable success in Mississippi since the war and Mr. Bixby was interested in chances for employment there. Mr. Davis had answered the letter, but his message, in essence, "Don't come here," was disappointing. So

(*Note:* the letter from Jefferson Davis, framed, hung on the wall of the Tuttle home for many
years, but has disappeared.)

The William K. Bixby estate, called Mohican Point

Home of William H. Bixby

Mr. Bixby had followed the Railroad to Texas and, in so doing, had laid the foundation of his own fortune.

Following the chance encounter over the chestnuts, Lillian saw Mr. Bixby often at her half-brother's house and, two years later, the young couple were married in San Antonio, Texas; soon after, they moved to St. Louis, Missouri. Mr. Bixby continued in the employ of the Railroad, making a spectacular success of the association. Ultimately, he became President of the American Car and Foundry Company.

Lillian never lost her love for the Lake George Country and its people, and they returned each summer, accompanied by an increasing number of children—there were seven in all. In the march of events normal for the times, they built a mansion, casually referred to as "the big house." As each person has an ancestry of those who have gone before, so houses have an ancestry. The immediate forerunner of the Bixby Mansion was the Mohican House, famous in its own way for over a hundred years.

Mohican Point lies just south of the village of Bolton Landing and here, in 1800, a tavern was built to accommodate travelers. An aura of mystery surrounded the operation of a store built on the property, and it was said that a trap door in the building led to a cellar where goods smuggled from Canada were stored. As a footnote to history, Dome Island lies opposite the site of the Mohican House half-way across the lake. On this island, Israel Putnam, hero of the French and Indian War, left his men while he went on to warn Ft. Edward's General Webb that an invading army from Canada was massing at Northwest Bay.

The tavern acquired further identity when, in 1824, it became Lyman's Tavern. In 1856, the tavern was purchased by Daniel Gale who, during the previous year, had remodeled the Fort William Henry Hotel at the head of Lake George. Gale made improvements on his purchase, and the tavern became a hotel, catering to the public. Guests started coming to Mohican Point from places as far away as New York City and Philadelphia, lured by reports of the game and fish dinners prepared at the lakeside hotel. It is said that Gale's two sons named the hotel, using the carved statue of a Mohican brave as their trademark. By 1873, the Mohican House was one of the famous hotels patronized by the vacationing public although it was much smaller than the average and could accommodate only 90 guests at full capacity. In contrast, the Fort William Henry could accept 600 guests at one time; at Saratoga, the United States Hotel hosted 1,200 guests simultaneously, and Congress Hall had rooms for 1,000.

By 1898, it became apparent that the Mohican House had outlived its period of usefulness. Gas, even electricity, was becoming usual for summer resorts; at the Mohican House, there were still kerosene lamps, and few of the niceties, or even the conveniences demanded by the public. Business dwindled, and in 1899, the Glens Falls Insurance Company foreclosed a mortgage of $13,000. The entire parcel embraced several tracts: the hotel itself was situated on 37 acres of lakefront property; 100 additional acres were included on Barker's Point just south of Clay Island, and 125 acres lay on the west side of Tongue Mountain. William K. Bixby of St. Louis purchased the entire tract. In addition, he bought the Spring lot on Potter Hill. Even the contents of the old hotel were included in the transaction.

At first, the Bixby family occupied the old Mohican House as their summer home hoping to save the structure, but since the timbers were decayed and worm-eaten, the building was torn down to make way for the big house. During construction of the mansion, in 1901–02, the family divided their summer between the Tuttle place on Federal Hill and the Sagamore Hotel on Green Island. The stately colonial-type house which arose on Mohican Point was, and still is, an imposing edifice. It was designed by Wilson Eyre of Philadelphia, whom Mr. Bixby had met on an ocean voyage. Massive white pillars support the roof with its several chimneys, and the visitor senses that this is an ancestral home built to last for generations.

In the heyday of the estate, a summer-house stood on the point where one might look far down the lake; a sandy bathing beach was a unique feature on the lake usually known for its rocky shoreline. There was a large boathouse and a formidable fleet: the 45-foot long "Forward" was a launch with two gasoline engines; an electric boat, the "St. Louis," carried 20 passengers then (and still carries the Bixbys' descendants today); the "Show-Me" was a then-modern hydroplane; the "Takonsie" was Mrs. Bixby's own electrically-driven boat; the "Weary" was used as a fishing boat, and there was a sailboat, and various canoes and row-boats.

The gardens and lawns with flowering bushes and shrubs were carefully tended by a corps of gardeners. Newly-planted elms lined the driveway, so spaced that in time their arching branches would touch overhead. A pond fed by springs reflected an ornamental bridge spanning its outlet to the lake. Part of the property was kept in a natural state and paths carpeted with pine needles wound through cool, dark woods where trees native to the land, of great age and size, stood untouched by civilization. Wild-flowers added their unexpected and transient beauty.

Near the house stood two trees which, in 1913, were mentioned in Samson's book "Mohican Point." One, a water-maple north of the house, was then twelve feet in diameter; the other, a locust to the south, fourteen feet in diameter. The water-maple died about 1970, but the locust still survives and now guards a stone with strange markings. The stone was removed from its original place and reset under the giant locust.

There is a legend told of this stone that first appeared in Stoddard's Guidebook published in the last century, and was repeated by Samson: Many years ago, a tribe of Mohican Indians lived in this area, and one day, a war party brought back from the northern tribes, a young Indian girl as prisoner. The chief's son fell in love with the beautiful maiden and wished to make her his bride, but the old women of the tribe had chosen another bride for him and agreed among themselves that the prisoner must die. When the chief's son had left for the hunt, the Indian women gathered together and, with the aid of the old men of the tribe, prepared to sacrifice the girl to their own ambitions. They tied her to a stake, piled fagots on the stone before her, and exulted savagely as the flames leaped upward.

When the fire was blazing its brightest, everyone was startled to see an apparition which appeared suddenly, swept the maiden up into its arms and disappeared. The ghostly visitor had seemed like one of their own tribe, but so quickly had it come and gone that none could be sure. Neither the girl nor her captor was ever heard of again, but every year afterward when harvest time came, one brave of the tribe was mysteriously slain and it became legend among them that for every hair on the girl's head touched by the flames, one brave would be sacrificed.

Thereafter, the stone assumed strange markings: discolorations said to resemble bloodstains, and the outlines of birds and animals appeared and are indelibly imprinted on the sacrificial stone. Even in these skeptical days, teachers still bring their pupils to view the stone and hear the story of the mysterious forces that have worked their magic upon it.

History has touched the entire area. South of the Bixby property was a site once owned by Ferdinand Thieriot, an early resident, who had erected a cottage, "Villa Matilda." Here, Winston Churchill, American cousin of the then-unknown hero of World War II fame, finished his first novel, "The Celebrity." The property was later purchased by Herman Broesel of New York who built a mansion in tune with the times and who became one of the founders of the Lake George Club. Mr. Broesel was a German-American, a fact which became uncomfortably evident as World War I drew closer to the United States and all with German names were under suspicion. There was a rumor that, on April 6, 1917, the day the U.S. declared war on Germany, house guests at the Broesel cottage included Franz Von Papen and Count Von Bernstorff. Von Papen, later Vice-Chancellor under Hitler, had been recalled to Germany at the request of President Wilson for "sinister activities against the United States." Von Bernstorff, as Ambassador, attempted to strengthen German-American relations until all contacts were broken off, irrevocably.

The Bixby family, too, made history. As residents of the Lake George-Bolton area, they touched many lives, from their humblest employee to the great and well-known people who were their guests. They were not only summer residents, but through Lillian Tuttle Bixby, had ties with the earliest settlers of the land. In 1903, Mr. Bixby bought property adjoining the estate and deeded a portion of it to the town of Bolton for use as a road to the lake. He served as president of the Lake George Club from 1911–1915, was on the golf committee from 1916–19, and gave a perpetual golf trophy which is still in the possession of the club. All the Bixby children lived successful and productive lives. One of the more

Former Broesel home—Hermstone

*Stone arch on property
of late W. H. Bixby*

169

*Detail of stone work,
former Broesel Estate—now Bixby*

spectacular achievers was Harold who was one of the sponsors of Lindbergh's flight to Paris and gave "The Spirit of St. Louis" its name. Harold Bixby went on to become a vice-president of Pan-American Airways and lived in China for many years establishing air routes in the Orient.

In past years Ralph, with his wife, Lucy restored the old Tuttle homestead on Federal Hill to its former glory; trees were cut so that Northwest Bay became visible from the hilltop, and stone fences again indicated boundaries. Mr. Bixby also privately published his mother's diary, covering the year she spent at Harrisena as a young girl; his own comments pay tribute to her as the wonderful person he called Mother.

Today, the big white house on Mohican Point is one of the few mansions remaining from a by-gone era. Perhaps it has survived because it has been adapted to the present-day needs of the Bixby clan, 150 strong, the descendants of William Keeney and Lillian Tuttle Bixby and their families. Inside the house, the spacious downstairs rooms remain much as they were; upstairs an architect son-in-law has created seven apartments, one for each branch of the family who come each summer from California, Texas, Kentucky, and St. Louis for joyous family reunions.

What will become of the great house on Mohican Point with its memories? Before his death in October, 1977, Ralph and Lucy Bixby often pondered this question in the Tuttle homestead on Federal Hill. Taxes and maintenance had become a heavy burden. Should the home be turned over to the public for its use? (But too often, public use means public destruction.) Shall this beautiful mansion, too, go down as so many others have fallen, sacrificed to expediency? Like the fated Indian maiden, the gracious house awaits the judgment of the future. In these swiftly-moving days, where is the power that can save it for posterity?

CHAPTER XVI

The Congers of Bra-Thole

The members of the Conger family and its branches should be grateful to Mary de Peyster Rutgers McCrea Conger Vanamee, for Mrs. Vanamee has placed her ancestors on a pedestal, disregarded any clay feet, and has told about them in a charming and rare book, *New York's Making—Seen Through the Eyes of My Ancestors.*

As she has recreated her family tree, lovingly and proudly, she has painted a picture of a star-studded ancestry where fabulously wealthy forebears share top billing with ancestors who figured in the most brilliant events of the American Revolution. Johannes de Peyster, early Dutch settler, was prospering when Manhattan was measured as "seven hours long and scarce an hour broad." His grandson, the son of Catherine de Peyster Rutgers, helped drive back the French at Lake George during the French and Indian War. Ancestor Stephen McCrea, a surgeon aboard Arnold's hospital ship, the Enterprise, served in the battle of Valcour Island; his brother, John, a lawyer, marched to Quebec with General Montgomery's regiment in the early days of the Revolution. And there was a sister, Jane . . .

The story of Mary de Peyster Rutgers McCrea Conger Vanamee is that of a little girl born into wealth who appreciated the unusual circumstances surrounding her and wrote about them. Like many streams pouring into a great lake, wealth had flowed from several branches of her family into the hands of her father, Clarence Conger. Consequently, his responsibilities were heavy.

At the turn of the century, there were a number of places which Mary called "home," but in New York City, home was a beautiful brownstone mansion on 20th Street "between Washington Square and Central Park." The household was patterned after an English style manor house with a definite division between master's and servants' quarters.

The servants' quarters with kitchens and dining-room were below the marble entrance hall of this palatial home. In this city home there were shining silver door-knobs on polished rosewood doors that swung on silver hinges. In the drawing-room, thick carpets with red roses softened the children's footsteps as they curtseyed to their mother and aunt. Crystal chandeliers with thousands of prisms sparkled in candlelight and firelight, and rooms were repeated in depth in ceiling-to-floor mirrors in gold frames. Heavy brocade draped the tall windows, muffling the traffic on 20th Street—the sound of horses' hooves, and the cry of vendors.

There was Dutch and English silver from de Peysters and Rutgers displayed behind glass; the china was Lowestoft and Willow; innumerable books, ranged neatly on shelves, were bound in brown leather mellowed with age. Symbolic of the Conger family's wealth and undoubted patriotism was a Gilbert Stuart painting of George Washington with his horse. The painting, heavily framed, covered an entire wall.

Going upstairs, little hands that could not span the wide, polished stair-railing, grasped the carved spindles, and little feet trudged upward past statues, each in its own niche holding friendly lamps to light the way. On the upper floor was the night nursery with a fireplace that often held a blazing log; there were four-poster beds with canopies in each bedroom, and in one, a mahogany cradle and a warming pan. On the next floor was the day nursery, and nearby, a playroom where each child kept his or her favorite toys; and up under the eaves, was a wonderful attic full of treasures in trunks and boxes. Some of the trunks held old-fashioned costumes, smelling of dust and lavender. The outmoded coats and dresses were too long and too big, but dressing up in them could turn a child into a miniature ancestor.

Mary's father, Clarence Repelje Conger, played a large part in her life, as well as in the lives of her brothers and sisters. An early photograph shows him to be fine-featured, obviously intelligent, with a self-assured bearing that would have made him an outstanding member of any generation. Mary was very proud of her father—of his good looks and distinguished appearance. In her narrative, she alludes to his fall from a horse which resulted in a slight injury. Later problems which he experienced could have stemmed from this injury. Educated for the Law, he was admitted to the bar, and it was anticipated that he would have a brilliant career before the public. His speech was elegant and he expressed his thoughts with a voice that could charm his listeners.

At the very beginning of Clarence Conger's career, a change in circumstances altered the whole tenor of his life. Accustomed to great wealth with its privileges and responsibilities and with every expectation that the status quo would continue, Clarence discovered that his father was on the brink of financial ruin; his mother's fortune, which could have bolstered their failing fortunes, was already half-spent, poured out in a futile attempt to cover the couple's unfortunate investments and heavy expenses. With this discovery, Clarence realized that he could not carry on plans for his own life. Family tradition demanded that he must take charge for the good of the family: his father's debts must be paid; his mother and her sisters must be cared for with no curtailment of their accustomed style. Going to Aunt Kate, his mother's sister, he laid the predicament before her. She, too, realized the seriousness of the situation, and her offer to help was immediate.

"I will give you half my fortune to pay up the debts," she told Clarence. "It will be yours anyway when I am through with it." Since Aunt Kate's fortune was equal to his mother's inheritance, Clarence could appreciate the enormity of his Aunt's sacrifice; her generosity saved his father from bankruptcy. Clarence now took over the business affairs of the family, working over books and records far into the night, and daily trying to placate his own brothers and sisters who often complained of his management of the family affairs.

"As a result of all this responsibility," Mary recalls, "Father got brain fever, and after that, he often had spells."

Aunt Kate's financial aid and Clarence's continued care of the family fortune meant that Grandmother and Grandfather Conger could continue to live in their big country house 30 miles from New York City, and that happily, the grandchildren could visit there. In spite of heavy losses, Grandmother's fortune was still very large, and she owned hundreds of acres of beautiful farming country. The country house was two miles from the village of Congers, which still retains the name of the family. Grandfather was a physician, but he never practiced anywhere else, confining his activities to his country estate and writing medical papers. During the Civil War, Grandfather had placed the family in an awkward position by favoring the cause of the South. Later, he reconciled his political differences and, in 1867, was elected to the State Senate. His speculations in Wall Street and his love of fast horses which had caused his financial losses in the first place, may have continued on a lesser scale as an avocation of the wealthy.

In Mary's word-picture of her father, he emerges as a complex character in which two opposite attitudes met and merged: he had the pioneer's feelings for the woods and streams of the wilderness where he felt at home; but he was just as much at home in the salons and drawing rooms of the wealthy and famous people of the period. He provided his children with the best tutors, boarding schools, and colleges; but he also taught them the art of survival through actual experience in the North Woods.

In the days when "idle" and "rich" were often synonomous, Clarence believed in physical education and took a daily swim in the Harlem River. As each child reached the age of 12, he or she was given a knife. Into the handle of this knife, eight other tools were folded, and the child was taught to use them. Each one received instructions in handling firearms and was presented with his own pistol. The children were taught to take care of themselves on land or in water, and could manage a sail-boat, swim, and dive. In the woods, they could climb trees 60 feet tall, and on recognizing poisonous snakes, both boys and girls were expected to kill them.

In estate business, he was a just and sympathetic landlord, and a friend to the immigrants who were swarming into the U.S. as the land of opportunity. He converted several city homes owned by the estate into tenements for the less fortunate, and never evicted a tenant for nonpayment of rent.

There were other homes in the Conger holdings besides the brownstone house on 20th Street. There was also a big house on Long Island

The Conger House, Bra-Thole

The Conger House today—Lamb's Lakeside Cabins

Stairs at Bra-Thole

Steps chiseled by Clarence Conger at Bra-Thole

near the ocean, with a white sand beach, and a big garden for flowers and vegetables. There was another house at Easthampton on the Atlantic Ocean. Overseeing the properties, managing them to produce profit and maintaining them, took most of Clarence's time; but there was still another house where the family went to enjoy the out-of-doors. This was the house at Lake George.

The days before their departure for the Lake were always busy, with servants packing clothes, necessities, and non-perishable food. Clarence, of course, saw to it that fishing rods and guns were properly packed. On the day of their departure, trunks and boxes were tied to the carriage, parents and children piled in, and they were off on cobbled streets for the Albany Night Boat moored in that part of the Hudson called the "North" River. The children were allowed to stay up until the boat had passed the Palisades; when they were put to bed and awakened in Albany.

From Albany, they traveled by train to Fort Edward were they changed for a train bound for Lake George. Here, at Fort Edward, the children knew that their ancestors, the McCreas, had written an important page in America's history. The story of beautiful Jane McCrea as told in the history books might differ in details from the legend which had come down to them; but *their* version had first been told by Dinah, the Negro servant who had been with their great-great-great Aunt Jane during her last tragic adventure. Nearness to the historic site was exciting but sobering as their father told the story once more.

It always started like one the make-believe stories their nurses told them, but this one was true. There was a beautiful girl named Jane who was in love with David Jones, a friend of her brothers'. It was at the time of the American Revolution, and David was on the wrong side of the war—the British side. The British were coming closer to Fort Edward and the Americans were leaving. (At this point, the little listeners were all ears.)

Jane and David wrote notes to each other, and they planned to be married as soon as the British Army came near Fort Edward. David had arranged to have a trusted Indian scout named Duluth meet Jane and Dinah with horses; and, as they neared the lines, Lady Ackland and Baroness Reidesel would ride out from the British Camp to greet them. (The children's eyes were wide and intense.)

Jane slipped away from her brother John and went to Mrs. McNeil's house in Fort Edward, taking Dinah with her. Suddenly, on looking out of Mrs. McNeil's window, they saw enemy Indians surrounding the house. (Gasps of fright from the young audience.)

Mrs. McNeil urged Jane and Dinah to hide in the cellar; she was too fat to get through the trap door herself. (The children laughed a little here, but immediately grew serious.) The Indians broke into the house, found Jane and Dinah and hurried them up the hill where Duluth was waiting with three horses. Mrs. McNeil followed more slowly with another Indian, as she was too fat to hurry. (Now there was no more laughter.) Duluth, the good Indian, tried to make the bad Indians release Jane, but they refused. Jane mounted the horse, and Duluth, still arguing with the other Indians, gave the horse a slap and it started off. (The children listened intently, even though they already knew the rest of the story.)

One of the bad Indians rushed after Jane and struck her with his tomahawk. (A chorus of o-o-o's.) The bad Indian took her scalp with its long, beautiful hair. (A little descendent patted her own smooth hair, and her eyes filled with tears.) The bad Indians took the scalp to the British lines and asked for payment. David Jones recognized Jane's hair; he wept for a long time and no one could comfort him. ("Poor great-Aunt Jane," a little girl whispered, "Poor David.")

But the Americans were so angry at what had happened to Jane that they all flocked to join the army; there was a great battle at Saratoga and the Americans won. The children were flushed with pride. Seeing the place where history had been made was like visiting Aunt Jane, and each time they heard the story, they felt that they knew her a little better; she was one of the Congers.

The train, passing through historic ground, reached the village of Lake George and, while the baggage was loaded on a paddle-wheel boat, the children played around the ruins of the old French & Indian fort, Fort William Henry, and climbed over stones at old Fort George. At the dock in Bolton, they were met by a horse-drawn carriage and driven through the tiny village at the Landing which then consisted of two stores, a post office, and a few weather-beaten inns. Then they came to the lodge at the entrance to the estate, Bra-Thole, passed through rows of pine trees, and once more, they were home.

The estate was extensive, covering a great part of the section which is now the business district of the village of Bolton Landing. The lakeshore home was very large, maintained in much the same style as their city residence, except that here the servants' quarters, their dining-room and kitchens were at the back of the house. Welcoming fires burned low in fireplaces in hall, dining-room and parlors as the children entered the house. Immediately, they rushed upstairs to the cupola on top of the house to see the mountains across the lake. "They're still here," a little boy announced with satisfaction.

They had to inspect the area under the eaves to see if the squirrels had managed to use them as hiding places for chestnuts; all closet doors had to be opened in the search for treasures that might have been left from the summer before.

Then they ran outside. The house was an architect's triumph, shaped in the form of a crescent to fit the huge rocks that lined the shore. Yearly, its shingled sides showed where northern storms had beaten against them during the past winter. Out on the broad verandah surrounding three sides of the house, light and shadow blended as the sun filtered through the chestnuts, oaks, and pines on the close-cropped lawns. There were always flowers in blossom when the children came, and under the pines and hemlocks, crisp leaves showed where the spring's arbutus had flowered. They climbed the chestnut trees to see if their skill had improved since last summer, and greeted the immovable boulders like old friends.

When they stopped chattering and exclaiming, even though briefly, a sudden silence fell on ears accustomed to the sounds of the city. With a sensitivity re-awakened, they became aware that everything was speaking to them, everything was in motion. The breeze moved the pine branches, mingling their fragrance with the spicy scent of sweet fern crushed underfoot; the waters of the lake lapped the shore rhythmically and gently; dry leaves rustled with the smallest step, and birds sang their well-remembered songs. Later, the children knew, if the summer day was hot, they would hear the metallic buzz of locusts, like singing wires.

Down by the shore, they could see life stirring under the water. Often, as they watched, the placid surface of the lake would be stirred by sudden gusts of wind. Rainy days were exciting, too, they recalled, when the winds raised waves that came crashing against the beach, vainly beating against the ancient rocks near the shore.

Their father often filled a knapsack with supplies and went deeper into the wilderness where he seemed to find peace in its solitude. Sometimes he would take the children. They would put on their back-packs, prudently filled with supplies for a week, and father and children would start off for an adventure in the wilderness. They learned how to make beds lined with balsam, and the heady fragrance ensured deep sleep after the day's trek. Sometimes, several of the children, accompanied by their father, paddled the canoe two miles across the lake where they camped on an island shaded by pine trees and lush with blueberry bushes. Crossing to the far side of the lake, they climbed mountains where, at the top as a reward for their efforts, there was a view of Lake George and Lake Champlain. On these occasions, they made their temporary home on the mountain top, learning about the wild life whose habitat they shared and, under their father's guidance, making the experience an exercise in survival.

They were happy among themselves, and when their father wished to be alone, they respected his choice. Often, they helped him clear unwanted growth on the estate, or watched silently as he chiseled steps on the rocks descending to the lake, realizing dimly that the stone steps would endure, even if everything else was swept away.

The name of the estate, Bra-Thole, puzzled people who often asked, "What does the name mean? Is it Welsh? Norwegian? French?" Those who asked the question, probably never got a satisfactory answer, because the name was Clarence's private joke. When his son and his nephews gathered at the Lake George house in the summer, full of energy, enthusiasm, and high spirits that often resulted in disaster, Clarence insisted that the place lived up to its real name, "Brat Hole."

In Clarence Conger's later years, his health failed and his once-brilliant mind was clouded. His elderly parents took him with them on their trips to Florida, Europe, or the Southern States—anything to keep him occupied and away from the tensions of New York City. But in spite of his family's care and concern, Clarence's hold on reality was lessening.

Now there was less money coming in, and some of the properties were rented or sold. One summer, the family could not go to Bra-Thole as the estate had been rented to the Chief Justice of the Supreme Court, Charles Evans Hughes. In 1903, the Town of Bolton had leased a strip of land on the Conger property for a public dock; now the rest of the Lake George property was sold, then divided and re-sold, as the site of business establishments.

The Congers took a smaller house in Brooklyn Heights and here Clarence received his friends, talking brilliantly on past civilizations; but he grew bitter on the subject of modern economics. Perhaps he realized dimly that the days of a landed aristocracy with its tradition of gracious living could endure no longer. From his window, he could watch the activity that powered the city of New York. Ships unloaded their cargoes from foreign ports; great steamers continued to bring immigrants from abroad who hoped to find in America a better life than they had known.

For these, "the tired—the poor," there would be opportunities to help them attain the good life. In the United States, a leveling-off process had begun: huge family fortunes were being broken up by taxation and economic pressures; the mansions of millionaires on Lake George and elsewhere were being bull-dozed out of existence to make way for the more-democratic motels and tourist businesses; the gap between master and servant, employer and employee, was closing.

For families like the de Peysters, Rutgers, McCreas, and Congers whose holdings had once been extensive, their dreams and strivings, their triumphs and defeats were now passing—into the romantic land of "once upon a time . . ."

CHAPTER XVII
Adolph S. Ochs

(Abenia)

Adolph S. Ochs, born March 12, 1858, possessed the ingredients for success in a developing America: he had more than a spark of genius which he fanned into a bright flame; he also had good parents. His father, Julius Ochs, who had come from Bavaria, became an officer in the Union Army during the Civil War. His mother, Bertha Levy, also from Bavaria, sympathized with the South, and even her marriage to a Northern Army man could not change her views. She put her convictions into action when she pushed a baby carriage along an Ohio river bridge. The carriage contained a baby, but the baby was sitting on a quantity of quinine, a medicine declared contraband by the Union Army. She was caught, but saved from punishment because of her husband's standing with the military. Each of the Ochs children thereafter vied for the honor of having been the baby who sat on the quinine—an honor denied to Adolph who was a few years too old for the escapade.

Adolph's parents were stern, but loving. Julius, although a mystic and a dreamer, spoke with authority; Bertha, intense and practical, was a woman of courage. Both parents raised their children with discipline tempered with love, and both were examples of an uncompromising devotion to duty. From them young Ochs learned that money is a poor measure of a person's true worth, and no substitute at all for character.

Following the close of the Civil War, the wagon trains moved westward; Julius chose to take his family South. No less a person than General William T. Sherman, who was definitely there, was advising the adventurous to go South where the struggling population had nothing and needed everything. The Ochs went to Knoxville, Tennessee, and Julius opened a store. They found a devastated land, unreconstructed rebels, and a bitterness now compounded by self-seeking politicians. In this setting, Julius as a merchant was doomed to failure from the start, and Adolph, aged 11, went to work.

As a carrier boy for the Knoxville *Chronicle*, he earned 25¢ a day, and somehow the family must have managed, for they stayed. As he grew in stature and responsibility, Adolph assumed other jobs around the newspaper office. He was a youngster who saw what had to be done and did it. During the next few years, there was a period when he spent nearly a year in Rhode Island, working in a relative's grocery store and attending business school at night. He returned to Knoxville and opportunity.

Resuming his work at the newspaper office, he was given a shift that ended at midnight. While Adolph was a person of undoubted courage, his imagination worked overtime: his route home took him past a cemetery and the combination of a cemetery and midnight was something he didn't care to face. Consequently, he formed the habit of staying two hours past midnight, waiting for a fellow worker who went his way. During those two hours, possibly to pass the time away, he started learning how to set type. This was a laborious method of setting up the form for each sheet by hand, and Adolph grew dexterous in the mechanics of printing. This new skill assured him knowledge of newspaper printing from the ground up; all his life, he was able to tell at a glance if there was a flaw in the make-up of a sheet. He went on to a job as journeyman printer and, since the newspaper was the repository of everything that went on locally, Adolph soon knew just about everybody in town.

At this time, he met J. T. MacGowan, another printer, and with the addition of another newspaperman, Franc Paul, the duo became a trio. Mr. Paul wanted to start a newspaper, so the three went to Chattanooga where they founded the *Dispatch*. This proved to be a journal with an uncertain present and no future, and it finally folded. Adolph was 19. Although his first business venture had been a disaster, being on his own was a heady experience, and he had no intention of returning home. Looking around for something to do, he decided that the growing city needed a directory, and persuaded the City Council to give him the job for the total sum of $50. With another young associate, they combed the city.

Chattanooga was, in many ways, a combination of a Northern and Southern city. It had been held by the Union during the Civil War and surrounded by Confederates. Its devastation had been caused by the big guns of both armies, so if there was bitterness, it was aimed in both directions. The city was building up again, and was, as it turned out, not a bad place for a young man to seek his fortune. The directory job, although it brought in little money, was another step in the right direction for young Adolph. As an investigator, he met everyone in town, both home-owners and business men, and at the end of his employment, he again had a wide acquaintance, and was at the center of everything that was going on in this busy town. He was convivial in the accepted sense; he had an eye for a pretty girl, and was a judge of good wines. He also had charm of manner and an active mind which readily threw off insults and injuries and tenaciously remembered kindnesses.

The story is told that, at a low point in his career, a woman took pity on his poverty and cut down a pair of her husband's trousers to fit him. Adolph never forgot her kindness. In later years when he had become wealthy, he heard that the woman, now a widow, was in need. He directed that a large check be sent to her, and that she receive a monthly pension as long as she lived. She outlived him, but the pension continued until her death. "That," it has been said, "was the most expensive pair of pants in history."

The fall of the *Dispatch* was not the disaster it had seemed, for Adolph learned a great lesson which guided his future newspaper work. He analyzed the failure and concluded that if he had had full control of the newspaper, he could have saved the entire venture. He never made that mistake again—although he made others.

He was currently in touch with a number of out-of-work printers, and with their encouragement, was looking for another opportunity to take over a newspaper. An editor on the Chattanooga *Times*, tired of his struggle, heard of the brash youth who was looking for this particular kind of trouble; he saw Adolph and proposed to sell the entire enterprise for $800. Adolph had nothing, and the bank, knowing the history of the newspaper, was reluctant to lend that much. The editor reduced the price to $500; for $250 cash, Adolph could purchase a half-interest and assume control of the newspaper. In two years, the remaining half-interest would be paid for at a price agreed upon by a board of arbitrators. Adolph accepted the terms and, two successful years later, the same Board awarded the former publisher $5500 for his half-interest. This was another valuable lesson, and Adolph made a mental note that in the future he would consider all the possibilities of a situation before signing anything.

On July 2, 1878, the Chattanooga *Times* first bore the name Adolph Ochs, publisher. He always used his full name, and an amusing story may throw some light on the reason. It was his first trip to the post office for his mail, and he asked if there was anything for "A. Ochs."

The clerk, not amused by this joker, looked at him coldly and said, "No, and there's none for 'A. Cow' either." Ninety-eight years later, the name and face of Adolph S. Ochs would circle the globe on a United States commemorative postage stamp.

Now that he was successful, he could send for his family: his father became treasurer of the enterprise, his brothers, on Adolph's insistence, were to be only part-time employees until they finished school.

Although Ochs was genial, his disposition was not all sweetness and light, and when his paper bombarded someone with the truth, it could hurt. These were violent days in the world of the press, and more than one editor was shot or threatened with horsewhipping for some misguided item in a newspaper; but there is only one instance when Ochs had a personal encounter with an irate citizen, and an eminent citizen, at that.

William Gibbs McAdoo was associated with an engineering company and Ochs' newspaper had taken exception to several contracts which the company had made in public works. McAdoo seethed with anger, but took no action until Ochs made a recommendation to President Cleveland regarding the appointment of a Federal Judge. He sincerely believed in the man's capabilities, but McAdoo, who had appeared before this Judge, felt less kindly disposed toward him. He therefore told the President that Ochs was taking a prejudiced view of the situation.

When Ochs heard this, he took it as an insult to his honesty and his temper flared. He instructed MacGowan to "lay on" McAdoo, and the chief did just that. Publication of the second attack soothed Ochs' feelings, and he considered the matter closed. Not so, McAdoo who now believed that the newspaper was bent on destroying him. Not long after, on entering a Pullman car at Knoxville, he saw Ochs already sitting there. Ochs, who had no personal animosity toward McAdoo, rose in greeting. The greeting he got was a blow to the jaw from his adversary's fist. He was knocked over the arm of the seat and into the cushions, but not seriously hurt. A conductor quickly separated them, and the affair was over.

There seems to have been no further enmity between the two men. Both rose to power: McAdoo as Wilson's Secretary of the Treasury, and Ochs as one of the country's leading publishers.

And then he met The Girl—lively, intelligent Iphigene (Effie), daughter of Rabbi Wise. The wedding was large and well-attended, testifying to his position in the community and the prominence of the family into which he had married. The couple was happy and, during a long married life, Ochs was completely devoted to Effie. Their first two children died in infancy; their third child, a daughter, survived and was the joy of her father's life.

The newspaper prospered; so did Chattanooga. Its iron ore was in great demand; real estate boomed; Ochs invested. Then the inevitable happened: new methods in the production of steel damaged the ore operation; values fell; and Ochs was $100,000 poorer. But he still looked for bigger newspaper worlds to conquer. He learned that the *New York Times* was for sale, and was interested. Behind that simple statement is a family uproar and the involvement of some of the keenest financial operators in the country.

On hearing that Adolph intended to purchase the New York Times, his mother was so incensed that she actually considered taking legal steps to prevent the transaction. Fortunately, she was dissuaded.

In the 90's, a newspaper war was being waged between giant publishers, and there were casualties. Joseph Pulitzer, owner of the World, had succeeded in humanizing his newspaper with items of interest to the average person. He also made his newspaper more colorful—literally—using a cartoon character wearing a blob of yellow ink to brighten up the text. The cartoon, known as the Yellow Kid, was later taken over by William Randolph Hearst of the Journal American, and became the insignia of what was known as Yellow Journalism.

Hearst had come from California, fortified by millions of dollars to wrest New York from the publishers who held the city in their grasp; several newspapers gave up after a brief struggle, Pulitzer waged a good fight and survived, but the Times, losing circulation, was in serious trouble. Besides the obvious rivalry of other newspapers, the Times, by favoring the reforms of Grover Cleveland had, incidentally, affronted readers who saw in presidential acts a threat to the labor movement. They retaliated by canceling their subscriptions in droves.

Charles R. Miller, editor of the Times, saw nothing ahead but complete capitulation and, badly defeated, decided that the newspaper must be sold. It was then that Adolph S. Ochs came upon the dismal scene. He had experience, high ideals, a working idea of how a newspaper should be run, but little money. He had paved the way with introduction from many persons of influence, including a letter from President Cleveland attesting to his ability and success as a publisher; so, Miller agreed to give him a few minutes of his time early one evening.

The minutes stretched into hours. The two men talked all night and Miller found his hopes reviving under the spell of this man with his courage and his ideals. The Times was definitely for sale—but could Ochs raise the necessary capital?

Ochs' next meeting was with Spencer Trask, leader of the stockholders of the New York Times. He made Ochs an offer: they would pay him a salary of $50,000 a year to publish the Times, but they, the stockholders, would retain control. The lesson learned on the *Dispatch* paid off: Ochs refused to surrender control for any amount of money and, in the end, had his way. He would purchase the newspaper for the $75,000 he had been able to raise, and would assume a large block of stock in the Company, and, he insisted, he would have sole responsibility for the publication. His offer was accepted and he was able to write gleefully to Effie that he had "captured Trask." Undoubtedly, both men got what they wanted: Ochs was granted full ownership of the Times; Trask, an able financier, would, in a few years, see his stock worth five times what he had paid for it.

The owners of other New York City newspapers were baffled by this relatively simple transaction, convinced that Ochs had a wealthy backer—probably one of the tycoons of the day. To them, the Times offered little in the way of a threat; its slogan was, and is, "All the News That's Fit to Print," whereas the Yellow Journalists offered well-paying sensationalism, often printing lurid drawings where the plain truth seemed dull. The Times bent its policy somewhat when it printed news of the murder of Stanford White by Harry K. Thaw, and Thaw's subsequent trial. This, Ochs believed, was justified by the eminence of the architect and the prominence of the Thaw family.

From his first day as publisher of the New York Times at age 37, Ochs was known as "The Old Man" to the office personnel; for good reason, he was also called "the little man who goes around turning off the lights." When he had demanded full control of the Times, he intended his responsibility to extend to every phase of getting out the newspaper, an attitude well described in a verse, author unknown, which circulated in the office,

Original Steamer Sagamore

Adolph S. Ochs,
publisher,
New York Times

> I am the Boss
> The Editor bold,
> And the Chief of the
> New York Times.
> The Big Ad Man,
> The Office Boy,
> And he who handles
> The Dimes.

He has been designated one of the most intelligent men of his day. Using his intellectual genius, he pulled the New York Times out of the doldrums into which it had sunk up to the point where its editorial policy formulated thinking from the humblest homes to world capitals. He surrounded himself with men of exceptional talent and exulted in their achievements. Although he dominated his associates, he was always a little in awe of them, and treated them with a certain formality. Salutations were always "Mr.," not "Joe" or "Charlie." A person of eminence himself, he was invited to gatherings of other prominent men, but always seemed a little bewildered by his own rise to power. For example, seated next to Carl Schurz, soldier, scholar, and statesman, he would wonder how he (Ochs) had arrived there. Incidentally, there was a bond between Ochs and Schurz which both men probably never realized: Schurz was a hero of the German Revolution of 1848; Ochs' mother, living through the same revolution, had also espoused the rebel cause and had gained local attention when she dipped her handkerchief in the blood of a martyred leader of the rebellion.

During the negotiations with Spencer Trask, Mr. Ochs had met George Foster Peabody who, although a partner with Trask, had taken only a small part in this particular transaction. The two men became fast friends and, thereafter, Mr. Peabody's letters to the Editor often appeared on the Editorial page of the Times. It was this friendship which brought Mr. Ochs to Lake George where, in 1914–15, he bought Abenia from Mr. Peabody and became a part-time resident of Millionaires' Row. Here he entertained the great and famous people of the day.

Abenia may have lived up to its name, meaning "House of Rest," but it was as often a place where Mr. Ochs enjoyed the nonsensical games he had missed in his working childhood. He loved the spontaneity and gaiety of children, and they were often at the Ochs' home attending his daughter's parties. These parties undoubtedly started off decorously enough with mothers hovering around their youngsters and warning,

"Don't run, Clara; it's not ladylike," or "No, John; you may not have another piece of cake."

As training for later social life, the children's parties fulfilled their function; that is, until their host arrived.

He came bearing gifts that mothers deplored, and children greeted with shouts of joy. Noisemakers, whistles, rattles, and bells came tumbling into their eager hands, and the calm of the summer day was broken by a wailing, screeching pandemonium. Ochs was the most gleeful of them all, and later, when the manufactured noise had subsided, might announce a squealing contest in which boys and girls, red-faced from excitement and exertion, attempted to outdo one another in the fine art of squealing. Dismayed though the mothers may have been, they withdrew with Effie, who had long ago discovered that nothing could stop her husband once he had set his mind on something he wanted to do.

Abenia knew fun of another kind when Mme. Marcella Sembrich, a Lake George neighbor, came to call. One of the greats of the Metropolitan Opera, Mme. Sembrich also taught singing to prospective opera stars at her studio on the lake. On summer evenings, she and her students often came to the Ochs' home for picnics or suppers. Mr. Ochs was unimpressed by opera, but fond of popular music with strong rhythms. Invariably, the opera starlets would find themselves involved in the syncopated rhythms of "Alexander's Ragtime Band," or the wailing of "Won't You Come Home, Bill Bailey?" Mme. Sembrich was, understandably, not delighted by the recital, but she was tolerant.

For years, Adolph had a valet, Jules, of whom he was very fond. One day, Jules, while serving Mr. Ochs, dropped dead in his presence. Shaken by the experience, Mr. Ochs went to the Catholic priest in Lake George Village and asked him to conduct the burial service for Jules. Since it was evident to the priest that Jules had not attended church regularly, he was reluctant to honor Mr. Ochs' request. Faced with this obstacle, Adolph contacted his friend, Cardinal Hayes who ordered the priest to conduct the funeral.

The ceremony was conducted grudgingly by the priest, who took the opportunity to speak his mind freely about some parishioners who failed to attend church regularly, interspersing his remarks with threats of purgatory and hell.

As the body was being lowered into the grave, Mr. Ochs, apparently dissatisfied with the priest's rendition of the service, suddenly whipped a Jewish prayer book out of his pocket and read the Hebrew burial service. So, buried in the Lake George Cemetery, lies a man named Jules, who was interred with the assistance of both the Catholic and Hebrew burial services.

From his mansion on Millionaires' Row, Mr. Ochs often made the relatively short trip to the famous race track at Saratoga. Here he delighted in entertaining friends, herding them into his box where there was an unobstructed view of the track. Concerned for his friends' complete happiness, his custom was to place all bets himself. He usually wagered $5 on each horse, and never bet on the favorite. He then allocated a horse to each of his guests, so that there was always a winner in his box, and a celebration invariably took place after each race. No losses were possible, since all bets were paid for by the host himself.

The Ochs publishing empire was but little affected by the panic and subsequent depression that struck in 1929. Now the New York Times, one of the leading newspapers of the world, seemed more important than ever; its daily appearance became one sure factor in an uncertain existence.

Through his publishing company, Mr. Ochs made innumerable contributions to the cause of culture, advancing $200,000 to cover the expense of editing Thomas Jefferson's papers, and $532,000 toward publication of the Dictionary of American Biography, a work in which his own biography is modestly understated. He was deeply interested in the explorations of Commander Richard E. Byrd, and in Little America, lakes and glaciers bearing the names of members of the Ochs family attest to this interest.

In 1930, Ochs bought another palatial home. This time, his choice fell on White Plains near New York City, where he purchased a 57-acre estate. Even larger than Abenia on Lake George, this mansion was distinguished by a ballroom and—final touch of luxury—17 bathrooms. The estate was easily accessible from his New York office and he enjoyed this extension of his holdings.

Although the lawns and gardens were carefully tended, there was one corner of the estate which remained untouched by the gardener's hand. Wild flowers grew there, and birds sang in a tangle of unspoiled wilderness lying along a country lane. This was Mr. Ochs' refuge, a memory of other days, simply lived.

From this time on, he gradually slackened his hold on business affairs, making only accasional visits to his office. Nostalgia crept in, and at 4 o'clock, one fall day, while he was ill in bed, he telephoned Karl Abbott, manager of the Sagamore Hotel on Lake George. No, there was nothing special, he was just wondering—Had the leaves turned color yet? Was a late-afternoon breeze rippling the lake? How high did the hemlocks grow around the boathouse this year? Mr. Abbott talked to the sick man for half an hour, describing as well as he could, the scene from the large window fronting the lake.

In the spring, Nostalgia—perhaps, this time—a sense of urgency, sent him back to Chattanooga, scene of his former struggles and triumphs. On April 8, 1935, having made a comfortable trip by train with his granddaughter and a nurse, he arrived in the southern city and called on his brother, now in charge of his former newspaper there. He expressed interest in all details of the publishing operation, greeted old friends, asked innumerable questions, and noted with satisfaction that circulation was up. At 1 o'clock, he and his brother went to a nearby restaurant for lunch. Both were studying the menu. Having decided, his brother looked up with the query,

"What are you having, Adolph?"

There was no answer, and there would be none. Adolph Ochs had slumped forward in his chair, unconscious.

He was rushed to the hospital, but never regained consciousness, dying that afternoon at 4:10. Great honors were paid to him: the business affairs of the world paused momentarily in deference to his passing. On the day of the funeral, the wires of the Associated Press were silenced for two minutes; every business office and factory in Chattanooga closed for the day; in New York City, the flags were at half-mast; and President Roosevelt sent a large wreath in honor of the man who had never supported him.

During a productive lifetime, Adolph S. Ochs had earned and enjoyed fame, power, and prestige; but as he neared the end of his journey, his memories were of the people and places that had meant the most to him, of his family, the friends who had stood by him, and of bright days at Lake George with the sun shining on its blue waters.

In 1976, 41 years after his death, the U.S. Post Office issued a commemorative stamp in honor of "Adolph S. Ochs, publisher."

CHAPTER XVIII
John Boulton Simpson and Family

(Nirvana)

John Boulton Simpson, it could have been said, was born with a gold spoon in his mouth; and, although the proverbial spoon was second-hand, it was definitely solid gold. Gold spoons were not rare in the hock-shop run by John's great-uncle, William Simpson, nor were hockshops unique in England. The first pawnbroker recorded in London was a man named Sympson who, in 1590, was a gold- and silver-smith. No doubt he also loaned money as was the custom of all silversmiths. The business progressed for several hundred years until, at the time of George IV, the incumbent William Simpson unwisely loaned considerable money to the noblemen who surrounded the king. When the shop-keeper dared to ask his debtors for his money, they rallied to the cause and threatened him with bodily harm if he persisted in the crazy notion of trying to collect debts incurred by the King's men. Besieged by danger from all sides, William Simpson left for America, and in the hospitable city of New York, in 1822, opened another Simpson's near the site of the future Brooklyn Bridge.

Simpson's Hockshop was available to patrons at every hour of the day or night; often blue-bloods who had run up gambling debts in the small hours of the night, stopped at Simpson's where the proprietor, a light sleeper, was ready to serve them. His method of taking care of late customers was unique, but practical: the pawnbroker attached a basket to a rope and dropped it down to the borrower; the latter placed his collateral in the basket; Simpson hauled it up, and after examination, let the basket down again, either with a pawnshop ticket, or the article itself if it had been rejected.

By 1826, business had grown to the extent that more help was needed, and since Mr. Simpson's own sons were not interested in the business, he sent for two nephews in London, John and Joseph Simpson. Five or six years later, he sent for two more nephews, William and John Bolton Simpson. The four nephews earned money both for themselves and for their uncle, and, incidentally, invented a slang phrase. Whenever an article somewhat out of the ordinary was brought in for appraisal, one of the nephews, not trusting his own judgment, was sure to say, "I'll have to ask my uncle." The Hockshop was located in the theater district of New York City, and the comedians who were frequent customers, begin using the word "uncle" to refer to a pawn-broker. "Seeing my uncle," be-

190

came the slang equivalent to pawning personal property, and it is still a dictionary term.

Simpson's was far more than the average pawnshop and, at any given time, the articles pledged for cash would have stocked a museum with rare objects and works of art. For example, the shop loaned money on the Hope Diamond to finance Mrs. Evalyn McLean's vain attempt to ransom the kidnapped Lindbergh baby. Simpson's also accepted a Stradivarius as collateral for a loan; loaned money on priceless paintings by Old Masters; and took in illuminated manuscripts dating from the middle ages. This aristocrat of pawnshops showed steady profits to the extent that each of the nephews became a millionaire. One of the nephews, John Bolton Simpson, Sr., bought, with his brother, 132 acres of land in the Bronx which could only increase in value and did so, handsomely.

His son, John Bolton Simpson, Jr., enjoyed circumstances that were equally fortunate, but on a different level. Born in New York City at 121st Street and the East River, he attended Collegiate School and began his prestigious career by becoming a member of the Union League, the Columbia Yacht Club, and the New York Athletic Club.

The first rift in family solidarity came in 1872 when John Bolton Simpson, Jr., married Miss Fanny Collins Shilton. Miss Shilton had become a school teacher in order to help her younger sister with her education, and while she appreciated the value of hard work, she took a very dim view of the pawnbroker business.

The rest of the family were aghast at this estimate of a business service which had paid off so lucratively. But John Bolton Simpson, Sr., rose to the emergency and purchased for his son the American Agency of the Estey Piano Company. From that time, John, Jr. was known to the rest of the family as "Piano Johnny." When he began spelling his middle name "Boulton" with a "u," there were some raised eyebrows, but the family was now beyond shock.

Home for the John Boulton Simpsons, Jr., was 11 Mt. Morris Park West, in fashionable Harlem, a place of early brownstone houses and tiny gardens. A later address was 988 Fifth Avenue. Mrs. Simpson always preferred the Harlem address, and they sometimes rented the Fifth Avenue house.

By 1877, they had discovered Bolton Landing on Lake George where they stayed at the Mohican House. At this time, four millionaires from Philadelphia, Robert Glendenning, William C. Bement, George Burnham, and E. Burgess Warren, had formed the Green Island Improvement Company for the purpose of building a luxurious summer hotel. Mr. Simpson joined the group and became its president, giving rise to a local saying that "five millionaires were involved in the Sagamore Hotel." As soon as the huge summer hotel was ready for occupancy, the Simpsons moved in until their own mansion, Nirvana on Green Island, was completed. The addition of Nirvana Farm on the mainland supplied the estate with dairy and garden product.

Along with the Simpson's business and social success, they endured family tragedy. In the Bolton Cemetery they buried "Our Baby," little Roy, aged 2 years, 8 months. The depth of their grief is chiseled in the pathetic inscription on the small monument of "Our Baby." "I'se so tired, mamma; I want to rest a little while." Another son, John Boulton, Jr., "Our Boy," died at the age of 14. In the intervening years, two girls were born: Frances Proddow Simpson arrived in 1881, and Helen was born in 1890.

Helen's birth was quaintly noted in the local newspaper as "the first white child born on Green Island." The approximately nine years that separated the two Simpson girls were translated into affection between Fanny and "The Kid," as she referred to Helen. Like many younger sisters, Helen, while admiring this older sister, may have been dazzled and overshadowed by her outgoing personality.

Fanny attended Miss Brown's Fifth Avenue School in New York City as preparation for Vassar College; at Miss Brown's, wealthy fathers gladly paid $1,000 per year for the proper education of their daughters. This exclusive school numbered among its patrons Seth Low, president of Columbia University; J. Pierpont Morgan, Wall Street financier; the Rev. Edward Everett Hale, great preacher of Boston; and the ex-Governor of New York State, the Honorable Roswell P. Flower. Helen also attended school in New York City, and letters written by Fanny, now in Vassar, to her mother show sisterly concern over "the Kid's" education, and the advisability of her transfer from Mrs. Schoonmaker's School to Miss Spence's School.

The Simpsons divided their time between New York City where Mr. Simpson's office was at 97 Fifth Avenue, and Bolton Landing, either at their own "cottage," Nirvana, or at the Sagamore. Mr. Simpson was a joiner, and it soon became known that his presence on a committee insured its success. Wealthy and influential, it seemed that everything planned for the betterment of the Lake George area bore the name of John Boulton Simpson. If the Regatta Committee was foundering, all that was needed was his hand at the helm. When the Lake George Club became more than wishful thinking, he joined with the organizers and accepted an office. Taking an active interest in the recently-built Episcopal Church at Bolton Landing, Mr. Simpson became its first warden, second only to the rector in influence; he held this position for 40 years. In a booklet issued by the church in 1892, he was thanked for securing a handsome Estey Chapel organ for the church, two choir seats, cushions and railings, carpeting for the entire church, painting and decorating of the rectory on the inside, and furnishing the paint for the outside, a handsome parish register, and an annual gift to the Christmas tree. He had become a member of the Board of Trustees in 1886, "in place of the Rev. Mr. Lancaster, resigned."

Vitally interested in the founding of the Lake George Club, he was Treasurer of the Organization Committee, and was one of the Directors appointed in the Certificate of Incorporation on November 16, 1908. He was first vice-president of the Lake George Club for the years 1910–11, and later was named Vice-Commander of the Yacht Club.

The Simpsons' island home, Nirvana, was a show-place, and their steam yacht, the Fanita, was a show-piece. The boat was 80 feet long, 11 feet in the beam, and capable of attaining a speed of 16 miles an hour. The Fanita was renowned for its luxury and its speed. Fanny, the older daughter, graciously accepted the luxury of several palatial homes and a yacht, and delighted in sharing them with her friends; "the Kid," Helen, seemed more interested in outdoor sports than in a luxurious and glamorous life.

Fanny reveled in social life, both at Miss Brown's School and at Vassar. She loved the girls who clustered around her, enjoyed their successes and sympathized with their many troubles. Her room in the college dormitory was an ex officio center of life at Vassar where her friends gathered to exchange confidences, or often only to enjoy her effervescent spirits. Fanny wrote letters home—so many of them that the reader wonders how she found time to study. Several hundred of these letters have been edited and made into a book by her daughter, Frances Townsend Marshall. The book, titled "The Turn of the Century Group," gives a vivid picture of college life at the turn of the century as lived by a very vivacious and very privileged young lady. A few letters were written to her busy father at his office on Fifth Avenue, but the great majority of them were written to her mother, and the letters overflow with her exuberance, closing one with "Love to daddy and the kid. Mostly your mostest lovingest sweetheart daughter."

In her letters, Fanny often mentioned Nirvana, their summer home, as a place for entertaining her friends; for using the "horrible green shelves" which she wanted replaced in her room at college, or when she wrote home indignantly,

> "I like daddy's nerve, exchanging our pool table when I wanted it up at the lake."

Planning one of her numerous house-parties at Nirvana, she wrote,

> "A lot of the college girls can come to the lake in September before college opens, but the trouble is that the lake isn't so gay then and I could not give them so good a time."

She compromised by having ten girls at Lake George the last few days of vacation. When men were included in the festivities at Nirvana, Mother made arrangements for them to stay at the Sagamore Hotel.

Evidently, Mother was Fanny's willing slave; if she ever rebelled, there is no letter to prove it, but there are many letters in which Fanny asks her mother to do errands for her; some of these errands must have cut very deeply into her activities. Since Mother was in New York City, and daughter Fanny was at college on the Hudson at a place called

"Nirvana"—cottage home of Mr. J. B. Simpson, Green Island, Lake George

Commodore John Boulton
Simpson of the Sagamore

The Fanita, John Boulton Simpson

Mrs. Leo Campbell poses with steering wheel of the Simpson's Fanita. Her father, Charles Moses Finkle was captain of the yacht for many years

Poughkeepsie, it seemed only natural to Fanny that Mother should be an emissary between her and the shops and theaters of the city.

From the first of each college year until the last, Mother shared Fanny's college life through her letters, contributing time and money in sending on curtains, rugs, pillows, soap, lots of food, also wallpaper, matting, and paint for Fanny's room. She willingly sent Fanny her own party cape; arranged to have her numerous friends as house guests either at the New York house or at Lake George; bought theater tickets for Fanny's visits home, always with friends; shopped for necessities or luxuries; exchanged articles already bought, and filled one request which may have topped them all by sending up to Vassar College dinner for twelve guests, complete with strawberries.

On one occasion, Mother's attention lagged briefly, possibly from sheer exhaustion. This situation brought a stiff rebuke from daughter Fanny who wrote,

> "Dearest my Mother,
>
> Why don't you answer what I ask you? You have never mentioned our going down to see Helen off and have not said that you would meet me in Peekskill with my white gloves, and please dear read my letters more carefully. I asked you if you could find out the particulars of Maude's operation.
>
> Mammy, I asked you if you would please ask Dad to get the courtesies of the port for us to see Helen off. She sails on the Patricia. I think it's on the Holland-American line, but I'm not sure . . ."

Generally, Fanny's daily requests were made so charmingly that her mother, who was obviously devoted to her, obeyed her orders without question or complaint. Probably she enjoyed a vicarious thrill from her daughter's enthusiasms, her bright, breezy accounts of college events, her frank, free discussions of friends and beaux.

Since even a hint of romance travels far, one of the eligible young men must have given the dowagers, rocking on the Sagamore porch, food for gossip, as:

1st lady—I hear the the Beardsley boy was visiting Vassar and called on—guess who—Fanny Simpson.

2nd lady—Beardsley? Doesn't his father own Fourteen-Mile Island? I believe the boy's name is Sterling; he's about Fanny's age.

1st lady—It would certainly be a suitable match; there's money in both families. William Beardsley is President of The Florida East Coast Railroad, you know.

3rd lady (interrupting)—But I heard that young Beardsley was calling on Eleanor Sampson, too. What do you make of *that*?

The ladies immediately made something of that, too; and the surmises went on.

But even Mother, knowing her daughter well, must have wondered about Fanny, absorbed in her many friends, her endless house-parties at

Lake George, her frequent theater parties with the bevy of girls she brought to New York, and her visits with friends in other parts of the country. When did she study? How could she possibly find time to complete the work necessary for graduation from that prestigious college? Such worries were groundless, as later events proved.

During her college years, Fanny's immediate concern was for "the Kid," and sisterly interest in Helen flows through her letters: she was delighted that the Kid had a pony cart; who would drive it? She was concerned about Helen's school; wondered if the Kid had the measles, and in one letter to her mother writes, "Maul that kid sister for me, will you? Tell her that she is getting entirely too frisky, skipping a class—the freak."

The letters to the Kid are full of affectionate teasing: such as, "My dear little bit of a tiny slip of a kid sister, how is your cough? I hope that by the time I get home you will be your lovely self once more . . . Ha! ha!" In a letter to her mother, Fanny writes, "The Kid wrote me such a dear, sweet, funny letter. Give her a kiss for me." And on the occasion of Helen's visit to Vassar, Fanny wrote, "The Kid was so good she'll have to come up again and stay two or three days. I'd give her a good time."

Fanny's restlessness erupted in criticism of the family's plans for the summer, and she wrote:

> "Well, of all hopeless families, the Simpsons are the most hopeless. They just get in a rut and stay there. They go to the same place every summer. (I don't object to that except that I would like to go to Europe sometime . . . I, for one, am tired of Atlantic City. I would prefer some other place, say Old Point Comfort.)"

She was sure that a trip to Old Point Comfort was just what her hardworking father needed, too. But Fanny's life was hardly dull; another letter referred to a trip on a friend's yacht to West Point for a game with Trinity.

Fanny had become concerned over her father's frequent headaches, as reported to her by Mother. Her cousin, Robert Proddow, actively engaged in the Estey Piano Company with her father, evidently had suggested that Mr. Simpson's headaches were due to his over-dedication to work. Cousin Robert probably did not tell her of certain business difficulties which eventually came to the attention of the public. It was a situation all-too familiar in financial manipulations of the day.

> "Mr. Simpson was one of the directors of the Traders' Fire Insurance Company. The Board included John Jacob Astor, Chauncey Depew, Edwin Gould, and others. Unknown to most of these directors, the annual statements falsified the amount of cash in the bank, overstated by 50% the premiums collected, and understated the losses in the same proportion. Mr. Simpson feared he might have a large fine and/or be imprisoned. The newspapers gave the fraud much publicity but as was generally the case in such matters, the directors were not implicated."

While Mother faithfully answered Fanny's numerous letters, the latter became concerned over her use of the embossed writing paper and reproved her in a letter, "Mammy dear, you give me a fit, always writing to me on 988 Fifth Avenue paper. You must have used up two or three quires writing to me on it. I wish you'd purchase some plain paper and write to me on that."

If her concern was over the expense of the paper used, it was hardly realistic; soon after, she listed the names of ten girls invited to 988 Fifth Avenue, asking her mother to purchase theater tickets for all to see *The Gay Lord Quex.*

In Fanny's Senior Year at Vassar, there was more responsibility for Mother: Fanny was one of a group chosen to decorate the Senior Parlor, evidently a college tradition, and Mother was called upon to assist as buyer for the project. In this capacity, she had to consider curtains 11 feet long, the number and size of oriental rugs, the selection of certain articles of furniture; and further had to withstand a threat from Fanny that she would raid both Nirvana and 988 (Fifth Avenue) in the search for furnishings.

Mother seldom made a mistake in filling her daughter's requests, but of one monumental error, Fanny wrote:

"... Mammy, you must have misunderstood me a lot about invitations. Do let me explain. In the first place, commencement on Wednesday is awfully stupid. It is in the chapel and consists of fool speeches, giving of diplomas, etc. Nobody asks anybody but their own families. The chapel is always hot and each girl gets four invitations. On my four, I have you, Dad, the Kid, and Aunt. NO ONE ELSE. I wouldn't have Dr. Stires there for the world; what did you ask him for? It's admittedly the stupidest thing we have during the entire week. I wouldn't have him come down from the lake for that for anything. It would be stupid for him and I WOULD HATE IT. So I'll have to write him and explain your mistake . . . and speaking of ministers, I want him and Dr. and Mrs. Van de Water to be here surely for the Dickens-Shakespeare boat ride Monday afternoon the 9th. That's about the most fun of all . . . Thanks for the food. Isn't it hot?"

Fanny's graduation from Vassar went off brilliantly; as first speaker on the program, she gave a dissertation on "Aristotle's Idea of Democracy"; the essay was printed in the Poughkeepsie Daily Eagle on June 12, 1902. With several other students who had attained the highest rank, she was awarded Phi Beta Kappa.

Several years after graduation, Fanny married Edward Perry Townsend, a founder-member of the Lake George Club. The big wedding held at Lake George included all the excited preparations, friends, family, decorations, and ceremony obtainable at great expense. Her letter to her mother, written only a few hours after the wedding, obviously came from a heart full of happiness. Written "on board the SS Fanita cruising from Bolton Landing to Rogers Rock, Saturday evening, September 16, 1905,"

Nirvana today

Nirvana, John Boulton Simpson

the letter began, "Mother darling, I love you; you are a trump," and continued with thanks to the guests for coming to the wedding, special thanks to her mother and dad for everything and for the glorious house party of the previous week. She also thanked Mother and Father Townsend for the "so generous wedding present of the up-coming trip abroad." She sent special love to the maid-of-honor, bridesmaids, best man, ushers, family of the groom and of the bride, and closed with the joyous declaration, "I just *love* Ed. Ed just *loves* me. We are very happy. Always your loving daughter, Fanny Townsend."

Eventually, a baby girl, Frances, their only child, was born. And now, Fanny, who had so much love to give—to her family, her friends and associates, gave that love to the whole world. During World War I, she headed the Vassar College Unit engaged in French War Relief, and her mementoes include medals and thanks "en l'aidant dans l'assistance aux enfants de la ville de Verdun." Her love for her classmates at Vassar blossomed into loving service with the Young Women's Christian Association of New York City; in 1967, she was honored for her 50 years of devoted service to that organization as member of the Board of Directors, for serving on many committees, and as President of the Board. She was made an honorary member of the Board of Directors in 1970.

And what of Helen, the Kid?

On Saturday, August 6, 1898, a very significant paragraph appeared in the *Lake George Mirror*.

> "Miss Helen Simpson gave a party aboard the "Fanita" one day last week in celebration of her eighteenth (sic) birthday (typographical error, should be "eighth") Refreshments were served on board . . ."

The list of young guests included "Master" Robert Proddow, cousin of the young hostess; years later, he became her father's associate in the Estey Piano Company. The article continues,

> "They were chaperoned by Mrs. J. B. Simpson, Mrs. Howe, and Miss Simpson. Miss Helen received some very pretty and costly presents, but she seems to take the most pleasure in a new set of golf sticks."

In Helen Simpson's later years, she was an avid sportswoman, both on the tennis court and on the golf links. Graduating from Vassar in 1912, she spend much of her time on outdoor sports. She swam every day of her life, was chairman of the Tennis Committee at the Lake George Club from 1916–49, was on the Board of Directors, and from 1946–50, served as 1st Vice-President of the Club. As late as 1967, she was continuing her civic career as President of the Garden Club of Lake George. Deeply interested in the welfare of children, she was active for many years on the Board of Education of the Bolton Schools. Of quiet pride to her was the success of her God-child, Hugh Allen Wilson, who has become eminent as an organist.

She never married. There was a pervasive rumor of a frustrated romance, but no one mentioned it either in her presence or out of it. Her emotions were controlled and concealed; people respected her as a person to whom privacy was of the utmost importance.

She gave carefully and consistently to worthy causes, giving of herself to enduring friendships, and always remembering the unfortunate nearby.

"She was a wonderful friend," recalls one who enjoyed her companionship. "Once you were her friend, it was forever . . . She visited the County Home often bringing useful gifts—books, magazines—things to make the patients' lives brighter. She gave graciously and with imagination, doing the little, kindly things that other people would never think of doing."

She gave without fanfare, and there are not many who know of her assistance to needy townspeople. Living quietly, helping where help was needed, active and athletic as long as her physical condition permitted, she lived into her 80's using Nirvana Farms as her residence.

Those who knew Helen Simpson well, speak of her as kind, sympathetic and generous with both her time and resources wherever she could be of assistance. Those who stood a little in awe of her, believe that her graciousness was tinged with more than a hint of the imperiousness often associated with her wealthy and dominating father, John Boulton Simpson.

But those who knew her best, insist that beneath the exterior of this kind-hearted, sometimes formidable woman, still lurked an image of "The Kid," impish, lovable—and wistful.

CHAPTER XIX
Alfred Stieglitz and Georgia O'Keeffe

(The Hill)

Alfred Stieglitz was born on January 1, 1864, in Hoboken, New Jersey. His father was a woolen merchant who had come from Hanover-Murden, Germany, ten years before and had become a lieutenant in the American Civil War. He resigned from the army—a privilege reserved to Foreign-born officers, and married in 1863.

From the first, Alfred was marked for greatness. His mind was clear, keen, and incisive, and his self-confidence was never marred by doubt. His home surroundings were comfortable, even affluent, with his father's woolen business attracting steady customers such as A. T. Stewart and Marshall Field.

In 1871, the family moved to New York City where they took up their residence in a brownstone house on 60th Street. Mr. Stieglitz was a bon vivant with a love of life, friends, art, good company, and the delicacies of the table. He was interested in sports of all kinds, owned horses, and was the only Jewish member of the exclusive Jockey Club. He was also a talented amateur painter. His jovial personality attracted many friends, and Sunday afternoons were given over to festive gatherings in the Stieglitz parlor. It was a matter of pride to young Alfred that his father entrusted him with the key to the wine cellar. Life flowed around the boy with a quick and fascinating tempo. At an early age, he shared his father's love of life, but there was a volatile essence within him which would surface in his later years.

Mr. Stieglitz' financial status enabled him to give his family uncommon advantages. To those who could afford it, these advantages included a sojourn at one of the Lake George summer resorts. The year when Alfred was nine years old, the family took their annual trip to Lake George, staying at the elegant Fort William Henry Hotel. The porch of this hotel was famous: twenty-five feet wide, it extended along the entire front of the huge hotel, and was the gathering place of the resort's wealthy visitors.

On a memorable summer day in 1873, the large number of guests who were "taking the air" on the porch included Alfred and a group of boys. The game which the boys were playing was Alfred's invention and involved moving miniature horses on a playing board. The adults, numbering among others, the Honorable John Alden Dix, Governor of New

York State, also became interested, and crowded around the players, cheering them on. At the end of the game, someone remarked,

"That's a fine game. The young gentlemen should have their pictures taken showing the game-board."

The idea caught fire immediately. Alfred packed up the pieces of his game and, with the other young players following, sought out the village tintyper. Alfred was fascinated by the photographic process and asked permission to enter the developing booth. Permission was granted, and thereafter he was a frequent visitor at the tintyper's establishment during his parents' stay at the resort. His career was chosen.

A major change in the Stieglitz' life-style came when Mr. Stieglitz sold his woolen business for a half-million. His fortune now freed him to pursue his hobbies: sports, the arts, and the sponsoring of artists. He could raise his six children in a creditable manner, and sustain sundry dependent relatives. Now he was able to build a summer home, Oak Lawn, at Lake George on Millionaires' Row and maintain extensive grounds. With plenty of servants, he could entertain as many as 30 guests at one time for dinner. His wife took readily to their expanded social life. She was a cultured woman who enjoyed company and when left to her own devices, read novels—sometimes as many as a hundred in a year. Her concentration was remarkable, and she could recall the plots, characters, and incidents in those novels years after reading them.

In New York City, Alfred attended Charlier Institute until 1877, and then went to public school. He did little studying, but managed to keep up without it, pursuing his intense interest in billiards, baseball, and the piano. He also spent a year at City College of New York. That same year, the family went to Europe where Alfred, now 21, was to study engineering. He spent the next year at Karlsrube Realgymnasium; then studied mechanical engineering at Berlin Polytechnical Institute. Here he discovered extracurricular activities that occupied much of his time.

Students then attending German Universities were not required to attend the courses for which they had registered, nor take examinations. With the spare time at his disposal, Alfred attended plays; he was enthralled by opera, seeing *Tristan* and *Carmen* one hundred times each. He devoured books written by Russian and German authors, and enjoyed the work of the humorist, Mark Twain, the only American author who seemed to be taken seriously at the time.

Then, one day, something happened; the event was casual enough, but it focused all the interests of his life. He saw a camera in a shop window and bought it. The next logical step in the fulfillment of his life-work was enrollment in a photo-chemistry course. His teacher, Professor Vogel, was not favorably impressed by this pupil who, by his very diligence, spent too much time on details when the rest of the class was progressing to the larger aspects of the subject.

Praise or blame never moved Alfred very much; he was interested in working out his own ideas and if, in the process, he failed to approximate the norm, he was unconcerned. He improvised his own darkroom by opening a door, making a triangle against the wall and covering the open space with a blanket. Although his future success in photography was spectacular, he never had a real darkroom until he was 70 years old.

The word "impossible" meant little to him. For example: it was accepted as an axiom that the camera could operate only in daylight. To disprove this theory, Alfred conducted an experiment in a cellar lighted only by one small electric light powered by a built-over dynamo. After a 24-hour exposure, he found, as he had expected, that he had produced a perfect negative.

In those years, some of the best work was being done by Americans. Possibly, as has been suggested, the speed of the photographic process was suited to their quick, nervous temperament. In America, events of historic importance were being recorded by photographers such as Matthew Brady. This great photographer, born north of Lake George Village, was producing a graphic record of the important people and events of those turbulent years. Through photography, Stieglitz, the artist, would record as his contribution, the evanescent wonder and beauty of life.

In 1887, he visited Italy, later entering a competition in London where he won first prize, a medal, and a purse. His work was attracting wide attention, both from those who merely liked what they saw, and those who analyzed and dissected the photographer's method. Once when one of these critics asked Stieglitz where he had learned the laws of composition, he was amused. He had never studied these laws formally; his response was to the laws of nature which he perceived as always operating to achieve a balance. Inevitably, there was a clash of viewpoints between the artist who, using emphasis, distortion, and imaginative coloring created a beautiful picture, and the photographer, working in black and white, who achieved an unqualified merging with the forces of nature.

"Don't ever be afraid to tell the truth," Alfred's father had advised him. The advice was unnecessary. Alfred Stieglitz was basically honest, integrated, dedicated to truth and its expression in beauty. The method of expression was the point where artist and photographer differed.

A chance remark such as "Your painting looks like a photograph," could fill an artist with despair; whereas, to a photographer, the comment "Your photograph looks like a painting," was a triumph, implying the creation of an individual impression through line, form, and composition.

Stieglitz was convinced that there was common ground between the artist and photographer. Undoubtedly, history was on the side of the artist, and traditionally had been, ever since the first caveman drew his story of the hunt on the walls of a cave. New and mechanical, photography was anathema to the artist who feared the further mechanization of his world. Stieglitz believed implicitly in the merging of art and photography, and devoted his life to establishing this medium as an artistic means of expression.

After years of roving over Europe with a camera, he was called back to New York City by the death of a sister. He found the city, in 1890, depressing: dirt, squalor, the greed of ambitious politicians, were ruining the city he had previously known and loved. Tenements were springing up everywhere, desecrating the countryside and blocking what remained of a view; but there were compensations: Eleanora Duse was appearing on Broadway in *Camille,* and he saw every performance. Realizing his obligation to become a solid, substantial citizen, he married Emmeline Obermeyer and established a home. With two brothers-in-law, he founded a business called the Heliochrome Corporation, but the business details bored him, distracting him from an insistent life-purpose. Simultaneously, he became editor of the *American Amateur Photographer,* taking pictures by day and printing them evenings at the Camera Club. He lost money on this venture; his father, re-entering the woolen business, also lost part of his fortune. Stieglitz became ill, depressed and disillusioned. Making a desperate, but wise, decision, he decided to retire from business and devote all his time to art, and to the art of photography.

Other camera-artists with similar beliefs joined him. The machine, with all its benefits, had dehumanized the worker; through another machine, the camera, the camera-artist would enlarge the worker's horizon and humanize his existence. Stieglitz continued to work for recognition of the camera as a art medium; prints from his studio appeared in all galleries of the world. With unselfish zeal, he promoted the work of others as well as his own, earning more than 150 medals wherever art was recognized. He published CAMERA NOTES, then CAMERA WORLD, the latter enduring 20 years before its last edition appeared.

In these formative years of American photography, the leaders of the Inner Circle formed an association called Photo-Secession, based on the modern art movement originating in Munich. Inevitably, Stieglitz was considered the international leader of this group. During the early 1900's, he founded an innovative gallery at 291 Fifth Avenue for the exhibition of advanced painting, as well as the best in photography. Cubism, impressionism, and pointilism had already arisen among European artists, but the American public was not ready for a sudden departure from the usual. It was 1908, before Stieglitz' gallery had a showing of the great innovator, Matisse.

The Stieglitz place at Lake George continued to be a fertile field for Alfred's imagination. Recently, the estate had been enlarged for esthetic reasons. On the hill above the estate was an established farm, and on the farm were pigs. Due to the time-honored custom of feeding garbage to pigs, the fresh, clean air of Lake George had become foul in that quarter. Happily, the Stieglitz family acquired the farm, reclaimed the farmhouse, and named their new addition "The Hill." Evidently, The Hill was a poor relation to the big house where, a photograph shows, luxurious confusion was the custom.

And now, into the stimulating, challenging life of Alfred Stieglitz, came Georgia O'Keeffe, an artist, who was stimulating and challenging in her own right.

When Georgia O'Keeffe arrived on earth in 1887, Alfred Stieglitz was roving over Europe, demonstrating the camera as a new medium of the artist's craft. No evidence suggests that Georgia ever considered the camera in her particular phase of art, but later it became useful in bringing her own art to millions.

She was born in Sun Prairie, Wisconsin; her father was Irish, her mother Hungarian and Dutch. There were six other children in the family to alternately encourage and annoy her, but encouragement and pride in Georgia's achievement were uppermost. She drew as soon as she could hold a pencil, and by the age of 10, had decided to become an artist. In 1905, at the age of 18, she entered the Art Institute of Chicago.

Her life at this period seems to have been motivated by seeking: for a sympathetic teacher, for the right locale for her work, and sometimes, for an answer to the question Should she really become an artist at all? After six months at the Chicago Institute, she returned home. In 1907, she started out again, this time enrolling in the Art Students' League in New York City.

If Georgia O'Keeffe had attended the showing of Matisse at 291, the experience could have been a revelation; but again she returned home, this time in discouragement. At the low point in her career, she felt that everything in painting had already been done, and that she would only add the work of just another painter to the world. Everything in her that cried out for expression seemed of little value in a world where art was standing still. She spent the next year doing commercial art in Chicago; possibly the discipline of the work was helpful in crystallizing her objective.

In 1912, the O'Keeffes moved to Charlottesville, the site of the University of Virginia. This move proved to be another segment of the zig-zag course she was pursuing—a course often followed by those who are driven to create. Often, theirs is not a straight course to their goal, but a series of by-passes and blind alleys which may, ultimately guide one to his own destiny.

Georgia had decided to give up painting; however, to please her sister, she visited a summer art class at the University; becoming interested again, she enrolled. Her teacher, Alon Bement, was a pupil of Arthur Dow, head of the Fine Arts Department of Teachers' College, Columbia University. Dow's enthusiasm for modern painters had communicated itself to his disciple and, through a chain of influence, to Georgia.

She decided to teach—a sure way of ingesting principles; she became supervisor of art in the public schools of Amarillo, Texas. Summers, she taught at the University of Virginia, then, for two years, went on to study with Arthur Dow himself at Columbia. Of this teacher, she has said,

"It was Arthur Dow who helped me to find something of my own . . . this man had one dominating idea . . . to fill a space in a beautiful way . . ."

Her next teaching experience was at the State Normal School in West Texas where she found the character of the country analogous to her own. For her, there was kinship with the vast Texas plains and the wide skies unbroken by mountains. The wind blew unchecked and, in the winter months, the temperature dropped to freezing. There was no green grass or trees, and the plains were so dry that no flowers grew. But the artist responded to this off-beat climate with deepened emotions expressed in depth, distance, and broad bands of color. Of this experience, she said, "That was my country—terrible winds and a wonderful emptiness."

The year 1915 found Georgia teaching at a small college in South Carolina with more time to paint, and more time for introspection. Her talent, she decided, was going stale, and one day, she locked the door of her room, set up all her pictures and studied them impersonally. She was forced to admit, with complete honesty, that everything she was doing showed the influence of some other school or painter. To the individualist that she was, this was intolerable. In that moment of self-revelation, she knew she must find and express that self which was not being represented.

Taking up watercolor, she found freedom from inhibition in the fluidity of the medium. In abstract painting, she reveled in shapes and colors, expressing emotions that could not be confined in words. Now the vitality of the creative urge within her seemed infinite. Where once her art had been earth-bound, now it partook of space and timelessness, and an ever-present light. But, although her creativity swung into the poetry and music of the space-age, her inspiration remained firmly rooted in Nature. Unlike the ethereal quality achieved by the impressionists, the edges of her concepts were sharp and firm. It was the idea behind the form that suggested continuity.

She had been corresponding with a young woman whom she had met when both were art students in New York City, and one day, on impulse, she sent several drawings to her with the warning, "Don't show these to anyone."

The friend, recognizing that here was great talent, showed the drawings to Stieglitz whose reaction was summed up in his remark, "Finally, a woman on paper."

Wanting to be sure his first impression had been valid, Stieglitz studied the drawings for months and sought the opinion of competent critics. Their judgment coincided with his: this was a rare talent. He then included her work in an exhibit along with two other painters. Georgia was not pleased. Back at Columbia for further study, she came to 291 and demanded that her pictures be taken down. In the argument that followed, Stieglitz won, and the pictures stayed.

In 1917, Stieglitz arranged her first one-woman showing. She was

Georgia O'Keefe at Lake George

Steiglitz and camera

Clouds over Lake George, photo by Alfred Stieglitz

The Hill, cottage occupied by Alfred Stieglitz and Georgia O'Keefe

The Bread Box, where Stieglitz-Georgia O'Keefe and Mrs. Stieglitz took their meals

teaching in Texas and came east for the exhibit. The pictures had already been taken down when she arrived, but Stieglitz had them rehung for her. This was the last exhibit shown at 291, as the building was to be torn down, a common occurrence in the restless life of the City.

The next year, Georgia returned to New York, accepting Stieglitz' offer of a year in which she would be free to paint. Thus began an association which lasted the rest of Stieglitz' lifetime.

Georgia O'Keeffe, the artist and the personality, became for Stieglitz an extension of his life-work, and during the next 20 years, he took about 500 camera-portraits of her. He was developing a theory that one might have a continuous portrait taken early in life and continued through the years of maturity. His idea encompassed more than a head-and-shoulders study, and included detailed concentration on parts of the body to express the inner life; i.e., hands, arms, feet, changes in bodily weight. A camera-study which he made of Georgia suggests in her face the qualities found in her paintings: there is strength of line; intellect indicated by the broad forehead; determination in the round chin; a direct penetrating gaze; laugh-lines around the eyes denoting a sense of humor, and hair severely arranged. Hers was a face radiating intellect and imagination, strong, sincere, and without pretensions. This was the face of a woman who could not be turned from her goal by either flattery or sincere praise. To the feminists of the day, Georgia, unconventional in her life and individual in her work, became a symbol of women's liberation.

In February, 1921, the life-work of Stieglitz was displayed at the Anderson Galleries and the exhibit evoked lyrical praise from appreciative critics. Due to his speaking, writing, and exhibiting camera work, and to his own artistic integrity there was a growing acceptance of photography as an art form. His future work would add strength and substance to the new concept.

On January 7, 1924, the Royal Photographic Society of Great Britain conferred upon him their highest honor, the Progress Medal, with the Citation:

> "... (for) services rendered in founding and fostering Pictorial Photography in America, and particularly for your initiation and publication of *Camera Work*, the most artistic record of Photography ever attempted."

In 1925, he established the Intimate Gallery, succeeded by the American Place. Both he and Georgia sponsored an exhibit of John Marin watercolors at the Montross Galleries. The acclaim which followed established Marin as one of the great water-colorists of all time, equalling the Chinese, masters of the medium.

Stieglitz and Georgia O'Keeffe had been married in 1924. At the time, he had passed his 60th birthday. His silver hair framed a face that had become serene in the contemplation of beauty. His eyes glowed with hidden fire; his lips never lost the definite curves of youth, and his voice was musical and resonant. The profile was distinctive, a broken nose giving a different aspect to each side of his face. He was a small man, but well-proportioned, and his entire bearing was composed and dignified. He was always talking, gesturing with those capable hands, always drawing people to him who crowded around him and followed him.

In the 20's, they lived in the Shelton Hotel on the 30th floor and Georgia painted 15 scenes of the city. They are realistic, but not photographic. Her geometric style, while precise, is softened by lights and shadows, with a luminous quality evident even in her drawings.

Both Stieglitz and O'Keeffe liked simplicity to the point of austerity. The New York studio in which they lived and worked was small, the walls stark white as though both wished no other image to intrude on their own creations. Later, Stieglitz' brother offered them rooms on the top floor of his New York City home. The only luxury was red carpeting on the floors; there was a couch, a few chairs, but the artists, writers, and musicians who came there, sat on the floor, paying homage to the artist and the artist-photographer. Of Stieglitz, the painter, Arthur G. Dove, has said, "Without a doubt, he is the one who has done the most for art in America."

During the summers spent at Lake George, Georgia painted flowers; Stieglitz caught and fixed the intricacies and delicacy of weeds. His photographs ranged from views easily recognizable as the wide expanse of Lake George, to fragmented objects that could be found anywhere by a discerning eye.

Georgia's flower paintings were, in some ways, analagous to Stieglitz' concept of a lifelong portrait. She painted flowers in series, from the entire magnified blossom to separate studies of its intricate parts, concentrating on each detail. In 1924, Freudian concepts were widespread, and critics claimed that Georgia's flowers revealed sexual fantasies. She vehemently disclaimed the analysis, insisting,

"Well, I made you take time to look at what I saw and when you took time to really notice my flowers, you hung all your own associations with flowers on my flower and you write about my flower as if I think and see what you think and see of the flower—and I don't."

Until Georgia discovered New Mexico, she was at Lake George every summer from April until fall and her paintings are of the area as she saw it: one of her works suggests plant-life seen through water. Many of her Lake George pictures are done in blacks, greys, sombre colors, in contrast to the flaming colors of her Texas days. The lake pictures are quiet, subdued; the mountains loom over the water, dark and eternal; black crows are etched against a clouded sky.

Essentially, the two artists were surrounded by beauty; materially, the depression of 1929 had cut deeply into their resources, and The Hill, rather than the big house became their home. It was simply furnished: deep chairs offered rest and contemplation. There were no curtains at the windows to shut out the view of majestic trees, an old red barn, the lake blue in the distance, hazy- or sharply-defined mountains, and above, the endlessly forming clouds.

Stieglitz studied the clouds at Lake George, photographing them in varied formations. He called the series "Songs of the Skies," and hoped that some day a symphony would be written around them.

To one who did not know of the deep sense of life pervading the house on the hill, their existence at Lake George would have seemed isolated. Sometimes, Stieglitz emerged from the retreat, walking to the village, wearing a pork-pie hat and a long, black cloak which swirled about him. Residents still remember that cloak; to them, it added a certain flair to the wearer; to the children, it seemed sinister, making a mystery of the Man on the Hill.

Following Stieglitz' death in 1946, Georgia gave her attention and her art to the deserts of New Mexico. She found beauty in the dry and weathered bones of animals found in the desert. Pelvis bones, polished by windswept sand, and with holes that framed the sky, were models for her brush. Her paintings of animal skulls startled viewers and became her best-known work. She herself seemed indestructible. In 1961, she took a hazardous trip down the Colorado River on a rubber raft; airplanes took her between New York City and New Mexico, and she rejoiced in being so close to the sky.

During Stieglitz' brilliant career, he had failed to write his biography, leaving that task to others. He often said that he had been too busy living his life to write about it, adding,

"If I could really put down the line of the mountain and sky as they touch, as I have seen it at Lake George from my house on The Hill, it would include all my life."

CHAPTER XX

Charles Evans Hughes

He was born April 11, 1862, in a house that stood on Maple Street in Glens Falls, New York, and although his family moved away when he was a year old, in later years he often visited Glens Falls and spent several summers at nearby Lake George. From a modest beginning, he became wealthy, although never to the extent attained by the tycoons on Millionaires' Row, nor did he wish it. He never bought or built an estate in the Lake George area, but such is his eminence that his presence there marked him as a resident, and the resort area claimed him as their own.

His father started life in a part of England bordering Wales. As a young man, he emigrated to America and by study and perseverance was ordained a minister in the Wesleyan Church; Charles was born during his father's first pastorate—the Baptist Church in Glens Falls.

His mother was intellectual with a deep desire to use her mental gifts. She studied at several prominent institutes of learning, including the Fort Edward Institute, and started her own school in Kingston, New York, her hometown. She looked deceptively frail, as though she were already living in the realm of the spirit, and Charles was once admonished by his father,

"You must never speak to your mother in that way; she will not be with us very long." Contrary to expectations, her strength carried her to the age of 84.

The Rev. Mr. and Mrs. Hughes were of contrasting temperaments: he, warm and outgoing, generous, living life eagerly; she, frail and delicate, rather reserved, with a gentle strength and a pervasive influence. In their son, heredity showed, and he seemed to possess the contrasting traits of both parents which he adopted almost at will, suiting his temperament and response to the need of the moment.

Charles, an only child, may not have shown the spontaneity of one raised with other children, but there were compensations: his parents were devoted to each other and included him in their circle of devotion. They taught him the value of honesty and integrity and a respect for his mind, instilling in him the desire to excel. Both parents believed strongly in discipline, and their guide-lines became in him a self-discipline and mastery that was the foundation of his character.

At one point in Charles' young life, he overheard his parents discussing the adoption of a child in order to give him companionship. Greatly concerned, he delivered one of his first speeches and convinced his parents that it was more important to educate their only child than to give him a companion.

It is difficult not to think of him as a prodigy, but he never claimed that distinction, insisting that the climate of love in which he was raised was the reason for his early mental development. He read at the age of 3½; before the age of 6, he read and recited verses from the New Testament. The next year, he was a student of French and German and began Greek. Before the age of 9, he had read Bunyan, Moore, Byron, and Shakespeare. He started school at 6, but became convinced that it was a waste of time and persuaded his parents to let him study at home. He had his own plan of study and arose early to complete his assignments with the result that he progressed faster at home than he could have at school.

The Rev. Mr. Hughes was called to other parishes, and in rather quick succession, the family moved from Glens Falls to Hudson Falls, to Oswego, Newark, Brooklyn, and New York City. At Oswego, the winds caused Charles to develop a sinus condition; in New Jersey, their home was near swamps, and he came down with fevers. To his mother's despair, Charles refused to eat a variety of foods, but got along well on milk, honey, and cereals. His eyes were weak, and he was obliged to read the New Testament and Psalms in large type. In later years, his eyesight improved, possibly because of a more varied diet, and throughout the rest of his life he used glasses only for reading.

Charles finally entered public school and earned grades of 97–100%. At the age of 11, he became a pupil in the high school at Newark where the family were then living. In spite of his learning and the depth of his mental processes, Charles was a normal boy with a boy's love of mischief. He played cops and robbers with the boys, hit a few homers on the baseball lot, hooked his sled on the back of a horse-drawn sleigh, and generally played as intensely as he studied. When he was home alone, he played "travel," riding a huge wooden horse in his playroom, and "visiting" all the countries he had read about.

At Newark, a game ended in disaster for him. The boys were playing red lion—a rough game where the players making a human chain with linked hands sweep up other players who become part of the chain. This time the leaders whipped the center boy into a stone post; the center was Charles. He lost two front teeth and was otherwise injured. This ended his education in Newark.

The Hughes' next move was to New York City and Charles entered School #35, a high school with a reputation for scholastic excellence. This was his senior year in High School. He was 13 when he graduated, gave the salutatorian's address and received a silver medal for composition. Too young for college, he studied at home another year, then at the age of 14, entered Madison College, later known as Colgate, eager to develop his talents further and to start his career. Devoted to his parents though he was, he seemed to sense that he must strike out on his own and loosen the ties that bound him to the family. He wrote home frequently, long, descriptive letters that brought his parents within the sphere of his

Charles Evans Hughes 215

college life where, incidentally, he was making great progress. Through his letters runs always the influence of a religious home, a reliance on God, and frequent references to Christian living.

At Madison, he excelled in his studies with near-perfect grades. All his life, his power of concentration was remarkable. His memory was photographic, and after a few readings, he could deliver a long speech verbatim. Long before the term "speed reading" was introduced, Charles practiced it, and it was said of him that he could read a paragraph at a glance—a roomful of newspapers in a week.

As a college Freshman, he learned to play whist, a game which he enjoyed all his life, and he tried smoking, a pastime which did not appear in his letters home. He joined the Delta Upsilon fraternity and, knowing that a fraternity demanded more expenditure in the pursuit of social graces, offered to help his parents with his expenses, tutoring at 20¢ an hour. At this time, he had his first introduction at Lake George. His father's friend, Marcus Allen of Hudson Falls, established a camp on the lake, and with other members of his fraternity, Charles enjoyed tenting and a modified "roughing it" with good fellowship, good food, and especially, good talk.

Later, as a delegate to a Delta Upsilon convention, he was deeply impressed by the caliber of the men he met there, unconsciously recognizing his own affinity for those destined for greatness.

After two years at Madison, deciding that he wanted to attend a larger institute of learning, he transferred to Brown University. Brown concentrated on the classics and on literature with less attention to science, but the curriculum, the professors, and the college life were all Charles could have wished. With graduation from Brown, came the question of what he should do with his life. He considered medicine, teaching, and finally, the law. Naturally, the ministry was his parents' preference, but he admitted ruefully that he felt no call to that profession.

The legal profession finally won his allegiance, but in order to carry on his studies, he accepted a teaching position at the Delaware Academy, Delhi, New York. That same year, he studied law in the office of a local lawyer and in the following summer had his first experience with a shady transaction.

Answering an advertisement of the Gill Rapid Transit Company headed by a man named Gray, he found what seemed to be certain opportunity for advancement. The salary was a princely $200 a month, and Charles was asked, as a matter of course, to make a small investment in the company "so he would feel identified with it." After making inquiries, the Rev. Mr. Hughes borrowed money from a parishioner and made a small investment in the Transit Company in his son's behalf.

As a clerk, it became Charles' responsibility to go over Gray's personal papers, and what he saw caused him considerable uneasiness. In addition, he found that Gray was forging his name, and making appointments in the name of Hughes instead of Gray. The proprietor had

Honorable Charles Evans Hughes

Birthplace of Charles E. Hughes, Chief Justice United State Supreme Court,
Glens Falls, N.Y.

Stebbins House rented by Charles Evans Hughes

IN HONOR OF
CHARLES EVANS HUGHES
BORN IN GLENS FALLS, N.Y.
APRIL 11, 1862
GOVERNOR OF NEW YORK STATE
1907 – 1910
JUSTICE OF U. S. SUPREME COURT
1910 – 1916
SECRETARY OF STATE OF THE U.S.
1921 – 1925
CHIEF JUSTICE OF THE UNITED STATES
1930 – 1941
DIED AUGUST 27, 1948

Memorial Plaque in honor of Charles Evans Hughes, Glens Falls, N.Y.

chosen his assistant unwisely. Charles began an investigation and found that his employer was operating under an assumed name, and was actually a notorious character. Previously employed by a Wall Street Banking firm, "Gray" had raised checks to the amount of $300,000 and had left the country, re-appearing in London as one of the worldly-wise members of the fashionable set who clustered around the Prince of Wales.

Armed with incriminating evidence, the young lawyer confronted Gray and was able to retrieve the money his father had invested. It was an enlightening experience, and he had learned a lesson not printed in his law books. Entering Columbia Law School for a two-year course, he enrolled for the afternoon sessions and spent his mornings reading in the Law Institute Library.

He now realized that he should affiliate with a law firm and chose the prestigious New York firm of Chamberlain, Carter, and Hornblower as a start. Here he met Walter S. Carter, senior partner, who immediately became interested in him and offered him a position. As an employee of the firm, Hughes became one of a group of brilliant young men recruited by Carter. At the same time, he pursued his law study at Columbia Law School and after graduation two years later, a prize fellowship of $500 a year for the next three years was awarded to him with the provision that he would consent to tutor at Law School. He took the bar examination of New York County in June, 1884, and was admitted to that professional organization. It was 60 years before he learned of his mark on that examination—it was 99%.

Like a hero in the Alger books so popular at that time, Charles Evans Hughes now had his foot on the ladder of success: he was a law clerk in a prestigious New York Law firm; he had already gained a measure of prominence, and he was destined to marry "the boss's" daughter, Antoinette Carter. The implication of marrying the boss's daughter for advantage was a sensitive point with Hughes. Actually, he did not know that Mr. Carter had a daughter until he had been an employee of the firm for a year, and for two years thereafter, until he was a valued member of the Company, their relationship was only friendship on a now-and-then basis.

Antoinette Carter was tall and willowy with lovely and delicate features and a serenity of expression which the years could never dim. But Antoinette's delicacy was only on the surface: with another young woman, she had conducted a gymnasium in Rochester for girls and women. Later, her radiant health stood her in good stead during the birth of four children, mountain climbing trips, and the task of being the ever gracious hostess demanded by her husband's position.

The mutual attraction which brought them together deepened into devotion which never lost the romance of their first meeting. With their growing family—three girls and a boy, Hughes, sometimes considered cold and impersonal, could relax and show his affectionate, fun-loving qualities. To his children, he was an adored companion, playing games with them and reading children's stories in dialect. To his wife, he confided his deepest feelings—even the surprising revelation that he lacked confidence.

In his earlier years, his confidence may have faltered, but his courage did not. On one occasion, he represented his law firm in Oregon which involved the sale of the Oregon Pacific Railroad. The sale was unpopular with the public who saw Hughes as a symbol of their troubles, and a report came that the men of the town were massing in the barroom, threatening vengeance upon the upstart Eastern lawyer.

"Where is the barroom?" Hughes demanded, and armed with a confidence he hadn't suspected himself, he walked into the midst of the grumbling men with a cheerful, "Good evening, gentlemen; what will you have?" After putting in their order, he presented his case, talking man to man, subduing anger with reason.

His character was complex: possessed of intense drive and a critical faculty which took in the minutest detail, his intellect was at once penetrating and delicately balanced. As a consequence, his own driving force frequently pushed him to the point of a nervous breakdown. Fortunately, he realized the temper of his own mental processes and, to recover his equillibrium, took long vacations in the Swiss Alps where he climbed many of the famous peaks. At one period in his legal career, he became so physically and mentally depleted that he took two years away from his office to teach at Cornell—an experience which he found both restful and stimulating.

As a lawyer, he was relentless in his search for truth and justice. He worked with intense concentration, insisted on taking all the responsibility for a situation, and leaned on no one. He had trained himself to produce the greatest amount of work in the shortest possible time and, through adequate preparation and concentration, was able to dictate his briefs in such finished form that the first draft was usually the last. He had no close advisors, played no favorites, and confided in no other member of his profession. The public regarded him with admiration, trusted him, and were awed by him. Theodore Roosevelt once referred to him as a "bearded iceberg" but this was due only to his professional stance. He had a sense of humor which he kept under wraps when the occasion demanded, and he became sought after as a toastmaster for gatherings where his ready wit and sparkling remarks would enliven the occasion.

An event which thrust Hughes before the public was the Gas Inquiry; this happened in the early years of the century. Now that utilities were becoming relatively widespread, chances for corruption were many, and crooked politicians were amassing large fortunes through exorbitant rates and manipulation of stocks. In New York City, the New York World, representing organized groups of citizens and merchants' associations, was demanding an investigation. Tammany Hall, with its collective hands in the pockets of New Yorkers, controlled the gas lobby and successfully blocked an investigation until the legislature in Albany was finally forced to act.

Charles E. Hughes' name was immediately presented to the Committee as a lawyer well-qualified to lead the inquiry, but the members of the committee hesitated, preferring someone whose name was better known to the public. Eminent lawyers added their recommendations, and Hughes was offered the position. Now it was his turn to hesitate: he knew nothing about the gas business, had no experience in legislative investigation, and knew that the Hearst newspapers would be quick to turn any misstep into a scandal. Furthermore, with tongue-in-cheek, he told the committee, "I belong to the same church as Mr. Rockefeller."

The Committee was unconvinced, and Hughes, considering the offer carefully, decided that here was a chance for public service, and that to refuse it would be cowardly. As he had anticipated, the Hearst papers came out with a headline, "Friend of Rockefeller, Long a Fellow Trustee of his Church, Leader in His Son's Sunday School Class, Counsel for Gas Investigators." The article described Hughes' impersonal attitude as "hard, cold, and flinty," with a suitable recreation of "climbing icy crags." Thus Hughes' public image was fixed as someone cold, aloof, and forbidding.

Undaunted, he went ahead and within a week, the revelations which he presented to the public were astonishing. Hearst's yellow journals which had blasted Hughes in order to stimulate newspaper sales, now found enough sensationalism in the truth. At the end of the investigation which proved that the people had been outrageously exploited, the newspapers were full of praise for the investigator, but Hughes took no time to enjoy the fruits of his victory. Taking a room at the Fifth Avenue Hotel, he worked constantly on his report, and at the end of a week, report in hand, he boarded the Empire State Express at 2 a.m. for Albany where he delivered his report to the committee. As soon as all details were completed, he took Mrs. Hughes and the children to Europe for mountain-climbing as an antidote to his gruelling fight.

Then the institution of life-insurance came under suspicion, and Hughes, in the Carinthian Alps, received the summons to return and head the investigation. The cablegram summoning him home was delivered while the family was at dinner following a day spent at a famous glacier. Early the next morning, they left the bracing air of the mountains and Hughes returned to public duty. But he found himself buoyed up by a sense of mission, and plunged into this assignment with great enthusiasm. The men opposing him were powerful, and Hughes found himself obliged to handle the investigation with little help. True to his determination to get at the truth, he brought from a reluctant witness, a J. P. Morgan partner and president of New York Life, the damning admission of a large bequest made to the Republican party—including $48,000 to T. R. Roosevelt's campaign. The contributions of other companies—Mutual and Equitable—were also disclosed.

"If no other or further information about the life insurance business were elicited by the Armstrong* Committee," said the *New York Times,* "the ordering of the inquiry would be fully justified." Since the Republican Party was Hughes' own political party, there was consternation among the party bosses. In a surprise move, they proposed Hughes' name as mayor of New York City. This, Hughes saw, was a shrewd move to sidetrack the investigation. He refused the nomination and on that day, took Mrs. Hughes to the theater.

On their return home, they saw a startling sight: the house was ablaze with lights, cabs thronged the driveway, and the house and grounds were crowded with people. Prominent and influential men seized him and demanded that he run for the office of mayor; he must run for the good of the public; it was his duty. Hearst begged him to run. The pressure was intense, but Hughes withstood the flattery, the demands, the pleas pressed upon him. Finally, in the small hours, the crowd went home hoping for a change in Hughes' decision. For two days he was besieged with telephone calls and telegrams, but when he issued his statement, he was firm in his refusal to accept the nomination, which he knew would jeopardize the insurance investigation.

The inquiry went on with disclosures of huge sums of money used for bribery, exorbitant salaries, even entertainment. Those who had profited at the expense of small investors were exposed, their offenses noted and their activities publicized in the newspapers. The sensational disclosures roused the indignation of the public, along with admiration for the investigator who was fair, persistent, and in complete control of the situation. At the end of the investigation, Hughes went into seclusion and for six weeks worked day and night on his report which included recommendations for legislation to control the insurance companies. He took his report to Albany, and the legislature incorporated his suggestions into laws that gave the United States "the best insurance legislation the world has ever known."

Hughes emerged from the Insurance Investigation widely acclaimed as a leader and champion of the public good. From the White House in Washington, Theodore Roosevelt had watched the proceedings with interest. Wherever Republicans gathered, the words "Hughes for Governor" were heard. Hughes himself did not respond to the swelling chorus. As he had often said, he would not seek public office, but he would serve wherever he was called.

The undercurrent of "Hughes for Governor" surfaced, and the subject of the demand learned at the University Club that he would be the Republican nominee and, further, that William Randolph Hearst, publisher, would oppose him on the Democratic ticket. Hughes was neither elated nor depressed, but watched the situation unfold almost dispas-

*Senator William M. Armstrong, Chairman of the Investigation Committee which numbered several other Senators and Assemblymen.

sionately. The convention was held that year at Saratoga Springs with Hughes favored by President Roosevelt. The party bosses were unconvinced as to the rightness of the choice, but bowed to the will of the President—and the obvious will of the people—and Hughes was nominated. At the Democratic Convention held in Buffalo, Hearst was nominated as the standard-bearer of his party. Previously, he had spent over a half million in a futile effort to secure the presidential nomination; he was now determined to achieve the governorship of New York State whatever the cost.

The Hearst newspapers tore into their opponent savagely. One cartoon depicted him as cold and unfeeling, coming home from Europe on a ship which was laden with ice, supposedly the result of his frosty presence. He was a human icicle, they asserted, devoid of human feeling. But all other newspapers were for Hughes: the *Sun*, Ochs' *New York Times*, and the *Evening Post;* with Joseph Pulitzer's *World* working the hardest. In his campaign speeches, Hughes' native humanity came out, and the public saw his warm, human, caring side; they learned and laughed over his amusing stories that pointed up his more serious views of government.

"I feel you are fighting the battle of civilization" wrote the President, mindful that Hughes' opponent, Hearst, was known as the country's worst rabble-rouser—one who appealed to hate and envy. When the President sent his cabinet officer, Root, to speak at Utica, setting forth his support of Hughes and distrust of Hearst, a gang from Tammany Hall that tried to break up the meeting were quelled by the audience.

On election day, Hughes won the governorship of New York State by a plurality of over 57,000 votes. Hearst, his political power broken, was no longer a threat, and Hughes assumed a responsibility made all the more burdensome by his basic honesty, devotion to duty, and uncompromising principles.

Governor Hughes began his term of office by asking for reforms in voting methods, limitation of a candidate's expenses, and a change in the power of the Commissioners of public utilities. The party bosses were indignant at this threat to their power and appointed anti-Hughes men in key positions in the legislature. Hughes was shocked and the public was outraged, but the fight was on. The President, a party man, was alarmed at Hughes' independence and, in time, coolness developed between the occupant of the White House and the governor at Albany, who obviously would oppose the highest authority if he believed he was right.

Another break with tradition came when Hughes opened an office in a large room of the Capitol where he saw all citizens who wished to be heard, regardless of rank or position. Hughes' housecleaning continued to the delight of the newspapers. He was determined to break the hold which political machines and big corporations held on the state, enriching themselves at the public's expense, but it was uphill work, with the legislature openly defiant, the President often out of sympathy, and former supporters who deserted. The suicide of one of his closest legal advisors who could not stand the pressure, emphasized his aloneness, and the pressures he would have to endure. Backed by the public, he pushed ahead relentlessly, and at the end of six months in office, had the satisfaction of knowing that he had surmounted the state machine and the party bosses, had overthrown privileged groups in the legislature, and had secured progressive legislation in the state government.

Pressures mounted with the financial panic of 1907, a development which most people, including Hughes, had not foreseen, and he appointed Luther Mott to head the Banking Department. The post proved too much for his appointee who broke under the strain and had to resign. In the crisis, Hughes chose eminent financiers to serve on a commission revising the state's banking laws; eventually, from their work came the Securities and Exchange Act.

In the executive mansion at Albany, Mrs. Hughes presided at state functions with grace and charm, winning friends for the governor and disarming his enemies. In 1907, their daughter Elizabeth was born, the first child born in the Executive Mansion. Hughes' heavy schedule prevented the trips abroad which had become a means for restoring his vitality; instead, during the summer he took a walking trip in the Adirondacks accompanied by his son. Taking the trail from Lake Placid through Indian Pass to Tahawus, they climbed Mt. Marcy, and on the heights, he renewed his perspective.

Hughes opened a war against gambling. He was not opposed to horse racing per se, but he knew the relation between gambling and its results in poverty and crime. Again, the public was with him, and even the Hearst newspapers applauded his stand. Prominent people including Seth Low, Oswald Garrison Villard, Spencer Trask, and Louis Wiley of the New York Times joined the crusade. At the height of the struggle, Hughes received a threat that his baby daughter would be kidnapped, but he persisted. The Agnew-Hart bill against race track betting was introduced and it was evident that the vote in the legislature would be a tie. On the day of the voting, one of the Senators who was gravely ill, insisted on taking his place in the legislature and casting his vote that outlawed race track betting. Such was the devotion inspired by Hughes and his idealistic program. There were no half-way measures where Hughes was concerned: those who were not for him were actively against him.

Hughes took an active interest in conservation, knowing that in a few years, without regulation, the country's natural resources would be exhausted. Under his governorship, the Workmen's Compensation Laws were passed, and he was hailed as the "greatest friend of labor that ever occupied the Governor's chair at Albany." He made a point of going to public gatherings including fairs where he could greet people, and they found him warmly human and sincerely interested in their problems.

At the end of two years as governor, Hughes found that he was $20,000 poorer than he had been at the beginning of his term. With the $10,000 salary he received as governor, he could not manage to keep his family and undertake all the entertaining demanded by his position, and he had drawn heavily on the modest fortune he had earned as a lawyer. An offer of the Presidency of Cornell University came to him and he was tempted to accept; Taft wanted him to run as his Vice-President; but the unfinished business at the state level held him, and he accepted his party's re-nomination, winning over Lewis Chanler, his former lieutenant governor.

During the next year, Hughes was faced by decisions that involved life and death. In one famous case, a murder had been committed at Big Moose Lake in the Adirondacks where a young man, Chester Gillette, had been convicted of drowning his girl friend. Since the evidence was circumstantial, the young man's mother and his friends were making frantic efforts to save him and asked Hughes to intervene as governor. He went over the evidence in detail and listened to the pleas of Gillette's friends and relatives, but heard nothing that would upset the verdict of the Courts. He spent the day before the execution reviewing the case and struggling with his conscience. The next morning, he gave his opinion: the sentence must be carried out as the Courts had decreed, and Gillette was executed. That evening, Hughes received a call from his secretary justifying his decision: before the execution, Gillette had confessed his guilt to his religious advisor.

With the goal of improving government's operations, Hughes submitted an annual budget, and brought about election reforms. He continued his fight against William Barnes, Jr., boss of the political system, and withstood a bitter public attack which Barnes launched. When he left the Executive Mansion on October 6, 1910, to take a seat on the bench of the Supreme Court of the United States, Hughes had rolled up a record of 56.6% of recommendations adopted—a record in New York State government.

He found that the work load of the Court was heavy, necessitating his working far into the night to get abreast of the day's business. As Justice, his annual pay was $12,500; evidently, the thought of service, not money, prompted him to accept the position as he could have easily earned $100,000 to $400,000 in private legal practice.

Socially, his new position demanded more of his time and energy than he felt justified in giving. Members of the Court were prized as guests by Washington hostesses, and invitations to "meet the president" could not be declined. He compromised by choosing carefully, making it a rule that he and Mrs. Hughes would leave social gatherings at 10 o'clock; several hours' work followed, taking him into the morning hours. Conserving his energy, he gave up his "nightcap," a highball, and eliminated cigars. Only by using every moment to its fullest, could he reduce the load of work. His mind worked like a computer; at a glance, he could pick up salient points, store them in his phenomenal memory and draw on them when needed. Unfortunately, the austere habits which he was forced to adopt, further deepened the public's image of his aloofness.

As the 1912 election approached, Hughes realized that the rift between Theodore Roosevelt and Taft had widened and was becoming a threat to the Republican Party. Keeping the Supreme Court out of politics, Hughes watched the three-way contest in which Woodrow Wilson captured the presidency from Taft and Roosevelt.

During Wilson's presidency, War broke out in Europe; Roosevelt and Taft faded out of the picture, and once more Hughes was named as a presidential contender. While he hesitated, his mind was made up by a curious turn of events. Chief Justice White, ready for retirement, told Hughes that Wilson intended to name him (Hughes) as Chief Justice. This was embarrassing, to say the least: if Hughes refused to run for the presidency and accepted the Court's highest appointment, the public would believe that a deal had been made. To avoid the suspicion of collusion, he reluctantly agreed to be the Republican standard-bearer. At the National Convention, he was nominated with far more votes than the required number. Wilson, disturbed, decided, it is said, that if Hughes were elected, he would resign immediately.

Hughes began campaigning calmly and dispassionately, and as he became known to the public, his popularity grew. However, an incident in California blunted his efforts: Governor Hiram Johnson of California was campaigning for the Senate on both the Progressive and Republican tickets. In spite of the fact that the Old Guard of the Republican Party opposed Johnson, he favored Hughes. The latter, however, refused to give his support to Johnson, fearing the charge of political expediency, and coolness developed. The impasse grew larger when Hughes failed to meet Johnson when both were guests at the Virginia Hotel in Long Beach. This omission dealt a fatal blow to Hughes' campaign.

On the evening of election day, Times Square in New York City was thronged with people awaiting the results of the presidential election. The Hughes apartment was nearby, and Mrs. Hughes, awakening little Elizabeth, took her to the window to see the historic sight. What the child saw was an electric sign which was flashing the election of Hughes based on return coming over the wires of the *New York Times*.

For several days, Hughes was hailed as President-elect, but when the final count was made public, the electoral vote was 254 for Wilson, and 227 for Hughes. More votes had been cast in this election than in any to date, but cross-currents of opinion had swept away Hughes' chances for success. Later, realizing that the task of guiding the country through the War Years could have broken him as it finally broke Wilson, he was grateful for defeat.

He resumed his law practice with enthusiasm, and again found himself serving the public. When the Declaration of War against Germany was signed on April 6, 1917, Hughes became one of the most fiery supporters of America's war effort. Fighting to prove the constitutionality of the Draft Law, he coined the phrase, "a fighting constitution," a phrase used again in World War II. Governor Whitman appointed him chairman of the District Draft Appeals Board for New York City; the Board handled a thousand cases every day. Offering his services to the President, he was given an assignment to investigate the Aircraft Board, a move which resulted in increased production. He refused the fee of $100,000 which was offered to him. At the War's end, he fought against the hysteria visited on innocent people who were persecuted as German sympathizers. Although he approved of the League of Nations, he objected to the Article which would have involved the United States in future European altercations. Wilson refused to compromise, and the League of Nations was defeated, leaving Wilson a bitterly disappointed invalid.

With Europe closed to travelers, the Hughes family re-discovered Lake George, renting the Stebbins cottage on Cannon Point. Here there was much to claim Hughes' attention and interest: the mountains surrounding the lake were hills compared to the Alpine peaks, but he enjoyed their well-worn trails along with the High Peaks of the Adirondacks further north. It is known that at one time the Hughes family also rented the Conger Place with its stone steps leading down to the shore—the steps which Clarence Conger had chiseled out long ago.

There were good friend here including Mr. and Mrs. Maurice Hoopes and their daughter Mary (Polly) of Glens Falls and their neighbors, the musical Homers. Hughes' daughter Elizabeth, played with the Homer twins; and one memorable summer, Mr. and Mrs. Hughes took Elizabeth and her friend, Polly Hoopes to Italy, Switzerland, France, England, and Scotland; and they climbed Mt. Vesuvius. The older Hughes children, Catherine, Helen, and Charles, made frequent visits to the summer place and it became "home" as so many other places were when the family was together.

Their daughter Helen, active in volunteer work, had become a member of the YWCA War Work Council in Boston. When the influenza epidemic became rampant, she fell ill and, later, developed pneumonia. After a few days' absence, she insisted on returning to work.

She was attending a YWCA Conference at Silver Bay on Lake George when a recurrence of her illness forced her to stop working and she went home to her family at Lake George. After ten days, her illness was diagnosed as tuberculosis. Her parents were shocked, realizing the seriousness of the disease.

When fall came, the Hughes rented a house on Warren Street in nearby Glens Falls, as Helen was too ill to move further. With Catherine at Wellesley and Elizabeth attending the Glens Falls Academy, Mrs. Hughes cared for Helen with help from her youngest daughter; but it was evident that Helen was gradually slipping away from them. Hughes, grief-stricken, occupied the family apartment in New York City during the week, and spent week-ends with his ailing daughter, knowing that her illness was terminal. After her death, a chapel was built in her memory at Silver Bay on Lake George.

Again Hughes was approached on the possibility of running for President of the United States. He refused, asserting that his heart was broken over the loss of his daughter and he no longer cared for an elective office.

Later, when President Harding offered him the post of Secretary of State, he accepted and, pushing down his grief, found that it was good to be back in Washington, serving his country in the way he knew best. He held the position from 1921–25, serving with distinction. He resigned soon after Coolidge took office.

In 1928, he accepted leadership of the Permanent Court of International Justice at the Hague. All nations represented in the Court praised his selection for the position. He took up the work with enthusiasm, interpreting international law as it applied to the nations of the world, and seeing with satisfaction the emergency of reason and justice and the continued prestige of the Court in World order. He enjoyed the wide scope of the work and would have accepted another term except for one little word uttered by Mrs. Hughes.

The word was "No." She had continued for years to acquiesce gracefully, and had finally decided that she wanted a home and family with some degree of permanence. On February 15, 1930, Hughes resigned, regretfully, from the World Court. The regret was short-lived: already he had been nominated as Chief Justice of the United States under President Hoover; he replaced William H. Taft who resigned because of illness.

The choice of Hughes as Chief Justice was widely applauded both in American and throughout the world, and tributes to him poured in calling him "the most distinguished private citizen" and "the greatest lawyer in the world."

He had not anticipated the bitter reception which awaited him from members of Congress. In a futile attempt to block his nomination, several Congressmen loosed a flood of invective, baseless accusations, and charges of fraud in previous cases which his accusers had never even investigated. Hughes, who had carefully built his career on justice and veneration for the truth, was anguished by this attack on his character which amounted to a public inquisition. The attack finally subsided and Hughes was voted in with 26 Congressmen from both parties opposing his nomination. The bitterness directed at Hughes has been interpreted as resentment toward former Administrations for creating the Great Depression—a circumstance for which Hughes had become a symbol. Resolutely putting the struggle behind him, the "most distinguished private citizen" put on his judicial robes and prepared to uphold the "greatest judicial office in the world."

One of his most difficult tasks was a personal one: it became his duty to notify Oliver Wendell Holmes that, having passed his 90th year, he would have to leave his position on the Supreme Court. The two men had shared a devoted friendship for years and Hughes approached his assignment with reluctance; but Holmes, with innate nobility, made Hughes' task easier by anticipating his own removal.

President Franklin Roosevelt's New Deal was a challenge to the Supreme Court which was obliged to review and assess the legality of many recovery acts which were new and untried. With the public and their representatives anxious that quick action be taken on every measure proposed, the Justices became watchdogs over the Constitution, concerned with the integrity of the government and loyalty to constitutional principles. As a result of their deliberations, the Court declared that the NRA (National Recovery Act) was unconstitutional. President Roosevelt who termed his NRA bill the most important Act since the Dred Scott Decision of pre-Civil War Days, was infuriated at the Court's action. Undaunted, the Justices found the Home Owner's Loan Act of 1933 and the AAA (Agricultural Adjustment Act) also unconstitutional, although other Acts were found to be within the legal limits of the Constitution. Hughes thus found himself in a position between an administration which was bending the Constitution to attain economic recovery, and a body of Justices sworn to uphold its basic principles.

Rumors of Court-packing by FDR began to circulate. The President asserted he wanted "new blood" on the bench, instead of the incumbent "nine old men" who were blocking his program. In addition, he felt that the Court had snubbed him in not paying him a traditional visit; and so resentments multiplied.

In 1936, FDR was returned to office for another term. Interpreting his victory as a mandate from the people, he introduced his bill to change the make-up of the Court which could raise the personnel from 9 to 15 judges.

The press and radio alerted the public to the dangers of infringing on the Constitution. The Justices were silent, but mail to government representatives started pouring in, favoring the Court as it existed. FDR made the Court issue the subject of one of his Fireside Chats, criticizing the Justices and their supposed ineptness. Opposing Congressmen organized to block the President's plan. Hughes spoke defending the system and proved that court cases were not behind as charged. Ultimately, the Court-packing ruse was dropped by the Administration. The Justices had won, and they proceeded to pass on other phases of the New Deal, declaring that the Social Security and Unemployment Insurance Acts were within constitutional limits.

In 1939, Hughes' iron physique started failing, and it was found that he had a duodenal ulcer; he announced his retirement on July 1, 1941. He was relatively affluent, having amassed a fortune of over a million dollars from private practice. A flood of tributes came from the greatest men and women throughout the world, as well as the little people for whom he had labored. He had worked with a succession of Presidents during his years of service: Theodore Roosevelt, William H. Taft, Woodrow Wilson, Warren G. Harding, Calvin Coolidge, Herbert C. Hoover;

and had administered the oath of office to Franklin D. Roosevelt three times.

In 1945, Antoinette Hughes died at the age of 80. Hughes and his beloved wife had been together for 57 years, and although he found a large measure of comfort in the children and grandchildren who surrounded him, he never recovered from her death. His last President, Harry Truman, telephoned on April 11, 1947, to wish him a Happy Birthday. The following year, his ulcer recurred and he passed away after a short illness. By order of President Truman, flags were flown at half-mast for this distinguished public servant who had been called one of the great minds of the century. In 1962, a 4¢ Commemorative Stamp was issued in tribute to this eminent man.

On June 2, 1976, Charles Evans Hughes Day was celebrated in Glens Falls, New York, the place of his birth, and a plaque was affixed to the house where he was born. The ceremony was sponsored by the Daughters of the American Revolution, Chepontuc Chapter, with Mrs. Colgate Phillips as regent. Mrs. William T. Gosset (Elizabeth) of Bloomfield Hills, Michigan, daughter of the former Chief Justice, was also present. Placing the plaque would finally end all controversy as to the Hughes birthplace. The site of the home where Charles E. Hughes was born was on Maple Street where a boulder in front of the library marks the former location of the house; the house itself was moved and now stands at 20 Center Street.

In making the dedication speech, Dr. Charles H. Eisenhart, president of Adirondack Community College, told of events in Hughes' life, closing with the words,

"Hughes stood tall in integrity, courage, and intellect. He was an undefeated champion of the people and of Right."

The plaque reads:

Birthplace of Charles Evans Hughes, April 11, 1862–August 27, 1948. Governor of New York State 1907–1910. Justice of the U. S. Supreme Court 1910–1916. Secretary of State of the U. S. 1921–1925. Chief Justice of the United States 1930–1941.

Erected by the Chepontuc Chapter, D.A.R., Glens Falls, New York 1976

CHAPTER XXI

The Finch Pruyn Family and
The Hyde Collection

Charlotte Pruyn, eldest of the three daughters of Mr. and Mrs. Samuel Pruyn, was born on December 10, 1867, in the village of Glens Falls, New York. Mary followed in 1870, and Nell arrived in 1875. Their first home, a rambling white house, stood near the business center of the village on an L-shaped lot. The south end of the lot faced Maple Street across from a house which the Rev. Hughes, his wife, and infant son Charles had vacated four years before. Later, Charlotte and Charles would meet when the Honorable Charles Evans Hughes had grown to be a world-figure, and Charlotte herself had become a collector of great works of art.

The house where Charlotte spent her early years was called a farm-house, but the subsequent building of houses on each side had placed No. 11 Bay Street within the village. It was a progressive village: elms and maples set out in 1840, shaded the streets; plank sidewalks, installed at central locations in 1853, covered the mud and dust of walkways; by 1854, gas lights were brightening the business district; in 1869, the railroad came, bringing Glens Falls and the rest of the world closer together. Water was piped into the village in 1873.

The natural setting of the village—on the north bank of the Hudson River, in the foothills of the Adirondacks—insured its prosperity. During its course through Warren County, the river drops 850 feet resulting in the "Great Falls" of history. While the river, because of the falls, could not be used for transportation, it had been used for many years to float logs, and a canal around the falls had been built as early as the 1820's. These fortunate circumstances became the destiny of Samuel Pruyn.

Born June 19, 1820 on a farm in Washington County, New York, Samuel Pruyn had left home at the age of 30 for work in a Stillwater lumber mill. After three years' employment, he came to Glens Falls and obtained work with the Cheney & Arms Company, dealers in lumber, at their Michigan Lumber Camp.

Armed with several more years' practical knowledge from the lumber camps he returned to Glens Falls, a move which promised advancement, married and, in 1865 when opportunity knocked, was ready to open the door. A partnership which he formed with Jeremiah W. and Daniel J. Finch, bought the Glens Falls Company, dealers in lumber, lime, and black marble. The next year, they purchased a sawmill from Abraham Wing, III, and began sawing logs which the Finches had confined upriver. With this latest purchase, the partners controlled all mills on the north side of the river, and the Finch Pruyn Company was established as a leader in the economy of the village.

Samuel Pruyn was a tough, sturdy pioneer with the resilience to weather both prosperity and depression. It is said that he loved horses, and many were used to draw the lumber wagons at the mills. These were the strong, steady, dependable horses in contrast to the unpredictable, nervous type found at races, or the high-steppers harnessed to fashionable carriages. He was interested in education, possibly because of his own lack of formal training, and became a member of the Board of Education. The village then operated a good public school, and several private schools were available, including the Glens Falls Academy. Like an English School, this institute had a headmaster, was strictly run, and offered an education in the classics. There is evidence that the three Pruyn girls graduated from the Academy; they also attended the Presbyterian Church on Warren Street. An old photograph shows the church surrounded by a picket fence with the Finch Pruyn mill, deceptively small, in the background.

There were a number of wealthy families in the village, and long before the turn of the century, large and imposing houses dominated the main street. Prosperity continued its sweep north up Glen Street, and mansions built to last for generations, each with its own barn for horses and carriages, lined both sides of the elm-shaded street. These great houses, solidly constructed of granite, brick, or stucco, were ornate on the outside, and inside were luxurious with the choicest of native woods elaborately carved. Parquet floors, carved woodwork, and intricate mouldings blended the skills of architect and builder. Marble was widely used in interiors, with Glens Falls-mined black marble the favorite for mantle-pieces.

One who resisted the grand march up Glen Street was T. S. Coolidge who built his home with its extensive grounds downtown on the corner of Elm and Cross Streets.* Located one block west of the Glen Street business district, the new home was, in 1876, in the neighborhood of old and established residences which included the home of Dr. A. W. Holden, local historian and famous as a doctor in the Civil War. Further south on Elm Street stood the Elmwood Seminary where favored daughters of Glens Falls families attended finishing school. As part of their training, each day at 4 o'clock, the young ladies of the seminary assembled for a two-by-two march through the center of the village. Formally dressed, with the required accompaniment of hat and gloves, all took the afternoon promenade, ignoring the mashers on street corners with ladylike disdain.

When Mr. Coolidge started building his residence, he could not foresee the gathering depression which struck the country with full force in

*now Clinton Avenue.

1873 and lasted several years thereafter. For financial reasons, he decided to sell his palatial home, cut down living expenses and invest in a substantial local business. Mr. Pruyn, mindful of the closely-knit and interdependent character of the business structure in the growing community, was ready to help a fellow businessman. For $6,800, plus the house at 11 Bay Street, he and Mr. Coolidge exchanged properties.

The new house was only two blocks away from the former Pruyn home, but in size and prestige it was a whole world away. The three-story mansion was constructed of fawn-colored brick with a dark-brown trim. The house and grounds occupied an entire city block, with gardens, icehouse, carriage-house, and a home for the caretaker. The main building was enclosed by an ornamental iron fence, joined on the Cross Street side by a high board fence which effectively excluded observers. Within the house, woodwork and inlaid floors of top-grade Adirondack lumber shone with a deep polish. Several years' work had gone into the building of the house; nature had been preparing the basic materials for centuries.

But even in surroundings that indicated a certain affluence, life was lived quietly and conservatively in accordance with the wishes of the new owners. Ostentation, a mode of living that distinguished the period, was not found in this household. Here, levels of accomplishment were recognized; in the highest stratum were those who had made the greatest contribution to the economic growth of the community, with education and culture cresting the wave of influence.

Charlotte was perceptive and thoughtful, and she had begun to realize and enjoy the color, form, and vitality of art. From her father and mother, she had absorbed the conviction that wealth and talents were given only to be shared; but what, she may have wondered, should she do with the years ahead? She did not choose an early marriage, and she did not take "teacher training," the profession reserved for young ladies. At this point in her life, like many other young men and women of the day, she was irresistibly drawn to the city of Boston, the "Athens of America," where music, art, and literature were being born and nourished.

The year 1887 was a memorable one for Charlotte Pruyn: she enrolled in Miss Hersey's School in Boston; she lived at Mrs. Smith's boarding house, and she made new friends. Among those who gathered at Mrs. Smith's table for food and conversation was a young man named Louis Fiske Hyde, a student at Harvard. The College, a center of learning, radiated its influence over a wide area, and days and evenings were filled with concerts, lectures and visits to museums. Boston, then the literary center of the United States, was distinguished by the presence—or influence—of authors Ralph Waldo Emerson, Nathaniel Hawthorne, James Russell Lowell, Henry W. Longfellow, John Greenleaf Whittier, Henry Thoreau, and historian Francis Parkman with many others who had attained success, and many more still struggling and hoping. It was Bostonian Oliver Wendell Holmes who had called Boston "the hub of the solar system."

In conservative Boston, American Art was in a state of ferment. A few artists, while acknowledging their debt to the Old Masters of Europe had formed an avant garde, introducing the French moderns. Painters George Innes, Alexander Helwig Wyant, Homer Dodge Martin, James A. Whistler, John Singer Sargent and their contemporaries were influencing the forward direction of American Art. Winslow Homer painted with a vital realism; Thomas Eakins' forte was an unadorned and sober presentation of the life he experienced.

For four years, Charlotte lived the stimulating life of a student in Boston. Following graduation, she took her first trip to Europe, visiting the Louvre in Paris and sight-seeing in Switzerland. In the same period, Louis Hyde was granted his M.A. and LL.D. from Harvard; shortly after, he was appointed attorney for the Boston West End Railroad and the Elevated Railway of Boston.

During the next ten years, Charlotte, whose official residence was the family home in Glens Falls, traveled to Europe as she wished, viewed some of the world's great art and, each year, spent some time in Boston. To her, as to many others devoted to the arts, the city had become a second home. In addition, Louis Hyde was there to share her interests. He was a warm and friendly person, scholarly and meticulous in all he undertook, innately kind and considerate—qualities which Charlotte appreciated. They were married in June 1901, and set up housekeeping in Hingham near Boston; and life became even more meaningful because it was shared. Later, a daughter, Mary Van Ness, added another dimension to their lives.

Always keeping in close touch with home, the Hydes learned that the mining of black marble had ceased due to the cheaper importation of Italian marble, that the marble mill had been dismantled, and that pulp and paper mills were being built. They also realized that a new era of prosperity—and responsibility—was beginning.

Meanwhile, a significant event was occurring in Boston: on January 1, 1903, Mrs. Isabella Stewart Gardner, heiress and art-lover, opened her Museum on the Fenway. The Museum, built in the style of a Venetian Palace, was also her home, and contained priceless paintings, sculptures, fountains, and objects of art. The venture had been incorporated as a museum by the State of Massachusetts with the requirement that it be open to the public.

The Hydes were entranced by Mrs. Gardner's art collection and its setting, but for them, serious art collecting was far in the future. The heavy obligations which awaited them back in New York State included building a home, and they knew that it would be a home that expressed their own interests as this house expressed Mrs. Gardner's.

The extravagance and imagination that characterized buildings of that period were well illustrated by the work of the eminent architect, Stanford White. Elegant and impressive buildings to the credit of McKim, Mead, and White included a French Renaissance Villa for the Oelriches of the Comstock Lode, the Casino, and other show places at

Christ of the Folded Arms,
Hyde Collection—Glens Falls

Head of a negro
from Hyde Collection

Home of the Hyde Collection, Mrs. Hyde was the former Charlotte Pruyn

A "Winslow Homer" from the Hyde Collection, Sidney and Winslow Homer were cousins

*From the Hyde Collection,
Glens Falls*

Newport. In New York City, notable buildings from the famed architect's drawing board included the residences of Henry Villard and J. Pierpont Morgan, the Columbia University Library, and the ill-starred Madison Square Garden. Others were the Boston Public Library and campus buildings at the University of Virginia. The quest for classic elegance had spread to the exclusive summer resorts, including Saratoga. Later, Charlotte would add to her treasured possessions two pieces of Renaissance Italian sculpture purchased from a home in Saratoga designed by Stanford White, and destroyed by fire. At Lake George, villas and mansions were replacing the rustic homes and sprawling hotels that had flourished there for generations. Elegance and distinction were the hallmarks of those who had arrived.

In 1906, Charles Evans Hughes, Governor of New York State, signed the document that made Glens Falls a City. Other, and more personal, changes were taking place in the newly-designated city. Samuel Pruyn was nearing 90 and failing in health. The time had come for the Hyde family to return to Glens Falls; Louis Hyde became associated with the family industry, and the Elm Street house was their home for the next few years.

As business spread to former residential areas, the social pendulum swung in the direction of Warren Street which paralelled the Finch Pruyn holdings. Here, it was decided, Samuel Pruyn's three daughters would build their homes: Mary and her husband, Maurice Hoopes, planned to build a gray stucco home; another sister, Nell (later, Mrs. Cunningham), would build a similar home and ceramic studio nearby. Charlotte and Louis Hyde decided that their home, also of gray stucco, would stand between the other two. A street fronting the canal which also paralelled the property reduced the depth of the site, so Mr. Pruyn arranged to have the street moved further south. His death occurred in 1908. By 1909, Maurice Hoopes, Mary's husband, had been elected President of the Finch, Pruyn Company, with Louis F. Hyde as Vice-President.

Some years before, Mr. Hoopes, while working as an electrical engineer in Lynn, Massachusetts, had met Mr. Bigelow of the firm Bigelow and Wadsworth, Architects. His admiration for the architect's work prompted him in 1905 to appoint Mr. Bigelow to design his new home. A few years later, about 1910, the same architect was engaged to design the Hyde house and the stone building at the foot of Glen Street hill where the administration of the Finch Pruyn interests is carried on.

These years also marked the entrance of Mr. Hoopes, Mr. Hyde and their families into the life of the summer colony at Lake George. The 60th Anniversary Year Book of the Lake George Club lists both men as original founder members. Louis Hyde was Treasurer of the Club from 1911–15; Mr. Hoopes' term as Treasurer followed his. Louis Hyde went on to become 1st Vice-President, then President of the Club. Mrs. Hyde was one of the founders of the Garden Club of Lake George.

Construction progressed on the home on Warren Street. Italian workmen, familiar with the appearance of ancient buildings in Italy, set the antique tile. The house, built strong enough to withstand a siege, was Florentine Renaissance with a two-story court in the center. Here tropical plants reached for the skylight high above, and tall, vaulted windows painted pictures in sunlight on the walls. The atrium was set off from the court by marble pillars with rooms extending each side of the court. A graceful staircase led to the upper story where rooms opened on a balcony that overlooked the court. This was a home to be lived in—by those who appreciated the best which the Past could offer. All furnishings, purchased piece by piece, were from certain periods selected to harmonize with the decor of the home. Outside, the house was elegant, but unobtrusive, blending with the Hoopes' gray stucco house on one side, and on the other, with Miss Nell Pruyn's home—built to resemble a small Mexican Hotel which she had seen on her travels. Ornamental trees, planted at the time of construction, bordered the garden walk which ran at a lower level behind the three houses. Family solidarity had built this group of distinguished homes; the dedication of the men whom the two Pruyn daughters had married would continue the business success which Samuel Pruyn had begun. Collectively, their efforts would enrich a community, a country, a world.

Many talented individuals and organizations devoted to education and the arts benefitted from the generosity of the Hoopes and Hyde families, and Mrs. Nell Pruyn Cunningham; their giving became legend. They gave substantially to the "new" Presbyterian Church, the beautiful Gothic church in Glens Falls, completed in 1927. The Florentine cross of silver and gilt bronze which they gave to grace the Communion Table, is dated 1507—a symbol of ageless art and man's aspirations. The first organ, and the carved organ screen, a masterpiece in itself, were given by Mrs. Cunningham in memory of her parents, Samuel and Eliza Jane Pruyn. Both the great and the small knew their concerned giving—even the historic little stone church in Harrisena received light-fixtures from Mrs. Hyde.

At Lake George, Stillwater, the summer home of the Hoopes and Hyde families, stood on Fish Point near Homelands, the residence of Mr. and Mrs. Sidney Homer and their six remarkable children. Stillwater, acquired about 1917, was most often occupied by the Hoopes; less often by the Hydes. The latter had become home-based in Glens Falls, making short trips to fulfill their obligations at Lake George. They also made frequent trips to Europe, with summers in Germany—winters in New York. During their sojourns in Europe, they began to acquire art treasures. They purchased works of art that appealed to them personally; and, increasingly, it seemed that their judgment was based on sound artistic principles.

From the beginning of their interest in collecting, Mr. and Mrs. Hyde sought the advice of Bernard Berenson, conoisseur of art, who had graduated from Harvard with Mr. Hyde. Another advisor was Dr. W. R. Valentiner of the Metropolitan Museum of Art.

One of their greatest finds came to them as the result of the upheaval in foreign governments. Prior to 1917, the time of the Russian Revolution, masterpieces of art were secretly taken out of the country by friends of the aristocracy and hidden in Germany. Restlessness grew in Germany and, in 1933, as the ruthlessness of Hitler became more evident, word came to the United States that masterpieces of art, including a Rembrandt were for sale.

The Hydes were notified, possibly by one of their advisors, and went to Berlin where they held secret meetings with those who held Rembrandt's, "Christ with the Folded Arms." They purchased the masterpiece, and went through another period of anxiety before it was safely in place at the Hyde Collection. A photograph of Mr. and Mrs. Hyde taken at that time, suggests the usual tourist, with nothing to distinguish them as the Angels of Mercy, which they were. And so the Hyde Collection grew, through war and peace, prosperity and depression, well into the 20th century.

Louis Hyde died in 1934, his work unfinished. The Collection, as with all collections, was incomplete. He was writing a book on the history of the area which was completed later by William Hull of Fort Edward, using Mr. Hyde's own carefully-kept notes. Mrs. Hyde died in 1963. By the terms of her will, the Hyde Collection is open to the public, carrying on a tradition begun in ancient Athens and Alexandria where the public was given the opportunity to experience great art.

The organization of the Hyde Collection runs smoothly under competent, professional direction. A staff of more than 250 volunteers forms a link with the public as guides, hostesses, and clerical helpers. The guides (docents) go through an intensive course in art appreciation and the history of the collection. The hostesses are a "living presence" in each room; they protect the paintings and art objects, making sure that nothing delicate is touched. Unfortunately, many adults have never grown out of the child-like desire to handle something that stirs their admiration and wonder.

The court, a formal indoor garden, where a visit to the Hyde Collection begins and ends, sets the tone of the exhibit—and the tone is one of reverence for the art and artists of the past. The group of visitors is quiet, listening to the docent as she explains the significance of the art work they are viewing at the moment.

Visitors are shown the small room that was formerly Mrs. Hyde's bedroom. Like the rest of the house, it is furnished with antiques, the walls hung with exquisite works of art: Renoir, Van Gogh, Winslow Homer, Degas . . . The docent is saying, "I knew Mrs. Hyde; she was a small person with a sweet disposition, very modest and retiring." One can imagine Charlotte Hyde choosing these particular paintings for her own quiet enjoyment. A window in this room overlooks the courtyard, and the docent will tell you that Mrs. Hyde often watched with interest as young artists in the court below painted under the direction of the artist-curator. Another who knew her, agrees, adding that Charlotte Hyde was always vitally interested in everything about her.

The group learns that the oldest art object in the exhibit is probably an Etruscan vase about 3,000 years old. In the library, are books of great age; one of these, the Nuremberg Chronicle, printed in 1497, is a history of the then-known world; its 1,800 wood-cuts may have been the work of Durer. Two Books of the Hours, illuminated in color and gold leaf, are venerated creations from the past. Here is Rembrandt's "Christ with the Folded Arms," the great painting which has survived the destruction of war.

Visitors stand entranced before a drawing of the Mona Lisa, a study which preceded the portrait of the lady with the enigmatic smile, now in the Louvre. Da Vinci, it is said, worked on the portrait itself four years, and then announced that it was still unfinished.

Throughout the combined home and art collection, are works by masters of their art: Degas, who painted ballerinas in suspended animation; again, Rembrandt, who discerned the very soul of his model; Seurat, whose technique, the painting of microscopic dots, gives an impression of science wedded to art. On the stairway, are two panes of richly-colored stained glass from a French Cathedral of the 12th and 13th centuries. In the guest room is an appealing picture of the child Coco, painted by his father, Renoir. "Head of a Negro," by Rubens, is recognized by the many school children who come to the Hyde. The Finch Pruyn Company has made excellent color prints of a number of paintings, and has presented each school in the Glens Falls area with copies.

Three of Winslow Homer's water colors may remind the viewer that the artist was a cousin of Sidney Homer's, the composer. There is also a bronze abstract created by the well-known sculptress, Dorothy Dehner, known in Bolton Landing as the wife of David Smith, who is celebrated throughout the world as a sculptor in iron. Mr. Smith maintained a studio outside the village aptly called "The Terminal Iron Works."

The three Pruyn houses, with the Hyde House at the center, are now (1978) operated for the benefit of the public. On the uptown side, the former home of the late Maurice and Mary Hoopes has been recently conveyed to the Unitarian Universalist Society of Glens Falls by Mrs. Mary Hoopes Beeman and her husband, Lyman A. Beeman, Sr. On the other side of the central house, the home of the late Mrs. Nell Pruyn Cunningham, is used for art classes conducted for high school students and any interested person in the area. This trio of distinctive homes pays silent tribute to Samuel Pruyn, the pioneer who, long ago, left the farm to work in a lumber camp.

From the northern forests above Lake George, still come truckloads of selected logs to be converted, by the magic of industry and art, into books, magazines, perhaps into the pages of *this* book. Here, it may be noted that, with the possible exception of New York City galleries, the Old Masters section of "The Hyde" has been called the finest collection in the State.

But who can measure the unmeasurable, or put a price on the priceless? Above all, there is warmth and vitality in "The Hyde" in contrast to the often-sterile marble halls of the professional museum. It is the warmth of living bestowed on life by Charlotte and Louis Hyde. Through the sharing of their talents and their resources, others may enrich their own lives, glimpsing the vision which these two saw so clearly.

Little Anecdotes of People and Places on Millionaires' Row

BEMENT, WILLIAM—one of the Philadelphia millionaires who formed the Green Island Improvement Company; he was a partner in Miles, Bement, and Pond, builders of overhead cranes for moving machinery. He owned Belle Vue "cottage" on Green Island, and also purchased land from Otto Muller of Brooklyn, property on which Miss Henrietta Thieriot had first started her Sunday School.

BOOTH, EVANGELINE—daughter of William Booth who established the Christian Mission in London; this became the Salvation Army. The movement spread to North America, and Evangeline was named Commander in Canada, 1895–1904; Commander in the U.S., 1904–1934, and General, 1934–1939. For a number of years, she spent summers on the Bolton Road (Millionaires' Row), occupying an unpretentious gray house on the shore of Tea Island Bay. Evidently, she appreciated the importance of the titles she had received using them even in personal letters. On writing to a friend, Mrs. Anna Allen Wilson in Bolton Landing, under date of July 28, 1925, she signed her name "Evangeline Booth, Commander." Seventeen years later, she was signing her name as "General."

Photographs of this handsome and dignified woman show that she did indeed live in a cottage while at Lake George. This was not the "cottage" show-place, a term borrowed from Newport and Saratoga, but an unpretentious frame house. It was situated on the shore behind Rockledge Estate and seems inadequate for her world stature. Obviously she would not choose luxury while serving people who lived in poverty.

Her Christmas card of 1923 bears the message, "To show mercy, to forgive generously, to be a friend of the friendless, to render service to our fellows without recompense—this is Christmas."

BROESEL, HERMAN—purchased Villa Matilda, lakeshore house built by Ferdinand Thieriot and replaced the Villa with "Hermstone," in the style of an old-world chateau. It is said that he entertained Von Papen and Von Bernstorff here when they were en route to Germany at the outbreak of World War I. (However, since the United States declared war on Germany on April 6, 1917 and, according to a monument in the Bolton Rural Cemetery, Mr. Broesel departed this life in 1912, the discrepancy in dates rules out any such meeting.) The mansion, built of granite quarried at nearby Trout Lake, is an architectural marvel. The outer spiral steps are chiseled in a near-perfect curve, the work of some forgotten craftsman who loved his work. The construction of an archway shows rare skill in the selecting and fitting of stones. In later years, the mansion was purchased by W. H. Bixby who wished to live near his parents, Mr. and Mrs. William Keeney Bixby, at their residence on Mohican Point. Another rumor clings about this lovely old house. Several years ago, a Lake George resident, since deceased, told the writer that the daughter of a summer resident, well-known at the turn of the century, died suddenly on her wedding day. In memoriam, so goes the story, her family had a statue made of her and placed the statue on the family cemetery plot. Rumor connected the incident with several prominent names, but inquiry has failed to disclose anyone else who has heard the story of the girl's tragic death.

The evidence is this: in the Bolton Cemetery, stands a statue—not of an angel, but of an angelic girl. The figure is larger than life-size and exceptionally beautiful; the face is haunting in its loveliness; the folds of the robe flow in marble as fluently as in satin. The name on the family plot graced by this beautiful statue is Herman Broesel.

Was this the girl of the story, frozen into marble? This is one of the rumors which have proven difficult—so far, impossible—to identify. Somewhere, someone knows the answer.

BRERETON, H. E. H.—was State Senator and summer resident at Brereton Brook in the village of Diamond Point on Lake George. A sister, Miss Elizabeth Brereton, owned Westwoods with its beautiful gardens. She was president and charter member of the Garden Club of Lake George in 1924, following Miss Marianne Schurz, the first president. Miss Brereton gave to the Club a building on her property for their use, and members donated furnishings, china, and books on gardening. In 1928, the building burned and books, club records, and furnishings were destroyed.

A brother, Denny, was one of the organizers of the Lake George Club, serving as director, treasurer, and chairman of the golf committee, all in 1909–1910. It is said that the family's fortune came from Pittsburgh, where they owned property in the "Golden Triangle"—the business section of Pittsburgh located at the junction of the Allegheny and Monongahela Rivers.

BURNHAM, GEORGE—of Philadelphia. He was one of the founders of the Green Island Improvement Company whose members planned the erection of a great hotel on Green Island. Subsequently, the Sagamore Hotel was built and opened in 1883. Mr. Burnham built his own cottage on Green Island and called it "East Cottage."

Churches—Town of Bolton
The Blessed Sacrament Catholic Church, a relative newcomer, was built on Main Street in 1890. When a new edifice was built on Goodman

Avenue, the first church was given to the Town of Bolton, and the building became the property of the Bolton Historical Society for use as a museum. The shrine in memory of Father Isaac Jogues still stands near the building, honoring the priest who first saw Lake George in 1642.

A Congregational Church was built on Federal Hill in 1811 with the Rev. Reuben Armstrong as pastor. The building sometimes used as a school, survived two moves and finally came to rest on the Trout Lake Road. Used by the Free Methodists for many years, the property is now privately owned.

Emmanuel Methodist Church built 1905–08 in Bolton, became the church home for the congregation which, for many years, had met on the third floor of a store owned by William Barber. The Methodist Church at North Bolton, built in 1850, was discontinued in 1925, and the congregation was swelled by their number.

The First Baptist Church was organized in 1825, with the church building erected about 1830 on property owned by William Stewart. The church was not opened regularly, and during the coldest part of the year, the congregation gathered in homes of the members. Later improvements included a baptistery installed in 1950.

St. Sacrément Episcopal Church (see pp. 261, 262, 400)—THIERIOT, MISS HENRIETTA.

Village of Lake George

The Methodist Church, located on Montcalm Street, was built in 1884 by Henry Worden. The congregation has no resident minister, but conducts services on a sharing basis. Known as a family church, it has become well-known for its bake sales and family night suppers.

Presbyterian Church. In 1810, James Caldwell, owner of 7,000 acres of land bordering the lake, laid out the village of Lake George. He also built the first church overlooking Artillery Cove. Two years later, the Religious Society became the First Incorporated Presyterian Congregation in the Town of Caldwell. There was no permanent pastor until 1830 when the Rev. Edwin Hall and the Rev. Amos Savage held meetings to revitalize the church. The present church was built in 1855 on land donated by the heirs of James Caldwell. The first accredited library was started in this church.

Sacred Heart Roman Catholic Church was built by the Paulist Fathers. The interior was altered in 1925, with a walk of Cainstone and altar of summa marble. Wood carving and windows were done by Powell & Sons of London, England. Stained glass windows depict the life of Father Isaac Jogues on his way to Christianize the Mohawk Indians. A few weeks later, he was murdered at Auriesville. Father Jogues was beatified in 1925 and canonized in 1930.

St. James Episcopal Church—see p. 262, TUTTLE, REV. ISAACH.

Village of Diamond Point

The Community Church at Diamond Point. This church was begun

The late Mr. George H. Cramer, he had twenty-two gardeners

Blenhem on the lake, built by Royal C. Peabody

Depe Dene, Capt. D. S. Denison

in 1876 and dedicated in 1879. Built of native stone, the cost of building was around $3,000. In years past, it was considered part of the Methodist parish; then was claimed by the Episcopal Diocese. Its original designation, that of a community church, has been reestablished. In recent years, the church has been open for two months in the summer, with a visiting pastor officiating each month. Many notable clergymen have occupied the pulpit at various times in past years.

CRAMER, GEORGE—was at one time president of the Rensselaer and Saratoga Railroad before it became the Delaware and Hudson. He owned Trinity Rock, first mentioned in Stoddard's *Guidebook for Lake George, 1873,* as "the "lovely grounds and tasteful villa of G. H. Cramer of Troy. These "lovely grounds" were tended by twenty-two gardeners. Mr. Cramer's son, LeGrand Cramer, took a leading part in the social life of the summer colony.

Cramer Point, which faced a small island, was once the subject of a spectacular land annexation. According to Stoddard, "one night, the kind waves, or something equally efficacious, filled up the intervening space with earth. The island and the mainland clasped hands across the muddy chasm and the twain was made one flesh in that hereafter, no one was found to put them asunder."[1] It has been suggested that the "efficacious agency" referred to by Stoddard was a contractor named Edward N. Sanderson who sent 40 loads of rocks and soil to fill the gap between Cramer Point and the nearby island.

DEMUTH, MR. AND MRS. WILLIAM—had a large part in the social and cultural life of Lake George. Mr. Demuth, described in Tippetts' LAKE GEORGE as a "wealthy New York man," owned Bayview on Bolton Bay, a show-place with walks, drives, and flower beds. Mr. Demuth, it was said, spent a great deal of the summer on his handsome steam launch, The Geneva. The mansion, Bayview, continued its prominence by becoming home to Mme. Sembrich and her vocal students.

DENISON, CAPT. D.S.—graduate of West Point, Class of 1858. The dashing captain had a spectacular military career, and in 1876, made a pilgrimage to Mecca—a dangerous jaunt which could have cost him, as a non-Moslem, his life. He founded the magnificent estate, Depe Dene on Millionaires' Row, the name calling to mind the gently rolling topography of England. The house itself is notable for its Colonial architecture. He married Mrs. Idene Dayton Sherwood whose name, by coincidence, closely resembled the name of the 200-acre Estate. The house itself, 60 ft. square, with 244 ft. of piazza, 5 floors, and many balconies, is still standing, along with carriage house and gate house. A portion of the estate was later purchased by Mr. and Mrs. Wallace McCaw, Sr. Mr. McCaw was an executive of the Proctor & Gamble Company; rumor has it that the McCaw's black cook devised the formula for Crisco, a product known to ev-

[1]Lake George and Lake Champlain, 31st ed. 1901, p. 31, published by the author.

eryone who bakes. The Depe Dene Estate has been divded and now contains Echo Lane Motel, Lone Bull Restaurant, the main house, and several motel units.

EDMONDS, JUDGE JOHN WORTH—His home was called Cheronderoga and, in 1870, was located at the foot of Coolidge Hill, in the village of Diamond Point. The Judge had a daughter, Laura, who had special talent for the exercise of spiritualism, and perhaps it was her influence that caused the Judge to take up the practice of the Occult. It seems that, when he sat at dinner in his boarding house with other law officials, he would "talk" to his wife who had been dead for many years. Naturally, his colleagues were uneasy and concerned. It was rumored that the Judge lost his position in the New York Courts as a result of his interest in spiritual phenomena.

Judge Edmonds thought a great deal of Daniel Moore, grandfather of Mrs. Maude Sampson, her mother's father. He was responsible for the euology engraved on Mr. Moore's tombstone in the Bolton Rural Cemetery which ends ". . . Happy indeed must be his present lot. Go on, Uncle Dan, I'll soon follow. J.W.E." (John Worth Edmonds)

The Judge's daughter, Laura, married James Kirk Gilmour. She may have had some connection with the following premonition: Mr. Gilmour, a close friend of President James A. Garfield, was with him the night before his assassination. He reported that the President was depressed saying he had a premonition of something sinister about to happen. The next day an assassin ended his life.

Laura became internationally famous as a spiritualist medium, attracting people from all over the world who came to her for readings. It is told that a client from Greece came to see her and, Laura, going into a trance, talked to him fluently in Greek—a language which she had never studied. Her message to the Greek client was that his son was dead—this he had not known.

GATES, FREDERICK T.—owned and occupied Halcyon around the turn of the century; this property became part of the Tuttle Estate. As advisor to John D. Rockefeller, Sr., Mr. Gates held a position which affected the financial structure of the country and, ultimately, the entire population. Mr. Rockefeller, of Standard Oil, had amassed a billion dollars and his great concern was how he should invest it.

> "Your fortune is rolling up, rolling up like an avalanche," Mr. Gates told him. "You must distribute it faster than it grows. If you do not, it will crush you, and your children, and your children's children."[1]

Crushed by too much money, power, and influence? Mr. Rockefeller heeded the advice and, on his retirement in 1911, turned his attention to philanthropies: his gift of a half billion is the largest ever given by a single

[1]*Rockefeller: The Family Fortune Grows* Associated Press, The Glens Falls Post Star, July 14, 1978.

individual. His descendants have followed his example, and charitable organizations, the arts, special projects such as Colonial Williamsburg in Virginia, Rockefeller Center, and Chase Manhattan Bank have benefitted by the family's wealth—all sparked by the vision of one man, Frederick T. Gates.

GATESON, MARJORIE—the daughter of Mrs. Sophie Gateson Kennedy and step-daughter of the Rev. John D. Kennedy, became famous as an actress on Broadway. When her clergyman step-father visited her backstage in her dressing room, the New York newspapers viewed a visit from the clergy as scandalous and healined the incident. In 1914, she visited the Kennedy-Gateson cottage, "Summer Rest" at Bolton, and The Lake George Mirror, noting her presence in the community, wrote of her as the leading ingenue of "The Little Cafe" Company under management of Klaw and Erlanger.

GUERNSEY, H. W.—According to a Senior Citizen, the Guernsey family lived very simply during their summers at Lake George. It was generally believed that their mode of living was from choice rather than necessity, as it was known that Mr. Guernsey's income came from Chemical stocks. Possibly this was the reason he was sometimes called "Doctor." In 1909, a change came in the Guernsey living-style and, exchanging simplicity for luxury, they built a mansion, Woodhome, on Cotton Point. Ruth, a daughter, married Dr. Edwin Jenks. She was interested in the Swedenborgian religion; the Doctor, it was said, did not share her beliefs.

Active in the Lake George Club, Mr. Guernsey served as secretary, 1912–1914, vice-president in 1914, and as president, 1915–1924.

HAYDEN, HENRY W.—secretary of organization committee of Lake George Club; also member of Board of Directors. He was one of the founders of the Lake George Association, and president from 1908–1923.

In 1899 he succeeded in revising an old Patroon law which was a source of annoyance to early property owners. Up to that time, those who had purchased land from James Caldwell's 7,000-acre tract were obliged to make an annual payment of a shilling an acre first to Mr. Caldwell, later to his heirs.

Mr. Hayden was active in St. James Episcopal Church at Lake George, serving as vestryman and senior warden. In the village, he made his home in the old Caldwell mansion House, built in 1803. The Hayden property joined the Tuttle property on the north and lay on both sides of the road.

HOMER, LOUISE, JR.—daughter of Louise and Sidney Homer; she also sang and recorded with her famous mother. On April 12, 1921, she married Ernest Van Rensselaer Stires. Later, he studied for the ministry, and was, for many years, rector of the Episcopal Church in Lake George Village. At their New York City wedding, it is said that so many presents had come to them, that the gifts were packed in barrels and locked in a basement room of St. Thomas' Church at 5th Avenue and 53rd Street.

Rumor has transposed this incident to another couple and another house at Lake George, specifically the Charles J. Peabody Estate, but so far, no one has substantiated the story at this locale.

Louise's sister, Anne, wrote a beautiful and informative book, "Louise Homer and the Golden Age of Opera." Katherine, who married Dr. Fryer, wrote an important book about their daughter Kathy who was desperately ill with a so-called mysterious disease. During her illness, Kathy stayed with her aunt and uncle, the Rev. Ernest V. Stires and his wife, Louise. For several months, she lived with them in the small white Episcopalian rectory that stood near a "rushing brook." Kathy attended the Lake George School and wrote to her mother, "Lou and Ern are wonderful." But with all their care, the disease progressed.

HUSS, GEORGE J.—of New York City. He owned property called "The Uplands" and was one of an influential group which founded the Diamond Point Library. He was the father of Henry Holden Huss, well-known musician (violin and piano) who took music students; Mrs. H. H. Huss was a vocalist. They were well known to the summer colony, giving concerts at the big hotels.

JACOB, LAWRENCE—Wall Street Broker. Mr. Jacob was Founder-Member of the Lake George Club, and member of Board of Directors, 1908, and secretary, 1909–10. He bought Hill View Farm from General Tremaine and married the daughter of E. Luther Hamilton. The public dock was his gift to the village of Diamond Point.

KENNEDY, REV. MR. JOHN DAVID—the author's great-uncle, was for many years rector of St. Mark's Church in Brookyn; he often preached at St. Sacrement Church in Bolton Landing, and at the stone Church in Diamond Point.

He married Mrs. Sophie Gateson of Brooklyn, widowed mother of several children, and the family spent summer at the Kennedy-Gateson cottage, "Summer Rest," on Huddle Bay, cited by the author, Charles Dudley Warner, as "one of the most exquisite spots on Lake George," this cottage and adjoining properties were bought by Dr. William G. Beckers during the World War I years.

The WALTER GATES house, now located on the West side of the Bolton Road, is an example of the adjustments made necessary by the creation of the Beckers Estate. Formerly standing nearer the lakeshore, this house was one of the properties involved in the transaction which were either torn down or moved. It is said that, in this case, the Doctor purchased the land he required, bought another lot across the highway, and had the house moved to its new location, paying for the operation himself.

Following the sale of the cottage on Millionaires' Row, and the death

Old Horicon

Wapanak on Green Island, built by E. Burgess Warren

Lake George Club, Lake George, N.Y.

of Mrs. Kennedy, the Rev. Mr. Kennedy built two smaller cottages at Trout Lake, a lake which is 789 feet above sea level and about 470 feet above Lake George. Here he spear-headed a group of cottagers who, bringing suit against Dr. Beckers, charged that he was preparing to dam the lake for his own water supply. The case was decided against Dr. Beckers.

KNAUTH, PERCIVAL—owned an estate, "Waldeck," near the Mankowski property; his brother, Antonio, owned "High Point," sometimes called Felseck. The family fortune, it is said, was founded on tobacco. Antonio Knauth was a Founder-Member of the Lake George Club; his daughter-in-law, Mrs. Peter Knauth, is responsible for the suggestion to form the Garden Club during a meeting of the Bolton Improvement Association in the summer of 1922. The title "Baron" is still used for Percival Knauth for reasons unknown.

KRUMBHOLZ, T. E.—manager of the Sagamore Hotel around 1914. Evidently, he was a popular manager of this famous hostelry, but more than that, was a recognized leader among the sportsmen who flocked to Lake George during the summer.

At the Gold Challenge Cup Races, held at the Thousand Islands in 1913, it was he who was given custody of the cherished Gold Cup even before the last race was won. Mrs. Krumbholz and Miss Klara, their daughter, were also social favorites.

Mr. Krumbholz was an original Founder-Member of the Lake George Club.

LOINES, STEPHEN—wealthy New Yorker who made his fortune in marine insurance; his wife, it is said, was deeply involved in the Suffragette movement, then gathering momentum. There were three daughters, Elma, Hilda, Sylvia, and a son Russell, and the young people enjoyed wonderful days at Lake George. Russell married Katherine Conger, whose family were large land-owners in Bolton Landing. Miss Hilda Loines is remembered for her work with children in the vicinity, encouraging them to plant flowers and beautify their surroundings. Miss Elma is now the last of her immediate family and still maintains the Loines Summer home, Quarterdeck, at Northwest Bay. She also tends a lovely flower-garden near the lake, and is an active member of the Garden Club of Lake George.

A graduate of Bryn Mawr, Miss Elma has written several books, including the successful "The China Trade Post Bag." This book, published in 1952, is based on 75 letters written by her mother's two uncles who were in the China trade from 1829 to 1870.

LUDWIG, BERTHOLD ALFRED—came from Germany in the early days of this century. A chemical engineer, he became associated with the Allied Chemical Company and through his business and professional interests formed close ties with Dr. William G. Beckers. Finding success in his field, he came to Lake George and rented the residence originally called the "Lower Price Place" (now Carroll Estate). Later he purchased the Brereton property at Diamond Point, which still remains in the family under the name of Richard E. Ludwig.

MEYER, DR. WILLY—was considered one of the greatest surgeons of modern times; he was also one of the most famous experts on cancer and throat surgery. Born in 1858 in Westphalia, Germany, he demonstrated his musical talent early but chose the study of medicine. He was educated in German universities, and became a member of the University of Bonn faculty.

He was the son of Dr. Abraham Jacobi's brother-in-law by his first marriage, and it was on Dr. Jacobi's advice that he came to America. He continued his career as a brilliant surgeon and, in 1893, contributed his skill to his adopted country. On July 1 of that year, President Grover Cleveland, suffering from a malignant tumor of the upper left jaw, was brought aboard a yacht where Dr. Meyer and other surgeons were waiting. The operation was a success, but was kept secret for fear that a financial panic would break out if the facts were known. In 1914, several years after Cleveland's death, the story was told.

Dr. Meyer, a Founder-Member of the Lake George Club, built a home on Green Island and, with his family, took an active part in the life of the summer colony. His daughter, Marjorie, was a well-known concert singer.

OAKES—the surname adopted by some of the Ochs family when anti-German sentiment was rampant in the U.S. at the time of World War I. Adolph Ochs, publisher of the New York Times, kept his own name and weathered the storm.

PAXTON, THE REV. J. D., and his wife, HELEN—became close friends of Louise Beatty (Homer) when she was a vocal student in Philadelphia; Louise was also a secretary, transcribing the Rev. Paxton's sermons, and was soloist at the Spruce Street Church where he was rector. Louise had her first introduction to Lake George through the Paxtons who, with their Paxton relatives, owned several "cottages" (summer homes) on the west shore of Lake George. After Louise became engaged to Sidney Homer, she turned to Mrs. Paxton for advice on her trousseau. The friends met again in Paris where Dr. Paxton had charge of the services at the American Church and Louise was taking advanced vocal training.

The Homers' daughter, Helen Joy, was named for Mrs. Paxton. When the Paxtons came to the Metropolitan and saw Louise in *Orfeo e Euridice,* they must have been deeply moved, as they remembered the eager young music student of long ago.

PEABODY, CHARLES JONES—one of the three Peabody brothers (George F., Charles J., and Royal Canfield)—was a partner in the Spencer Trask Company. He was one of the original Founder-Members of the

Lake George Club and bought the Lower Price Place, an English Tudor Mansion on Millionaires' Row which he named Evelley. The house is now owned by the Paul Carroll Estate of Albany.

PEABODY, CHARLES SAMUEL—son of Royal C. Peabody and Founder-Member of the Lake George Club. Charles S. Peabody became an architect in the New York firm of Ludlow & Peabody. He designed his father's mansion, Wikiosco, and the Lake George Club. Observers may note similarities in the architecture of both buildings.

He was a favorite of his uncle, George Foster Peabody, who called him "Carlos."

PEABODY, FRED G.—son of Frederick Forrest Peabody—This young man, a speed boat enthusiast, was chosen by the Lake George Syndicate to drive the racing craft, Hawkeye, in the 1915 speed boat races at Lake George. Since a great deal depended on the Hawkeye's making a good showing, the choice of Fred G. Peabody marks him as an outstanding racing driver.

PEABODY, FREDERICK FORREST—1839–1929, was descended from Francis Peabody (Paybody) who came from England in 1635, became successful and gave land to the Commonwealth. This land was later incorporated with the site of Harvard College. Although Frederick Peabody and the three Peabody brothers, George Foster Peabody, Charles Jones Peabody, and Royal Canfield Peabody were not directly related, all were descended from this early settler and all became residents of Millionaires' Row.

From a humble beginning, Frederick F. Peabody became a partner in the Troy, New York, firm of Cluett and Peabody, manufacturers of shirts, cuffs, and collars. The business prospered; he became wealthy and influential, and was a Director of a number of Corporations. At the apex of his career, he purchased property on Cooper Point, Lake George, and engaged the Schermerhorn Construction Company of that village to build a 42-room mansion for his wife. Due to a break-up of the marriage, she never lived there. Mr. Peabody kept his Lake George residence for summer visits, and served as 1st vice president of the Lake George Club from 1915–18. When the estate was finally offered for sale, it was purchased by M. L. C. Wilmarth who bought it on speculation. The next purchasers were William T. Carter and Frankie Carter Randolph, et al., of Houston, Texas, who leased the mansion to Herbert H. Lehman, Governor of New York State, for two summers; The American and State flags flying from the flag-pole at Green Harbour, gave notice when the Governor was in residence. In 1934, the estate became the property of the Harold Pitcairn family of Bryn Athyn, Pennsylvania. Following the ownership of J. R. Earl, local businessman, the property was sold to Elio Micheli and Gene Black of Schenectady. It now bears a "For Sale" sign.

PEABODY, ROYAL C—with his brothers, George Foster Peabody and Charles Jones Peabody, came to Lake George about 1890 where the brothers established a summer home for their mother. All became members of St. James Episcopal Church and, with Charles Samuel Peabody, son of Royal, were Founder-Members of the Lake George Club. Royal Peabody's business interests included the founding of the Brooklyn Edison Company and the presidency of the Combustion Engineering Company. Following the death of Mrs. Peabody, their mother, Royal built a mansion northeast of his brother George's estate, Abenia, and named his own home Wikiosco, Home of Beautiful Waters.

The mansion, built to last for centuries, is one of the few remaining examples of the luxury, beauty, and art that flourished on Millionaires' Row at that time. The house contains an elevator, installed so that Mrs. Peabody, a wheel-chair invalid, could enjoy the outdoors and, within the house, could be part of all social gatherings. She loved to entertain, and this great house—which would have been lonely without people—was a center where artists, musicians, and theatrical people came for extended visits. It is said that at Wikiosco, life was one continual house-party from June to September.

After Mr. Peabody's ownership, first Nathan Proller, and later Charles R. Wood bought the property.

The last purchasers of the house were Mr. and Mrs. John Cullinan of New York City who, for twenty-four years, operated the mansion as Holiday House, a summer resort. Mr. Cullinan tells of an incident that occurred during those early years: One day a large limousine drove up to the porte cochere; the chauffeur entered and asked Mr. Cullinan to come out and greet his employer. Mr. Cullinan did so, and found that the big car held a single occupant, an elderly lady sitting stately and erect in the back seat. She was dressed in black, and wore a small black hat held firmly on top of her head. She explained softly that she was Mrs. Royal Peabody and had once lived in this house. No thank you; she was sure he would understand why she couldn't come in. She asked a few questions, seemed pleased that the present owners planned no major changes in the house, and thanking Mr. Cullinan, directed the chauffeur to drive on.

"She was the epitome of class," says Mr. Cullinan with a nostalgic sigh.

The old mansion: Wikiosco—Holiday House—and now Blenheim on the Lake, continues its distinguished career. Now operated as an elegant restaurant, it is under the management of Miss Jeanne Cullinan and John Cullinan, Jr., son and daughter of the former proprietors.

THE RUSSIANS

AUER, LEOPOLD—was born in Hungary and studied violin in Budapest, Vienna, and Hanover, Germany. He achieved early success and was called to the Imperial Conservatory of St. Petersburg, Russia, as Professor of Violin. Here he was soloist in the Czar's Court and Concert Director of the Imperial Russian Society of Music. He fled the Russian Revolution of 1917, and gave concerts in Europe. Famed as a teacher, his pupils included Mischa Elman, Efrem Zimbalist, and Jascha Heifetz. At his Lake George studio, he also taught, among others, George Porter Smith, director of the Nassau Symphony Orchestra of Long Island. Professor Auer was a welcome addition to Mme. Homer's Hymn Sings held at the Lake George Club.

ZIMBALIST, EFREM—born in Russia, 1889, he trained at the Imperial Conservatory in St. Petersburg under Leopold Auer. In 1907, his first appearance in Berlin with his playing of Johannes Brahms' Violin Concerto [was a sensation]. Although only 18 at the time, he was praised for the maturity of his playing, as well as for his exceptional technique. Received enthusiastically in Europe, he came to the United States where he received an equally warm welcome. His first appearance was in 1912 with the Boston Symphony. In 1914, he married Alma Gluck, former pupil of Mme. Sembrich and leading soprano of the Metropolitan.

Recognized as one of the world's great violinists, he was soloist with the Philharmonic and other symphony orchestras. He also composed for the violin, orchestra, and piano.

At Lake George, the Zimbalists lived in a small house on West Street in the Village. On adjoining property, a studio was built for Mr. Zimbalist; that studio in time was incorporated into the home of Mr. and Mrs. Christo G. Starche, and is now their living room. Although the great violinist and his opera star wife were not residents of Millionaires' Row per se, their talents gave them world-wide stature. Their son, Efrem Zimbalist, Jr., is making a career as an actor and has been seen in many TV plays. A daughter of Alma Gluck by a former marriage, writes under the name of Marcia Davenport.

THE SCIENTISTS—in early decades of the present century, famous scientists, too, came to Lake George. The group included Dr. Irving Langmuir, Dr. Charles Steinmetz, and Dr. John Apperson. The Nobel Prize in Chemistry was awarded to Dr. Langmuir twice; Dr. Steinmetz became famed for his research on lightning, building a generator for producing it artificially; Dr. Apperson, engineer, was interested in the forever wild theory; he suggested that the dam at Ticonderoga be removed—this was a very unpopular suggestion. He owned Dome Island for a while, later transferring it to the National Conservancy. Dr. Langmuir purchased Crown Island and Tongue Mountain property—a mountain famed for its rattlesnakes.

The scientists lived in cottages solidly built of chestnut on land extending from Huddle Beach Road to Bay Road. Nearby was the former Lakeview House between the old Bolton Road and the shore. Only the annex stands now; its windows, which once looked upon cleared land

Old Court House, Lake George Village

Bayview, owned by William Demuth, occupied by Madame Sembrich and pupils

with lawns and tennis grounds, now overlook the encroaching wilderness.

Further along the winding, single-lane road, on a wooded slope, is a succession of stone arches. Oddly out of place, they seem like the remains of a former civilization deep in a jungle. Actually, the arches formed the beginning of a mansion planned by members of the Theodore Roosevelt family. Disagreements among them resulted in an end to the mansion before it was properly begun.

SEXTON, PLINY T.—Born at Palmyra, New York, in 1840, educated at Palmyra and RPI, Troy, New York; graduated with L.L.B. from State and National Law School, Poughkeepsie, New York, 1859; admitted to New York Bar in 1861; became member of Supreme Court of the U.S. in 1882; Honorary Chancellor of Union University, Schenectady and Albany, New York, in 1893.

In the closing years of the 19th century, Dr. Sexton made his summer home at "The Hermitage," on Recluse Island in Lake George. There is a legend that a Jesuit priest, captured by the Indians, escaped and lived on this island. Rosary beads and an account of his experiences written on the leaves of a prayer book were, it is said, found under a stone.

In Stoddard's Guidebook "Lake George," published in 1873, he describes the setting on Recluse Island as,

> "The encircling belt of whitened stones, rustic vases and arbors, cozy seats, swinging hammocks, and pleasant flower-skirted walks winding about among the trees with many gay banners floating over it, make the little island-home beautiful as a dream of fairyland."

Recluse Island was the subject of a hoax in 1868 when it was reported in New York newspapers that, due to an earthquake, the Island had sunk 80 feet below the surface of the lake. The exact date of Dr. Sexton's arrival at Lake George is uncertain, but it is known that he was a summer resident here in the 1890's.

According to published accounts, Chancellor Sexton also owned Dome Island which he made available to Union College students for their picnics and parties. A Union College banner in garnet and white, 40 feet long, was used to announce the presence of the college men on the Island.

SOME SUMMER HOTELS

Hotels on Millionaires' Row, smaller than the Fort William Henry and the Sagamore, did a thriving business in the summertime. At the turn of the century, the *Lake George Mirror* and several guide books listed the following:

THE ANTLERS—stood on the West Shore (Millionaires' Row) 3½ miles north of Caldwell (Lake George Village). Built by Jerome Burton, it was

14 years before the hotel was ready for business. (Perhaps the demands of a family of 11 children might have had something to do with the delay.) As chronicled in 1898, Mr. Burton's hotel had accommodations for 100 guests with every room fronting on the lake. Rates were $2 per day. During the life of the hotel, the huge wooden structure burned; much later, cabins were built. Considerable changes have been made in recent years, and the site is now the Antlers Motel.

LAKEVIEW HOUSE—on Bolton Bay, offered a view of the Narrows and its clustering islands. The hotel contained a large music hall and equipment for billiards and bowling. Guests enjoyed a large fleet of boats, the tennis grounds, and the spring water. R. J. Brown was the proprietor of this hotel which accommodated 125 guests. Over the years, the main part of the wooden structure fell down; today, only the annex remains. (See Sidelights, "The Scientists.")

THE ALGONQUIN—on Bolton Bay was north of the Lakeview. Quoting from the *Lake George Mirror,* June 27, 1914, "One of the most popular locations on the lake with picturesque views and delightful surroundings . . . perfect sanitary plumbing and drainage . . . a fleet of cedar boats, lawn tennis, croquet, bathing and other amusements." A porter and free carriage met all boats at the Bolton dock. There were accommodations for 75; the season extended from June 15 to September 15. Rates were $2.50 to $3.50 per day. In 1901, the proprietor was E. G. Penfield. The hotel was destroyed by an arsonist in 1959. A restaurant and motel now occupy the site. (See Chapter VIII, *Harold Pitcairn.*)

THE MARION—also built by Jerome Burton, north of the Lake George Club, was one of the larger hotels and, in 1914, advertised, "This hotel has been greatly improved. Newly furnished rooms, with or without private baths. Service best obtainable. Livery, launch for parties always on hand." J. H. Marvel was manager. A few years later, the hotel was demolished; only the foundation is left.

MOHICAN HOUSE—Bolton-on-Lake George. In 1898, rates of board were from $10 to $15 per week according to size and location of rooms. Open throughout the year, Frank Clark was lessee. Stoddard's 31st edition of "Lake George and Lake Champlain," 1901, states, "The Mohican House as a hotel is no more. It has been purchased by W. K. Bixby of St. Louis, Missouri, president of the American Car and Foundry Company of that city, and converted into a dwelling place for summer occupancy." (See Chapter XV, *The Bixbys.*)

THE LAKE HOUSE at Caldwell (Lake George Village) was brought up to date by Otis Elevator Company in 1895. This Canada Street hotel, with accommodations for approximately 300 guests, offered all essential appointments from $12.50 to $21.50 per week (including cottages). Besides the usual comforts, the advertisement listed a fine orchestra, electric bells to hotel, and 700 electric lights in hotel and cottages. A. C. and M. L. Pike, manager, also ran the Fort William Henry. Ladies' pool-rooms, reception and writing rooms were featured and, according to the advertisement, there were no mosquitoes.

THE WORDEN—north of Lake House and facing east, accommodated 100 guests at $2.50 per day, $10 to $15 per week. THE ARLINGTON, adjoining the Worden, offered rooms for 60 people with free bus to train, E. J. Worden, proprietor. On October 25, 1978 these two buildings, known as the Lake George Hotel, burned to the ground.

STARR, FRANCES—well-known Broadway actress who married Haskell Coffin, celebrated artist. They lived at Diamond Point. Miss Starr often accompanied the artist when he painted portraits, busying herself with fancy-work. Among the many whose portraits he painted were Maurice Hoopes, of Glens Falls and the Bolton Road, and Mme. Sembrich, celebrated opera star.

THE STEAM BOAT ON LAKE GEORGE—In 1817, the Lake George Steam Boat Company was incorporated to handle commercial shipping on Lake George. Members of the Corporation were James Caldwell, Isaac Kelly, John Winans, Samuel Brown, and Halsey Rogers. The first steamboat to ply Lake George was the *James Caldwell,* built in 1817; the *Mountaineer,* painted red, white, and blue, followed in 1824. The "steam packet," the *William Caldwell,* built in 1834, left the "spacious Lake House" at Caldwell (early name for Lake George Village) at 8 a.m. for visits to the Ruins of Fort Ticonderoga. The *John Jay* (built in 1850) after six years' use on the lake, caught fire near Silver Bay and burned with the loss of several passengers.

Twelve days after the loss of the *John Jay,* the directors of the Corporation voted for its replacement, and the next year, the *Minne-ha-ha* was launched. The steamboat provided a whole day's adventure: leaving Caldwell at 7:45, the boat touched the docks of various resorts, with a longer stop at the foot of the lake. Here, stages from Baldwin's Landing were available to take passengers to the Ruins of Fort Ticonderoga. The *Minne-ha-ha* returned to her dock at 7 p.m. Fare was $3.00.

The *Ganouski,* built in 1869, took passengers through the Narrows, stopping at Fourteen Mile Island where there was a small hotel, with swings, picnic tables, and facilities for croquet and dancing. The boat returned to the Fort William Henry in time for dinner and the departure of the afternoon stage. Fare was $1.50.

The *Lillie M. Price,* built in 1871, also followed a shorter schedule and, leaving Caldwell at 3:30, cruised among the Hundred Islands, returning at 7 p.m. Fare was $1.50.

Other steamboats patronized by the travelers of the period were the *Horicon,* built in 1877; the *Ticonderoga,* 1884; the *Mohican,* 1894; the *Sag-*

amore, 1902. Second editions appeared as *Mohican II*, in 1908, and *Horican II*, 1911.

The question of what to do with old steamboats was partially solved during the last century when, in 1878, the aging *Minne-ha-ha* was sold and, for several years, used as a floating hotel before sinking to a watery grave. In 1886, the *Ganouski* was also demoted; its machinery was removed, the hull sold to Captain G. W. Howard and moored, as a floating cafe, near Big Burnt Island at the entrance to the Narrows. In the barroom, on a counter, was a unique feature: a large box with a glass top, full of rattlesnakes. It has been suggested that there was some connection between the snake exhibit and the "snakebite antidote" sold over the counter.

Steamboats in use today are the *Mohican II*, completed in 1908; the *M. V. Ticonderoga II*, 1944; and the paddlewheeler *Minne-ha-ha*, 1969.

STIRES, REV. DR. ERNEST MILMORE—born at Norfolk, Virginia on May 20, 1866; ordained deacon in 1891 and Priest in 1892. He served at West Point, Virginia, 1891–92 and, in 1893, was appointed to Christ Church, Chicago, where he remained until 1901. He married Sarah McKinne Hardwick in 1894; four sons were born to them. The Rev. Dr. Stires was rector of St. Thomas' Church, Fifth Avenue at 53rd Street, New York City, 1901–1925; and Bishop of Long Island from 1925–1951, the year of his death. When at Lake George, he lived at Brook Hill Farm, just above Bolton Landing; the site is now called Lagoon Manor, a tourist resort.

His son, Ernest Van Rensselaer Stires, an ambulance driver in France during World War I, married Louise Homer, Jr. Later, he received his theological training at Virginia Theological Seminary. His longest term of service was at St. James Episcopal Church of Lake George where he served the parish two distinct terms, totaling 41 years. Louise Homer Stires died in August 1970. The present Mrs. Stires was Nell Gunthorpe of Brunswick, Georgia.

TAUBE, COUNT HENNING G.—a native of Sweden and one of the area's resident nobility; the Count, a Founder-Member of the Lake George Club, was reported to be very wealthy. His property, south of the Club, was one of the largest privately owned tracts of land on Millionaires' Row. His daughter, Kierstin, was an interior designer and did the interior of Sagamore II. There was also a son, Ivig, about whom little is known.

THIERIOT, MISS HENRIETTA—daughter of Ferdinand Thieriot, it is said, had been disappointed in love. To forget her sorrow, she plunged into church work. The time was the early 1860's. A Sunday School was needed in Bolton Landing and she gathered up the children of the area, holding classes on the lakeshore, in a barn, or at her father's place, Villa

Matilda. Others became interested in her work and started a fund with which to erect a frame building to house the Sunday School. Miss Thieriot had a rough shed built on property owned by Otto Muller of Brooklyn and later (1892) purchased by William B. Bement. The shed also served for church services until the new church was completed. The fund grew and with sufficient funds, the group decided to build a stone church. The new edifice was given the name St. Sacrement in honor of Father Isaac Jogues, captive of the Indians. According to the priest's letters to his Superieur, he first saw the lake on the eve of Corpus Christi in the early 1600's, and named it Lac du Saint Sacrément in celebration of the holy day.

After the church was built, Miss Thieriot began collecting funds to build a rectory, and on her marriage to Charles H. Meade, gave the fund, amounting to a thousand dollars to the vestrymen to build a rectory next to the church. The vestrymen were assisted in organizing the Parish by the Rev. Dr. Isaac Tuttle, rector of St. Luke's in New York City . . . and summer rector of St. James in Lake George. The first wedding held in the new church at Bolton Landing was that of Miss Wilhelmina Myer, daughter of L. H. Myer of Staten Island and Bolton. The first year-round rector was the Rev. Clement Blanchet. The present clergyman is the Rev. Russell D. Smith (1977) who has held the position since 1959.

TREMAINE, GENERAL HENRY EDMUND—owned Hill View Farm on Hemlock Point. A veteran of the Civil War, he wrote "Last Years of Sheridan's Cavalry," in the closing years of the last century.

General Tremaine purchased a mile of lakeshore property from Grandfather Truesdale (Maude Sampson's grandfather, her father's father) for $8,000. Today the cost would be prohibitive if the property were available.

TUTTLE, REV. ISAAC H.—was fifth rector of St. Luke's in New York City* from 1850–1892. He was probably the first summer visitor, returning to Lake George annually from the 1840's on. His summer home, Rockledge, was the first mansion on Millionaires' Row. In 1852, he led a group of men in a religious service at the Court House in Lake George; there, several years later, a vestry was organized and a rector placed in charge. The first church, built in 1858 in Lake George Village, was constructed of wood. It is said that, in 1866, a tornado struck the village, completely destroying the church and carrying pieces of the steeple completely across the lake. Two years later, the present stone church, St. James, was erected on the same site. Dr. Tuttle assisted the Thieriot family in building the Episcopal Church at Bolton and, at times, conducted services at the stone church built by John J. Harris in 1869 in the commu-

*Footnote to history: Dr. Clement Clark Moore, born 1779, and writer of "The Visit of St. Nicholas," was one of the founders of St. Luke's in the Fields and its first senior warden. His whimsical poem was first published in 1823 in the Troy *Sentinel.*

nity of Harrisena. Mr. Harris was also a vestryman at St. James' Church in Lake George.

WARREN, E. BURGESS—built "Wapanak" on Green Island. A Founder-Member of the Lake George Club. He was one of the millionaires who formed the Green Island Improvement Company and built the Sagamore Hotel. Mr. Warren owned the *Ellide,* a steam yacht which, in 1898, was considered the fastest boat of its kind in the world. There is some question on its actual speed. According to the *Lake George Mirror,* in 1903, a speed of 25 miles per hour was improbable; other authorities have set 42 miles per hour as a top speed and probably the speed of the *Ellide.* In this connection, the *Lake George Mirror* on August 6, 1898, reports that Captain E. Burgess Warren entertained a small party aboard the steam yacht *Ellide* on a trip to Hague. (The party included Commander John Boulton Simpson.) Backing up the claim that the "yacht was going faster than the wind," the news reporter explains that, on the trip down the lake, the wind was from the south, and the flags were flying to the south.

Wapanak, the fortress-like home of the Warrens, still stands on the shores of Green Island, resembling a medieval castle. It is occupied during the summer by employees of the Sagamore.

WATROUS, HARRY—from New York City, and a Founder-Member of the Lake George Club. He spent summers with his family at Camp Inn, Clan-Amity Point (see *Lake George Mirror,* August 6, 1898) at Hague. Mr. Watrous was a well-known painter and at one time was President of the National Academy of Design. While his summer home is beyond the geographical limits of this book, he is mentioned because of a hoax which he perpetrated and which has become well-known at Lake George.

It seems that, in the summer of 1906, Col. W. D. Mann had constructed a large "wooden trout" in order to play a joke on his friend Watrous. Watrous retaliated by making a wooden sea-monster which he worked with a system of pulleys. "George, the Sea-Monster," first created panic among the summer visitors, then amusement. In 1962, George went to the Virgin Islands to become the property of Mrs. William Bailey.

WILMARTH, MARTIN LUTHER CLARENCE—a Founder-Member of the Lake George Club, bought Count Taube's extensive lakeshore property. Mr. Wilmarth, whose store in Glens Falls featured distinctive furnishings, played a large part in furnishing both Sagamore II and Sagamore III. His former property is now the site of five motels.

WILSON, MRS. ANNA ALLEN—an exceptional musician, she formed a link with the Great and the Gracious. Her piano teachers included Mrs. Clement Blanchet, wife of the rector of St. Sacrement Church; Mrs. William McCune of Glens Falls; Frank La Forge and Gottfried H. Federlein of New York City. Married to Clarence E. Wilson, Jr., they had one son, Hugh Allen Wilson, who is giving a magnificent account of his musical heritage. Mr. Wilson has his mother's album which contains invitations, notes, and programs from the famous people who summered at Lake George and wintered in New York City, including the Rev. Dr. Ernest Milmore Stires and Mrs. Stires, Sidney and Louise Homer, Mme. Sembrich, and Evangeline Booth, among others. There are invitations to receptions for Mme. Ernestine Schumann-Heink; for Mr. and Mrs. Lawrence Tibbett, and for Dr. Walter Damrosch. Cards from Miss Helen Simpson, daughter of John Boulton Simpson, and from Miss Marjorie F. Meyer, daughter of Dr. Willy Meyer, accept invitations to attend Miss Allen's social debut at 485 Park Avenue, New York City.

Anna Allen Wilson played the organ in the Church of St. Sacrement, Bolton Landing, for over 45 years.

WOODBURY, W. B.—came to Diamond Point on Lake George from Ohio more than a half-century ago. President of the Telephone Company in his home state, he transferred his energy to Lake George where he was influential from the day of his arrival. He took great interest in the Hillview Library and the Church, with particular involvement in Conservation. He served as President of the Lake George Club from 1929–1935, following Louis F. Hyde.

Mr. Woodbury's son, Cyrus, carried on his interests and continued his work as protector of the lake. Devoted to Conservation, Cyrus was concerned about water levels, pollution, and care of the lake's fish. His services covered 20 years as sanitary inspector for the Lake George Park Commission, and 28 years with the Lake George Association. He was active in securing passage of a Lake George anti-pollution law and was chairman of the Pollution and Water Resources Committee of the Adirondack Park Association. At the time of his death, he was secretary of the Lake George Club and had compiled its 60th Anniversary Year Book which lists many of the distinguished people covered in THE GREAT AND THE GRACIOUS.

The Location and
Present Owners of Estates
which are the subject of chapters

LAKE GEORGE
COTTAGE DIRECTORY
Cottagers on Lake George in 1900

•••••• ● ••••••

CALDWELL LAKE HOUSE COTTAGES.

Comptroller W. J. Morgan, Albany; G. F. Bayle, John H. Heller, N. Y.; W. H. Johnson, Albany; Walter Geissinger, New York; Dr. C. W. Gumbes, Philadelphia.

CALDWELL, EAST SHORE.

M. Van Zandt, New York; H. L. Leonard. Central Valley; Dr. Caryle, Albany; Mrs. Mathew Wilson, Peerless Point; Mrs. William Walter Phelps, Capt. John J. Phelps, Englewood, N. J., Overlook; Joseph Ladue, Schuyler Falls, N. Y.; Miss Lucy B. Moss, Philadelphia; Paulist Fathers New York, the Convent of St. Mary's of the Lake, William H. Burnett, Lenox Cottage; J. E. Mallman, Mr. Grosevnor, Plum Bay; J. C. Clirehugh, Elizabeth, N. J., Woodcroft; Rev. Geo. D. Hulst, Brooklyn, Dark Bay; G. M. Ferris, Glens Falls; Mrs. J. H. Havens, New York, Havenswood; Mrs. A. G. Brown, Mrs. W. H. Townsend, Brooklyn, Rock Top Cottage; Dr. Edward Eggleston, author, Joshua's Rock; Mrs. M. D. Wilbur, Guy's Cliff; Wm. H. Peckham, Edgewater.

LAKE GEORGE ASSEMBLY.

C. T. Sanford, New York city, "Ravenswood," Dr. D. S. Sanford, New York city, Island Home, Sanford's Islands; Frank Wait, Glens Falls, N. Y.; J. H. Bain, Glens Falls, "Caledonia;" Prof. Carl Frommel, Brooklyn, Oak Knoll; Mrs. Harris, Vineclad.

HORICON LODGE

(CLEVERDALE).

Judge A. D. Wait, Fort Edward, N. Y.; H. Colvin, Mrs. F. W. Sherwood, Weehawken, N. J., Idlewilde cottage; E. F. Freeman, Glens Falls, N. Y.; O. E. Finch, Glens Falls, N. Y., The Birches; H. A. Peck, Schenectady,; Smith Philley, Nelson Murray, Mrs. H. N. Clothier, Glens Falls.

KATTSKILL BAY.

Eber Richards, Sandy Hill, Phelps' Point; DeLong's cottage; Nesbitt's cottage, Forest Queen, C. A. Stevens, Salem, N. Y., Stevens' cottage; Mrs. Ralph A. Frost, Brooklyn, N. Y., Amsterdam; Mrs. Lindendoll, Fort Edward, Mayflower; A. R. King, Fort Edward; Amasa Howland, Sandy Hill; John J. Cunningham, Sandy Hill, "Birchcliff."

BOLTON ROAD.

Jas. A. Hayden, New York, Hayden Mansion; Edward Steiglitz, New York, Oak Lawn; Galloway C. Morris, Philadelphia, The Boulders; Mrs. P. T. Tuttle, New York; E. Thile, New York, Bonnie Nook; Rev. W. A. Holliday, New York, Woodcliff; Mrs. H. H. Hayden, Lowland Lodge; Rev. W. M. Paxton, Theological Seminary, N. J.; Rev. J. D. Paxton, Philadelphia; S. Alexander Orr, Troy, Oarlock; E. M. Shepard, New York, Erlowest; George F. Peabody, New York, Abenia; Geo. H. Cramer, Troy, LeGrand C. Cramer, Trinity Rock; Mrs. D. S. Dennison, Depe Dene; Mrs. M. A. Brereton, New York, "Brereton Brook;" Gen. Tremain, New York, Hill View Farm; George J. Huss, New York, "Onelgie;" Mrs. G. Federlein, New York; A. G. Davis, Baltimore, Wawbeek cottage.

BOLTON-ON-LAKE GEORGE.

W. K. Bixby, St. Louis, Mo., Mohican; Rev. J. D. Kennedy, Brooklyn, N. Y., Summer Rest; Pliny T. Sexton, Palmyra, Recluse Island, "The Hermitage;" William Demuth, New York city, Bay View; J. H. Palmatier, Chicago, Ill.; George A. Sawyer, U. S. N., Washington, D. C.; Dr. Jacobie, New York; C. Edward Benedict, Brooklyn, N. Y., "Ganouskie Place;" Carl Schurz, New York; Mr. Samuel J. Blatchford, New York, Bra-Thole; B. G. Ackerman, New York,

Mrs. H. T. White, Bell Point, Claremont, N. H.; Mrs. C. J. Billwiller, Yononte; George William Warren, Villa Solitude; Charles C. Bowen, Brooklyn, "The Maples," J. W. Moore, U. S. N., "The Moorings;" J. C. Knoblauch, New York city, Cranbrooke; Stephen Loines, Brooklyn, Northwest Bay; Percival Knauth, New York, Waldeck; Antonio Knauth, New York, Felseck.

SAGAMORE.

Comodore J. B. Simpson, New York city, Nirvana; E. Burgess Warren, Philadelphia, Pa., Wapanak, George Burnham, Philadelphia.

SHELVING ROCK.

George O. Knapp, Chicago; Dr. J. B. Knapp, New York; C. Ellis Stevens, Philadelphia, Edgemere.

ISLANDS.

Rev. A. C. Rose, Round Lake, South Island, Sanford's Island; James M. Patterson, Glens Falls, Ivanhoe Island; Dr. Delevan Bloodgood, U. S. N., "The Bungalow," Hen and Chickens Island; E. C. Smith, Albany, Turtle Island; Cold Water Club, Glen Island; James A. Holden, Dr. Lemon Thompson, Phantom Island; Wm. F. Ranger, New York, Ranger Island; C. M. Griswold, Edward Fassett, Arona Island; George W. Fackler, New York, Crown Island; Rev. G. W. Clowe, Hudson, N. Y., Belvoir Island; Colonel Wm. D'Alton Mann, New York, Waltonian Island; Paulist Fathers, Harbor Island.

HULETT'S LANDING.

Henry Darling, Schenectady; Mr. George H. Danforth, New York; Dr. C. O. Kimball, New York, Bitter Sweet; Mrs. James N. Osborne, Orange, N. J., Fern Cliff; Dr. Frank Hupp, Wheeling, West Va., Sunshine; H. B. Thurber, New York, Cedar Knoll; Mrs. Charles Kitchell, Newark, N. J.; Andrew Peters, "The Birches;" A. H. Balmer, Wheeling, West Va.; George H. Stockbridge, New York; Mrs. John Moore, New York, Cliff Cottage; Mr. C. S. Rhind, New York; Mrs. J. D. Hancock, Mrs. Alice Shirland, Schenectady, Woodbine; Wm. P. Ferguson, New York, Craig-Darrack; J. Pendleton Cruger, New York, Bluff Head; Prof. John Meigs, Pottstown, Pa.; Walter Gillette, Wigwam.

SILVER BAY, N. Y.

Mrs. Selah W. Strong, Twin Mt. Lodge, New Brunswick, N. J., Mrs. Robert Grier Strong, Cliff Cottage, Flatbush, L. I.; Mrs. W. S. Gillette, New York, Bluffhead Cottage; R. K. Quayle, Albany, Silver Bay, Knowl Cottage; E. J. Mercelus, Clifton, N. Y., Hotel Uncas, "Rest."

HAGUE-ON-LAKE GEORGE.

Mr. and Mrs. Harry Watrous, New York, Camp-Inn; Mrs. Slocum, New York, Camp-Us; Mrs. Rice, New York, Camp-Out; Mrs. Robinson, New York, Camp Comfort; Clan Amity Point; Mrs. R. H. Robinson, Staten Island, Lakeside Retreat; Robert M. Decker, New York; James F. Newell, Albany, Cosey Nook; Walter W. Watrous, New York; Benjamin Day, New York, Glen Day.

INDIAN KETTLES PARK COTTAGERS.

Mr. Edward Barr, Brooklyn, N. Y., "Cosy Corner;" Mr. Jay Nevin Schroeder, Lancaster, Pa.; Mr. Charles C. Clark, Rochester, N. Y.

ROGERS' ROCK, HEART BAY AND BALDWIN.

H. B. Moore, M. F. Smith, Brooklyn, N. Y.; W. W. D. Jeffers, Ticonderoga; Joseph Cook, "Cliff Seat."

62

266

Modern Mohican, going South on Lake George

Main Street, Village of Lake George, looking North

Lake George Village, looking North—1978—Fire destroyed the Lake George Hotel (large 3-story building) on October 25, 1978.

Main Street, Village of Lake George, looking south, yesterday

Lake George Village, looking South—1978

Minne-Ha-Ha—1800s

Modern Minne-Ha-Ha

Lake George Club

There was also a "Lower Price Place" built by William J. Price, son of the Colonel. This English Tudor-type mansion was purchased by Charles Jones Peabody, brother of George Foster Peabody, and named Evelley.

V   *Triuna Island,* off-shore from Bolton—the unique home of *Spencer and Katrina Trask.* Now owned by the Swire family of Schenectady, it has resumed its original name—Three Brothers. Other buildings associated with the Trasks are: Wiawaka on the east side of the lake, built as a low-cost summer place for working women, still follows the purpose of its founding, on a modified plan. Amitola, nearby, built for artists to pursue their craft, is now a summer resort for tourists.

VI   *Erlowest*—owned by Edward Morse Shepard. Considered one of the most beautiful mansions in a gilded age, it is now owned by Charles R. Wood, President of Wood Enterprises, and used as his residence. A deluxe motel also occupies the property.

VII *Wayside, Rockledge, Halcyon*—properties owned by the Rev. Isaac Tuttle and his descendants. Halcyon is used as a summer place by the Tuttle family; Rockledge the mansion is no longer owned by the Tuttles; a motel "Rockledge" is also on the property.

VIII *Green Harbour,* built by the Frankie Carter Randolph family from Texas, was purchased by Frederick Forrest Peabody, manufacturer of shirts and collars in Troy, N.Y. The estate was purchased by *Harold Pitcairn,* and is now owned by Gene Black and Elio Micheli who are advertising this 42-room mansion for sale.

IX   *Marcella Sembrich's* Studio at Bolton on Millionaires' Row is dedicated in her honor as a museum. A winding road takes the visitor to the studio; a foot path leads to the summer house on the promontory with an expansive view of the lake. The Museum is open to tourists during the summer months.

X   *Homeland,* built by *Sidney and Louise Homer* on Homer Point. It was formerly a wooded area on the Bixby property. The large shore-front home is now owned by Mrs. Huldah Kunker Heine.

XI

XII The home of the *Drs. Jacobi,* sometimes called *Juniper Hill,* stood less than a mile north of Bolton Landing at a site now called Kellem's Acres. The Jacobi house was completely destroyed by fire in 1918; only the foundation remains, overgrown by trees and brush, and no other structure was ever placed on the ruins.

The house which the Doctor built for *Carl Schurz* still stands somewhat southwest of the Jacobi foundation. Most prominent at the site is the mansion which the Doctor built for his daughter, Marjorie McAneny, with huge rooms and innumerable windows. Now painted a light blue, the house has a faded and nostalgic beauty. According to Ernest McAneny, Dr. Jacobi's grandson, his grandfather purposely built this house without a kitchen or dining room so that the McAneny family would always have their meals with him in his house.

XIII   The *Mankowski residence,* just above Bolton Landing, was named *Tallwoods* and, like all estates, had its own garages, boat house, and servants quarters. Following the Count's disappearance—or demise—(opinions differ) the property was sold. It is now owned by the Spatney family; a motel, the Contessa, stands on the south end of the property.

XIV   The *George Reis* place at Bolton Landing is built over the waters of Lake George, illustrating the interests of the man who won an enduring reputation as a skillful driver of motor craft. The home, now privately owned, is one of the lake's showplaces because of its unique location, and its association with famous speed boat races.

XV   The *Bixby Mansion* on Mohican Point is of Colonial design, and its gleaming whiteness attracts the attention of visitors. Bowing to modern living, six apartments have been installed on the second story for the use of the members of the Bixby Clan who still enjoy spending some time each summer at Lake George.

XVI
XX   *The Congers of Bra-Tholé*—property owned by this wealthy New York family has now become part of the village of Bolton Landing extending from the Bolton Free Library to the shop of Von Teck, hair-stylist. The only reminder of more opulent days is a flight of steps partly chiseled in rock by Clarence Conger. The *Hon. Charles Evans Hughes* rented this house for one or more summers. He also rented a home from the Stebbins family on Cannon Point; that house is now used as a clubhouse for the condominium on the property.

XVII   (See page 1)

XVIII *Nirvana* on Green Island, built by *John B. Simpson,* still stands flanked by the Sagamore Hotel. Nirvana Farms which supplied the big house with necessities and luxuries is located on the mainland.

XIX   *The Hill*—owned and occupied by Alfred Stieglitz, the artist/photographer, and the artist, Georgia O'Keeffe, is located a short distance north of Lake George Village overlooking Lakeshore Drive. The acreage formerly owned by the Stieglitz family is extensive, and now includes large tourist accommodations along with individually-owned homes. Lakeview Circle, that portion of the property fronting on the lake, is considered one of the area's most attractive developments.

The property is bisected by Route 9N and the upper part is reached by several sharply-ascending driveways. One roadway leads to the house on the hill. Formerly a guesthouse for the Stieglitz mansion, which has been razed, it consisted of six rooms opening into a central area, with no facilities for cooking or dining. The first Mrs. Stieglitz occupied a small cottage south of The Hill. It was customary for Alfred Stieglitz to call for his divorced wife each morning, and together they took an early-morning walk around the property. All three took their meals at the Bread-Box, a small building nearby with cooking and serving facilities.

The Stieglitz house is now occupied by Mr. and Mrs. Thaddeus C. Thomas who have remodeled the interior; the Bread-Box,, with added space, is occupied by Mr. and Mrs. Thomas Pratt.

XX   See page

XXI   *Stillwater* on Fish Point is maintained as a summer residence by Mr. and Mrs. Lyman Beeman, Sr. This home is the second edition of the family summer place. The former house was torn down in the 1970's, and the new Stillwater arose on the site.

POSTLUDE

At the Dedication of the Abraham Jacobi-Carl Schurz Memorial Park, Bolton Landing, Lake George, June 13, 1936, Dr. Dixon Ryan Fox of Schenectady, New York, President of Union University, said:

> "Places have power so long as and so far as they move the emotions of mankind. This place, this well remembered 'Schwartzwald,' has such power; these stately trees, this woodland beauty, make their contribution to the charm of this hill-girt lake, well known to us but not too well known throughout the world. Had a Wordsworth walked its shores, peered into the starlike flowers along its winding margins, surveyed its flashing waters and its forest walls, this lake would be as well known throughout the world as are the lakes of Cumberland across the sea. This grove has its part in the beauty of a lake all too insufficiently celebrated in song and story. But its chief charm and its chief power are not in the loveliness of nature. They come from its human associations."[1]

It is the human association that the author has sought to bring to the foregoing pages. If, through the reading of their story, one is moved to seek out the places where the Great and the Gracious once lived, to walk where they walked, and to see the lake as they saw it, the purpose of this book will be fulfilled.

THE AUTHOR

Rockledge Farm
Glens Falls, New York
November 7, 1977

[1]Dedication of the Abraham Jacobi-Carl Schurz Memorial Park, Library of the Johns Hopkins University; Collection of the William H. Welch Medical Library; Copyright American Medical Association, 1937, pp. 13 and 14.

BIBLIOGRAPHY

Abbot, Karl. *Open For the Season.* Garden City, New York, Doubleday and Company, 1950.

Amory, Cleveland. *The Last Resorts.* New York, Harper and Brothers, 1952.

The Autobiographical Notes of Charles Evans Hughes, edited by David J. Danelski and Joseph S. Tulchin, Cambridge, Massachusetts, Harvard University Press, 1973.

Beeman, Lyman A., Sr. *Finch, Pruyn, Inc., History and Control.* Ms. July, 1975.

Berger, Meyer. *The Story of "The New York Times," 1851–1951.* New York, Simon and Schuster, 1951.

Birmingham, Stephen. *The Right People.* Boston, Little, Brown and Company, 1968.

Bixby, Ralph F., ed. *Diary of Lillian Tuttle Bixby and the Tuttles of Bolton Landing,* New York, 1965.

Bolton Historical Society, Bolton Landing, New York. *Civic Directory of Bolton Landing.* Chicago, Women's Clubs Publishing Company, 1971.

Brown, William H., ed. *History of Warren County, New York.* Lake George, New York, The Warren County Board of Supervisors, 1963.

County Atlas of Warren, New York. From recent and actual surveys and records under the superintendence of F. W. Beers. New York, F. W. Beers and Company, 1876.

50th Anniversary Yearbook. The Garden Club of Lake George, 1922–1972.

Frank, Waldo and other editors. *America and Alfred Stieglitz;* a collective portrait with 120 illustrations. New York, Literary Guild and Doubleday, 1934.

Freud, Sigmund and William Christian Bullitt. *Thomas Woodrow Wilson, Twenty-eighth President of the United States; a psychological study.* Boston, Houghton Mifflin, 1967.

Fryer, Katharine Homer. *Kathy.* New York, Dutton, 1956.

Goodrich, Lloyd and Doris Bry. *Georgia O'Keeffe.* New York, Praeger Publishers, 1970.

Homer, Anne. *Louise Homer and the Golden Age of Opera.* New York, William Morrow and Company, 1974.

Homer, Sidney. *My Wife and I: the Story of Louise and Sidney Homer.* New York, the Macmillan Company, 1939.

Howe, Pamela. "Lake George—Once a Rich Man's Paradise," *Times-Union* (August 2, 1970) E-1-2, f., Albany, New York, Capital District Newspapers, Inc.

Hume, Ruth F. *Great Women of Medicine.* New York, Random House, 1964.

Johnson, Gerald White. *An Honorable Titan; a Biographical Study of Adolph S. Ochs.* New York, Harper and Brothers, 1946.

Knight, Arthur S., ed. *The Adirondacks: Guide and History.* Lake George, New York, 1921.

Lake George and Vicinity. (Memorial Gift Book), Book and Illustrations Copyrighted in 1929. Henrietta Hudson Press of Lake George Printing Company, Inc.

The Lake George Club, 60th Anniversary Yearbook, 1909–1969. Compiled by Cyrus Woodbury, Lake George, New York, Lake George Club, 1969.

Lake George Mirror, 1898–1936.

Lamb, Wallace E. *The Lake Champlain and Lake George Valleys,* Vol. III. New York, The American Historical Company, 1940.

Langford, Gerald. *The Murder of Stanford White.* Indianapolis, The Bobbs-Merrill Company, 1962.

Marshall, Frances Townsend. *The Turn of the Century Group.* Woodstock, Vermont, Phoenix Publishing, 1973.

Mason, Howard C. *Backward Glances*. Glens Falls, New York, Webster Mimeoprint Service, 1963, 1964, and 1965.

Mellon, Robert H. "Discovering the Hyde," *Adirondack Life*-4 (Spring 1973), 12.

Music Lovers' Handbook Section: *Biographical Dictionary of Musicians*. New York, The University Society, Copyright 1893 by Theo Presser; Copyright 1911 by the University Society, Inc.

175th Anniversary of the Founding of the Town of Bolton, 1799–1974.

Owen, H. Goddard. *A Recollection of Marcella Sembrich*. The Marcella Sembrich Memorial Association, 1950.

Perkins, Dexter and Glyndon G. Van Deusen. *The United States of America: a History*. New York, Macmillan, 1962.

Pusey, Merlo J. *Charles Evans Hughes*. New York, Macmillan, 1963.

Reid, W. Max. *Lake George and Lake Champlain*. G. P. Putnam's Sons. New York and London, Knickerbocker Press, 1910.

The Reminiscences of Carl Schurz. New York, The McClure Company, 1907.

Roosevelt, Elliott and James Brough. *An Untold Story: the Roosevelts of Hyde Park*. New York, G. P. Putnam's Sons, 1973.

Samson, W. H. *Mohican Point on Lake George, the Summer Home of Mr. and Mrs. W. K. Bixby of St. Louis, Missouri, With a Brief Glance at the History of the Lake*. New York, privately printed, 1913.

Sills, Beverly. *Bubbles: a Self-Portrait*. Indianapolis, Indiana, Bobbs-Merrill, 1976.

Simpson, William R. and Florence K. Simpson. *Hockshop*. New York, Random House, 1954.

Span, Paula. "The Duchy of Pitcairn," *Today* (September 21, 1975), 12–20. Philadelphia, Pennsylvania, Philadelphia Newspapers, Inc.

The Steamboats of Lake George, 1817–1832. Lake George, New York, The Lake George Steamboat Company, 1932.

Steinback, Elsa. *Sweet Peas and a White Bridge*. Burlington, Vermont, George Little Press, 1974.

Stoddard, Seneca Ray. *Lake George; a Book of Today*, 3rd ed. Glens Falls, New York, published by the author, 1873.

Stoddard, Seneca Ray. *Lake George; A Book of Today*, 31st ed. Glens Falls, New York, published by the author, 1901.

Talese, Gay. *The Kingdom and the Power*. Cleveland, Ohio, World Publishing Company, 1969.

Tippetts, W. H. *Lake George, State of New York . . . The Queen of American Lakes*. Caldwell, New York, published by the author, 1901.

Trask, Katrina. *Spencer Trask, December 31, 1909*. Published by the author.

Truax, Rhoda. *The Doctors Jacobi*. Boston, Little, Brown and Company, 1952.

Tuttle, Charles Henry. *Memorabilia For My Children*. Lake George, New York, Halcyon Press, 1966.

Tuttle, Charles Henry. *Supplement to Memorabilia For My Children*. Lake George, New York, Halcyon Press, 1967.

Tuttle, Mrs. H. Croswell. *History of Saint Luke's Church in the City of New York, 1820–1920*. Appeal Printing Company, New York, 1926.

Tuttle, Helene Wheeler. *On Our Way Rejoicing*. Lake George, New York, Halcyon Press, 1964.

Vanamee, Mary DePeyster Rutgers McCrea Conger. *New York's Making, Seen Through the Eyes of My Ancestors*. London, Methuen and Company, 1938.

Waite, Marjorie Peabody. *Yaddo, Yesterday and Today*. Saratoga Springs, New York, 1933.

Waller, George. *Saratoga, Saga of an Impious Era.* New York, Prentice-Hall, 1966.

Ware, Louise E. *George Foster Peabody: Banker, Philanthropist, Publicist.* Athens, Georgia, University of Georgia Press, 1951.

Wiawaka (pamphlet), undated.

Williams, Dorothy. *The Pruyn Family in the Glens Falls Area.* Undated Ms. in the Hyde Collection, Glens Falls, New York.